APPLIED SOCIAL PSYCHOLOGY
and ORGANIZATIONAL SETTINGS

APPLIED SOCIAL PSYCHOLOGY

A series of volumes edited by
Michael J. Saks and **Leonard Saxe**

CARROLL • Applied Social
Psychology and Organizational
Settings

APPLIED SOCIAL PSYCHOLOGY
and ORGANIZATIONAL SETTINGS

Edited by

John S. Carroll
Alfred P. Sloan School of Management
Massachusetts Institute of Technology

LEA *LAWRENCE ERLBAUM ASSOCIATES, PUBLISHERS*
1990   *Hillsdale, New Jersey*   *Hove and London*

Lawrence Erlbaum Associates, Inc., Publishers
365 Broadway
Hillsdale, New Jersey 07642

Library of Congress Cataloging-in-Publication Data

Applied social psychology and organizational settings / [edited by] John S. Carroll.
    p.   cm.
    Includes index.
    ISBN 0-8058-0541-9
    1. Psychology, Industrial.   2. Organizational behavior.
  3. Communication in organization. I. Carroll, John S., 1948–
    HF5548.8.A724   1990
    158.7—dc19   89-1624
                                                CIP

Printed in the United States of America
10 9 8 7 6 5 4 3 2 1

Contents

Preface

The historical development of social psychology can be written as the evolution of conceptual frameworks that embody our understanding of social behavior and its causes and consequences. This evolution is fueled by insight, careful empirical research, sensitivity to current social issues, and creative methodological invention. The seminal figures of social psychology in the 1940s enacted an integrated web of theory and practice, laboratory and field, qualitative and quantitative approaches.

In this spirit, our book presents work that bridges social psychology and organizations. The primary goal is understanding, but that goal has two mirror images: understanding organizations by bringing to bear the concepts and methods of social psychology (along with other social sciences), and understanding and developing social psychology by confronting it with the phenomena of actual organizational life.

As such, we break down some traditional stereotypical barriers between the academic world and the business world, between theoretical and applied research, between laboratory and field, and between various academic subdisciplines. The result is a series of challenging forays into new research domains from which provocative ideas and provocative phenomena emerge.

Max Bazerman and his colleagues tie together research on negotiation in two-person, multiperson, and market contexts. They point out that negotiation is becoming more central as organizations increase their internal and external interdependencies. Their chapter bridges social psychology, economics, and decision making and combines empirical descriptions of how conflicting parties behave with prescriptive insights for effective negotiation in organizations.

Two chapters examine issues relating to justice or fairness, and its central role in human interaction. Joel Brockner and Jerald Greenberg analyze the effects of layoffs on workers who remain in the organization. They argue that survivors' reactions depend on their perception of the way the layoff victims were treated and the degree to which they identify with the victims. They report both laboratory and field research supporting their ideas. Tom Tyler and Robert Bies argue that we need a broader concept of procedural justice that includes, for example, how managers treat people during the recruitment process and performance appraisals, and whether fair procedures were properly carried out. They deepen the discussion of formal procedures to include experiential and organizational components.

Two chapters look at group behavior, but break new ground in our conceptualizations of familiar phenomena and our ability to link theoretical concepts to organizational realities. Deborah Ancona analyzes top management teams in organizations. She points out that we cannot understand their functioning without extending beyond the traditional internal perspective of group dynamics to include an external perspective of how groups manage activities that cross the group boundaries. Through these combined perspectives, it is possible to analyze the kinds of skills needed by top management groups under a model of environmental demands. Robert Lord and Karen Maher reconceptualize leadership in terms of perceptions of leaders by followers, and of followers by leaders. Their perspective links cognitive processes and behavior, and provides new insights into the differences between lower level supervision and higher level leadership of organizations or polities.

Finally, two chapters examine a dynamic issue of our modern age: the impact of information technologies on our lives, on the workplace, and on human relationships. Arthur Shulman and his colleagues look at information technologies in relation to organizational communication. They argue that traditional empiricist methods must be combined with phenomenological approaches to the management and mismanagement of meaning. Their analyses of the meaning of information, communication, and technology reveal information technology as an aid to communication rather than a substitute for it. Jolene Galegher focuses on a specific use of information technology: the support of collaborative work such as joint authorship or joint design. She addresses the match between the needs of collaborators during initiation of a project, and during the coordination of work, and the capabilities of information technologies such as electronic mail and group decision support systems. Her analysis surfaces limitations in available technology, and suggests avenues for research and system development.

It is my hope that the next decade will continue this process of breaking barriers in a creative and useful way. The study of organizations offers one domain of interesting phenomena, rich with puzzles and possibilities. After all, adults spend much of their time at work, and all of us are deeply affected by the successes and failures of business and government organizations. The process of investigation promises new theoretical and methodological developments, and strategies for improvement of important institutions.

John S. Carroll

Social Psychology in Business Organizations

John S. Carroll
Alfred P. Sloan School of Management
Massachusetts Institute of Technology

More social psychologists are studying business organizations and business contexts. Increasingly, social psychologists are finding their academic home in business schools. Social psychologists are becoming a visible and important force among researchers interested in business organizations, marketing, and related domains. The purpose of this chapter is to present some brief ideas about *why* this is happening, and then to turn to the more important topics of *how* this can and should be done and *what* may come of it.

SOCIAL PSYCHOLOGISTS AND BUSINESS CONTEXTS

Times change. I was a college student in the 1960s when we struggled against the military–industrial "Establishment." Along with many other baby boomers, I went to graduate school in the early 1970s to make a career, work on interesting scientific questions, and improve society. Working for business or on business problems was somehow not what was dreamed of by long-haired, left-leaning students. After 10 years teaching in psychology departments I find myself one of a growing number of social psychologists who have made a permanent transition to business schools. This is an important change that should be viewed in its social and economic context.

Social Issues

During the 1970s, it became evident that social psychology was trying to deal with its conflicting orientations toward social problems and laboratory experiments. Shortly, we would be treated to pronouncements of a "crisis" in social psychology, and to the founding of the *Journal of Applied Social Psychology* and doctoral programs in applied social psychology that hoped to lead social psychologists out of the laboratory and toward institutions such as the schools, the courts, and the media.

In one sense, business has become a researchable social issue of the 1980s. In the mass media, the hot questions are global competition, productivity, computers in the workplace, the stock market, and the labor market. Popular culture is 110% consumerism; even Presidential candidates are marketed. Our social movements involve groups labeled *yuppies* and *dinks,* which refer to occupational classifications. The growth of two-earner households has placed working life as the focus of the modern family. As Barry Staw expressed in one of the interviews I conducted that is described shortly, "We've started being just as concerned with the efficiency and effectiveness of corporations as we wish to be with issues of discrimination and helping."

Maybe this explains why social psychologists are becoming interested in business organizations. It is an extension of a long tradition of involvement with social issues such as war and peace, racism and inequality, law and crime. Social psychologists have always been sensitive to the world around them, and that world is noticeably business-oriented.

Economic Issues

The movement of social psychologists into business schools and organizational psychology departments accelerated for partly economic reasons. Beginning in the mid-1970s, psychology departments have had decreasing enrollments as the numbers of college students fell off, and as students shifted to majors that promised easier employment. As a result, hiring of new faculty decreased, as did support for graduate training, salaries against inflation, and, to some extent, research support. At the same time, business school jobs have boomed, salaries have exploded, and the resources available to researchers in business schools have become superior in some ways (although frequently deficient in lab space and doctoral students).

As the financial inducements to social psychologists were increasing, the ideological barriers between left-wing academics and right-wing businessmen were softening. The protest movements quieted and businesses accommodated to the new generations of workers and managers they hired. The movement leaders of the 1960s became the entrepreneurs, the professional staff, and the managers of the 1980s. People in business shifted a bit more to center, and people in academia did also. Business became more open to having researchers on site, and even to paying for research that had dubious immediate benefits. Researchers found in business settings a rich set of social behaviors to stimulate theory and application.

SOCIAL PSYCHOLOGY IN BUSINESS ORGANIZATIONS

The issue of social psychology in business organizations brings up the same set of concerns that have always accompanied attempts at "application" or "relevance": How do we connect an academic discipline with a real-world context? But this turns out to be too narrow a frame: There is more than just the application of disciplinary knowledge and methods because basic advances in social psychology can be promoted in this context. Indeed, there is more at stake than the development of social psychology. Some fundamental insights about social behavior could emerge—important questions, approaches, concepts, methods, and theories—that reach out across disciplinary boundaries.

Because my own experience is limited, having spent most of my career working on issues in cognitive social psychology and law-psychology, I sought to broaden my thinking by holding discussions with colleagues who really know about social psychology in business organizations. I interviewed four academic "experts" whose careers and experiences give them a deep yet diverse viewpoint on social psychology in business organizations. They are:

J. Richard Hackman, head of the Joint Program in Psychology and Business at Harvard. After receiving his degree in social psychology from Illinois, Richard did seminal studies in job enrichment, work design, and group effectiveness. He has logged many miles in airplane cockpits watching real groups carry out their jobs, and placing his life in their hands at the same time.

Barry Staw, Director of the Organizational Behavior Program at the Graduate School of Business, University of California at Berkeley. After receiving his degree in organizational behavior from Northwestern, Barry did research on intrinsic motivation, the escalation of commitment, and job attitudes. He co-edits the preeminent annual series, *Research in Organizational Behavior*.

Harvey Hornstein, Professor and Director of Psychology and Education at Teachers College, Columbia University. Harvey received his degree in social psychology from Teachers College and went on to do research on prosocial behavior, organizational change, and conformity. He coauthored

Applied Social Psychology with Mort Deutsch. His most recent book is
Managerial Courage.

Madeline Heilman, Coordinator of the Industrial/Organizational Psychology Program at New York University. After receiving her degree in social
psychology from Teachers College, Madeline did research on attributions
and gender in the workplace. She was recently involved in the writing of
an American Psychological Association *Amicus* brief for a sex discrimination case soon to be heard by the U.S. Supreme Court.

I am sure there are more opinions out there, and more variety, than the
five of us could raise during our discussions. However, the similarities that
emerged and the overall picture warrants presentation. I trust that this will
provoke others to help broaden our viewpoint.

The Lewinian Legacy and the Later Laboratory Legions

Each of my colleagues spontaneously mentioned Kurt Lewin as the embodi-
ment of a desirable style of research and linkage between theory and application. The essence of this approach is that social psychology must "confront
the world," in the words of Hackman, who called himself an "unabashed
Lewinian." As Staw said, "social psychology was most, not just useful, but
interesting theoretically when it had its eyes and ears open to the outside and
was trying to solve social problems." Hornstein and Heilman suggested that
the challenge of social psychology was and is to do "scientifically rigorous
work on annoyingly soft problems."

When we look back to the time of Lewin in the 1940s and 1950s, we see a
time when social psychology and organizational psychology could not be told
apart. Dan Katz and Bob Kahn, Mort Deutsch, Ted Newcombe, others in the
Michigan group with John French and Doc Cartwright, and the various
students of Lewin were doing social psychology in organizations, whether
businesses, colleges, or summer camps. As Hackman put it, "Dan Katz was
on the one hand the coauthor of one of the first textbooks on the social
psychology of organizations and was also the editor of JPSP and that would be
very unusual to see now; at the time it was the most natural thing in the
world." Heilman suggested that, "when Mort [Deutsch] studied conflict, [and
when] people studied groups, communication . . . leadership, these things
were directly relevant to people's experience in organizations."

The social psychologists of this time were not simply trying to solve social
problems. In Hornstein's words, the goal was to find "essential issues" and to
investigate "theoretical questions implied by these issues" rather than to aim
only at solving applied problems. As Hackman said, their strategy was to do

"basic research trying to understand fundamental social processes." The stubborn phenomena of real contexts provide challenges that cannot be avoided by manipulating or selecting "subsets . . . that lend themselves . . . to our methodologies and existing theories."

With the development of laboratory experimental social psychology in the 1950s and 1960s, the field created a sociological phenomenon with at least two major features. First, laboratory experimentalists could out-compete fieldworkers on accepted criteria of scientific productivity. A researcher in a large university with hundreds of captive subjects and several graduate assistants could produce a high volume of publishable studies unmatched by any other method. These studies were clearly "scientific" because they had carefully developed theories and highly controlled methods. Second, once attracted into the lab, social psychologists gravitated toward studies and theories that were best suited to the lab, providing a major impetus to the already influential studies of cognitive processes.

What emerged was a "parting of the ways," in the words of Hackman, with organizational psychologists moving away from the core to management schools, education schools, and other places, while social psychology went cognitive. In their interviews, my colleagues described 1980s mainstream social psychology in terms such as *micro, narrow, remote,* and *insular,* but the organizational psychologists could easily be perceived as *soft* and *applied.*

One of the benefits of the growing rapprochement between the social psychology of the *Journal of Experimental Social Psychology* or the *Journal of Personality and Social Psychology* and the social psychology of Lewin and Deutsch would be a softening of the barriers separating different aspects of social psychology. Hackman argued that distinctions such as lab versus field or quantitative versus qualitative have us in a "Which camp are you in?" trap. Research questions should come first, with appropriate use of multiple methods and approaches following.

Social Psychology's Worldview

All of my colleagues expressed their belief that social psychological training was an excellent way to approach business organizations, or any sort of social behavior. Hornstein asserted that people trained in social psychology "have an approach that is exciting for people in organizations and forces them to ask questions that otherwise might not be asked." Heilman added that training in social psychology produces "special ways of thinking about social phenomena." Staw suggested that social psychology "is particularly useful for studying organizations in general." Hackman seemed sincere when he said, "I feel blessed by my social psychology training."

The analytical approach of experimental social psychology is "a search for causal, deductive theories using systematic, programmatic studies in precise, small steps," as Heilman stated. We generate "very detailed theories . . . [with] lots of information about moderator variables." Hornstein continued together with Heilman in suggesting that the "primary span in the bridge between research and application is theory, i.e., concepts, generalizations." Staw found it useful that social psychologists had "injected the experimental perspective into the field of organizations . . . [A realistic experiment] might tap some more general processes . . . which can have external validity; . . . it is absolutely ludicrous to think that you have external validity because you did a study in Sears." Conceptually, this training leads social psychologists to look for interactions; as Lewin said, "nothing happens across the board." Heilman stated that, "if you can figure out what the mediator is, then you can always figure out when it shouldn't happen . . . which is a tremendous game of mental discipline."

The substance of social psychology provides both a corpus of knowledge and a way of developing further understanding. The theories and frameworks are a "quiver with a bunch of arrows" (Staw), or a "backboard off which to bounce [ideas]" (Hackman), or the "conceptual grounding critical to organizational research" (Heilman). Staw felt that social psychology has a "broader perspective [than industrial psychology]" and is "more interdisciplinary [than sociology]" with "some appreciation of having to mix levels [from micro to macro]." The mix of topics such as attitudes, social influence, and groups seems central to any investigation of social systems. The "array of methods" (Hackman) is broad and really helpful.

However, the focus on real organizational problems suggests that researchers not limit themselves to the paradigms and ideas of one field. Staw argued that organizational behavior is a new basic field that is more interdisciplinary than social psychology, including micro (cognition) to macro (social structure) levels. He sees the study of organizations as a "potential growth point for the social sciences . . . one of the few areas where the various kinds of social sciences can all have something to say and . . . have to talk to each other." Hackman added that it is "hard to bound social psychology," because so much is shared with fields such as cognitive psychology and sociology. "If our methods and theories are inadequate [to deal with phenomena as they exist], then we should change them . . . and start doing social psychology that is congruent with the way the world works."

Application As a Goal

My colleagues seemed to agree about two major points in regard to the "application" of social psychology to business organizations. First, application was not their immediate goal. Instead, the development of basic knowledge, or comprehensive theory developed through rigorous research, was the key to understanding and to application. Second, to achieve a higher rate of application or knowledge transfer, we would have to change elements of our training or identify and nurture a different type of professional, a "translator," to facilitate the application process. Finally, my colleagues did not agree on what has already been applied.

Staw stated that organizational behavior is "not just applied social psychology; it is new basic knowledge." His goal was expressed by saying that "we understand rather than improve organizations." Hornstein suggested that social psychology "develops paradigms which encourage others to look at the world in ways that might be new and unfamiliar." One might add that new viewpoints can be painful: The difficulties of translating knowledge into action were illustrated in a story told by Staw about his attempt to extend his studies of escalating commitment to the tendency of banks to throw more money into bad loans. A big bank declined to participate in the proposed research project; the underlying reason was that they "did not want to know what the deficiencies of the system were . . . if it is not working well they will get fired. . . . They don't want anything that will highlight . . . bad loans." Thus, "room for improvement" is not simply an opportunity, it is also a threat to the "entrenched status quo."

Hornstein pointed out that our empirical data are sometimes irrelevant to management. "You can show up and down that no one can do a performance appraisal without distortion or bias. [Yet,] they have to do them anyway . . . We've got to promote people; we can't promote everybody; they have to decide."

For application to occur, in Hornstein's insightful analysis, there must be attention to the *precision* of theory and the *politics* of theory. The former depends on rigorous research and generalizable theories that attend to moderator variables in real contexts. Unfortunately, as Staw and Hackman suggested, social psychologists have shied away from some of the big issues such as authority structures, reward systems, task variables, and time constraints that are really central to organizations. Hackman noted that "playing in a real social system is hard, there are uncontrolled *strong* factors" that are ignored in many social psychological theories.

The politics of theory deals with practicality and analogy, or workable and communicatable ideas. Heilman observed that, "our solutions are very complicated. They are not like, 'take this pill.'" She and Hornstein added that social psychologists are trained to publish in JPSP, not to carry through the ideas or to communicate and sell these ideas to others. Without some analogy or connection to the organization, the idea is hard to sell: "work that lacks mundane reality or face validity is hard to disseminate, even if valid."

The most successful *translators* (Hackman's term) or *engineers* (as Heilman put it) are not necessarily mainstream social psychologists. Staw suggested that "consultants are the real innovators out there, and we haven't really capitalized enough on them." Hackman thought that "discipline-based people in the business schools" provide a bridge as one of their roles. Hornstein suggested that social psychologists are involved in "hands-on work in areas such as organizational development and human resource management" where they bring the social psychological paradigm but combine it with "clinical skills—know-how in working with people." Very few programs provide skills in working in such settings and successfully presenting ideas to others: Hornstein and Heilman listed a few programs that have internships such as Columbia and New York University.

Hackman most poignantly expressed the difficulties of bridging social psychology and organizational applications or problem solving. As head of a program integrating the managerially oriented Harvard Business School with the theoretically oriented psychology department, he has found there to be "two cultures" that are "hard to integrate." If anyone had thought there would be a "magic synergy," that image has given way to something more like "Which hat shall I put on?" Hopes that the students could create more integration on qualifying exams have led him to recognize that the faculty is "expecting more of our students than we would actually be capable of doing ourselves . . . You ask a business school faculty to read any topical issue of JPSP and they say, 'What do I need to read this for?' And you ask somebody over here to even pick up a *Harvard Business Review*. . . ."

The bottom line, at least from the viewpoint of business management, is what impact social psychology has already had on business organization. Staw said we have "had almost no influence on managerial practices . . . they are influenced by what's in the air, socially, culturally, economically." He later admitted that consultants "tend to pick up some" knowledge from academics and that we have "furthered some tendencies such as participative management." Hornstein suggested that *people* transfer, since "a lot of social psychologists are involved in hands-on work in organizations—organizational development and human resources," *ideas* such as group dynamics and employee participation transfer, and *technologies* transfer, such as marketing work on attitudes, survey methods, and evaluation research, and measurement technologies such as the Hackman Job Diagnostic Survey and the Vroom leadership model, but there is "minimal transfer of empirical research knowledge." Hackman said, "I am sure that it has, and constructively so, . . . but off the very tippy top of my head I can't think of a specific example."

Impact on Social Psychology

The interest in confronting social psychology with real problems stems in great measure from the goal of advancing social psychology. The Lewinian ideal generates "good theories" by the process of application. Staw expressed the concept that "when people came up against a complicated social problem, that's what stimulated interesting theory." Hornstein and Heilman suggested that problems taken from natural settings permit researchers to find "essential issues," investigate "theoretical questions implied by these issues," and "test ideas." The "input from outside . . . new problems and new challenges, are good for social psychology." Heilman added that "there are so many questions that can be raised for social psychologists as they look outside. . . . Everybody is feeding off each other without much coming from outside." Hackman asked plaintively, "what can we do to get social psychology out of the academy?" He gave examples in which laboratory-based research was enriched when it was taken into real settings, and criticized researchers who "alter or select phenomena to fit their theory. . . . We must confront phenomena as they exist."

Hot Topics

During our conversations, I tried to get some suggestions for what was seen as the most exciting work now going on in social psychology that might be applied or related to business contexts, and what business issues or problems would be stimulating for social psychologists to investigate.

Hackman suggested that the study of close interpersonal relationships could help greatly in our understanding of roles and interpersonal relationships. After all, the informal organization is built on personal relations, yet we have a "weak language" for expressing such issues. Staw suggested that social psychologists working on emotion and affect would have major impact on our understanding of job attitudes and satisfaction over the next 5 years, and maybe a later impact on business practice. Hornstein and Heilman suggested that the resurgence of groups, social phenomena in contrast to cognitive phenomena, and affect, would be helpful to the understanding of organizations.

Heilman called business organizations "a world, a microcosm, everything happens there." She added that the quality aspects of productivity, and crisis management during cataclysms such as mergers and layoffs posed interesting problems. Hackman suggested that organizations are seeking decentralized authority and effective ways to generate collective action without removing individual autonomy. Flatter organizations, more use of autonomous work teams, and other innovations create a fascinating set of issues to stimulate social psychologists. Staw identified computer-aided communications, the integration of work and family (seen more broadly than career success), and the social determinants of innovation, at individual, group and company levels, as critical business issues of interest to social psychologists. Finally,

Hornstein suggested the desirability of studying changes in the workforce—increasingly diverse populations inside organizations, and the apparent trends toward declining loyalty and commitment and increasing egocentrism. He also wondered how people developing, implementing, and supporting information systems build a relationship with internal clients, drawing upon the clients' ideas without overemphasizing their own "expert" role.

CHALLENGES FOR THE FUTURE

It seems as though there are sufficient challenges for the future. Paraphrasing a famous Chinese proverb, we live in "interesting times." Social psychology has had its "crises," but seems energetic and diverse as a discipline. The basic soundness of our orientation toward theory and empirical research, the rigor of our methodological training, and our valid interest in natural settings and institutions suggests a productive future for the field.

The interaction of social psychology and business organizations offers a healthy direction for both sides. There are challenges for social psychologists to understand real and important phenomena, to broaden our theories and methods, to work with social scientists from related disciplines, and to learn clinical skills for communicating and cooperating with managers, consultants, and other members of business organizations.

Much of our contribution to business organizations in the past has been as bearers of bad tidings. We tend to attack the justifiability of what practitioners "know." Our standards of proof are far higher than theirs, and when we use evaluation research to test a new innovation, we tend to find little evidence of improvement. Staw expressed his dream that "when we know something, it's implemented, and then evaluated *in situ.*" But for that to happen, social psychologists need to achieve a better understanding of the viewpoint of others. We need to "spend more time playing participant observer" or "walking around in organizations" and build into our graduate programs some of the clinical skills needed for dealing with people who live outside our academic "turf." We need to partner with practitioners, consultants, and "translators" who have the real-world knowledge and skills that we lack, without labeling them "unscientific" and therefore useless.

I think we are seeing the beginnings of a return to the curiosity and values of Lewin with the sophistication of the modern theorist and methodologist. Social psychologists in business organizations have an important job to do.

As a closing note, I would like to mention a story related by Staw about his teaching experience in China. Students asked whether the social scientists he mentioned in his lectures were advisors to President Reagan. They were "dumbfounded" to hear that none of these people had any policy role, and that the President's advisors were mostly lawyers and economists. The students said, "If we knew some of these things we would certainly use them." Barry suggested that in China ideology and social relations "are so pivotal to the culture and to the government decisions that they will first make decisions on what they think are the implications for the social structure and for interpersonal relations, with the economic aspects following. . . . Whereas in the United States basically we make most decisions on economic merit and then we . . . sweep up any social consequences with [corrective] programs." Perhaps we should be asking why there exist such deep divisions among the social sciences, and whether a more active and worldly stance would better serve our field, the social sciences, and society.

2

Negotiator Behavior and Decision Processes in Dyads, Groups, and Markets

Max H. Bazerman
Kellogg Graduate School of Management, Northwestern University

Elizabeth Mannix
University of Chicago and Northwestern University

Harris Sondak
Kellogg Graduate School of Management, Northwestern University

Leigh Thompson
Department of Psychology, University of Washington

Organizational and business settings inevitably involve conflict. Some of the most critical decisions facing actors in organizations involve how to behave in competitive situations. Negotiation is the process through which people who have conflicting interests jointly make decisions to resolve those conflicts. Actors in organizations must frequently negotiate with other individuals, in groups, and across larger social entities to accomplish their objectives. In this chapter, we examine decision making in competitive contexts that affect organizations and focus on how the social contexts of various competitive situations influence decision making and negotiated outcomes. We examine negotiations in dyadic relationships, group situations, and in a specific type of competitive market.

Developing the negotiation skills of organizational decision makers is increasingly important. The social structure of many organizations is becoming more lateral, and the decreased use of hierarchical decision structures requires individuals to negotiate within organizations (Brett & Rognes, 1986). Organizations are also becoming more dependent on other organizations and individuals, making negotiation a necessary process for resolving conflicts of interest between organizations.

Our approach to negotiation is both descriptive and prescriptive. Descriptively, we seek to identify systematic errors in negotiator judgment that affect

13

the quality of negotiation outcomes. Prescriptively, our focus is to develop methods to decrease these errors and improve negotiator performance. A key assumption of our analysis is that an optimal solution or a set of optimal solutions exist for a given situation. Simply put, some decisions and outcomes are better than others for all parties involved. We examine deviations from optimal negotiated agreements and discuss the factors that lead to suboptimal decision making behavior.

Economic Rationality

Fully rational behavior in individual decision making has been defined as maximizing expected utility (von Neumann & Morgenstern, 1947). Nash (1950) and Raiffa (1953; Luce & Raiffa, 1957) extended this economic definition of individual rationality to two-party contexts with their mathematical analyses of competition between fully rational actors. They noted that actors need to behave rationally, or consistently, and should also expect that the other party's behavior will be rational. Thus, competitors need to consider fully the decisions that their opponents will be making. According to these game-theoretic formulations, a fully rational negotiated agreement must be Pareto optimal so that there is no possible alternative agreement that would be preferred by both parties. In addition, game-theoretic solutions identify which Pareto optimal solution should emerge when all actors make the decisions to maximize their own utility (Nash, 1950).

We accept the game-theoretic definition of rationality. However, we do not suggest that maximizing one's own gain is an individual's only possible motivation. Rather, our discussion is restricted to social relations that involve social exchange (cf. Clark & Mills, 1979). In exchange relationships, an individual's primary concern is with his or her own stock of benefits; goods are given to others, for example, with the expectation that a debt is thereby incurred and that this debt will be repaid. In communal relationships, individuals are concerned with each other's welfare; goods are given to others because those others are in need. In this chapter we limit our discussion to relationships that are based on exchange because exchange relationships are common in contemporary society and because our focus is on negotiation in business settings, where exchange relationships are the rule.

Human Judgment and Decision Making

Despite the clarity of the economic model of rationality, a large body of research suggests that human judgment is not fully rational. Thirty years ago, Simon (1957; March & Simon, 1958) suggested that the economic model of decision making is not an accurate view of individual decision processes and that limitations in ability, knowledge, and time constrain the rationality of human judgment. Recent studies have demonstrated systematic and predictable ways in which judgment deviates from rationality (cf. Bazerman, 1986; Kahneman, Slovic, & Tversky, 1982; Nisbett & Ross, 1980).

The traditional assumption in economic models of two-person negotiation games is that bargainers know the entire set of possible outcomes and one another's utilities for each possible agreement and act rationally with this information. However, in most real-life contexts, and in some recent game-theoretic formulations, negotiators do not have complete information and instead negotiate under uncertainty. Raiffa (1982) recognized the need for negotiators to consider deviations from rationality in the behavior of their opponents. Not only does the behavior of opponents deviate from rationality, however, so does that of the focal negotiator. Experimental evidence shows that there are considerable discrepancies between negotiator behavior and the predictions of game theoretic models (for a review see Roth & Malouf, 1982).

Because game theory does not adequately describe the behavior of individuals in most social contexts, researchers have developed other models to describe competitive behavior. These approaches include personality and motivational models (cf. Greenhalgh, Neslin, & Gilkey, 1985; Pruitt & Rubin, 1986; Rubin & Brown, 1975); situational approaches (cf. Carnevale & Isen, 1986; Yukl, 1974); and decision-making approaches (cf. Bazerman & Neale, 1983; Thompson & Hastie, 1988a). The discussion in this chapter is based on a decision-making approach that addresses many limitations of game-theoretic models. In addition, the decision-making perspective explains negotiation behavior across a wide variety of persons and situations (Bazerman & Carroll, 1987). In contrast to most studies of decision making based on individual behavior in static, nonsocial settings (cf. Abelson & Levi, 1985), this chapter examines negotiator judgment in dynamic social settings.

The goals of the decision-making approach are to identify systematic errors in negotiators' judgments, determine the conditions that lead to faulty judgment, and examine the relationship between the accuracy of negotiators' judgments and behavior. The descriptive focus of the decision-making approach is to identify factors that lead negotiators to make errors in the perception, processing, and retrieval of information. Errors in perception include the tendency to ignore relevant information and to seek information selectively (Chapman & Chapman, 1967); errors in information processing include the tendency to misinterpret information and to draw invalid inferences (Ross, 1977; Ross, Green, & House, 1977); errors in the retrieval of information include selective and reconstructive retrieval of information (Snyder & Uranowitz, 1978). The prescriptive focus of the decision-making perspective is to develop methods to decrease negotiators' errors in judgment and to increase their performance.

In the sections that follow, we discuss competitive decision making in three social contexts: dyads, groups, and competitive markets. In each of these contexts, we identify optimal behaviors and outcomes, analyze how actual behavior in real situations deviates from optimal behavior, and examine the factors that lead to suboptimal competitive behavior. These three contexts are used to highlight the conceptual issues raised as we move from examining rationality in the individual to examining rationality in more complex social settings. Throughout our discussion, we refer to fictitious situations faced by Chris Carlson, a manager of a profit center in a large electronics firm. The nature of Carlson's job, like that of most managers, includes a variety of negotiations.

NEGOTIATOR BEHAVIOR IN DYADS

> Chris Carlson is the head of the audio products division of a large electronics firm. Recently, in developing a new sound system, Carlson's division discovered a magnetic material that will improve the quality of a variety of audio products. Even more important, there exists the potential for a huge market for the magnetic material itself. However, the audio products division cannot make magnets as efficiently as the magnetics division. Thus, it is in the best interest of the corporation for the magnetics division to manufacture the magnetic material. Further, the audio products division is barred by company charter from selling magnets outside the company; this right belongs to the magnetics division. The conflict that Carlson faces is how to negotiate a mutually acceptable agreement with the head of the magnetics division concerning the development and sale of the magnetic material.

Dyadic negotiations involve disputes between two parties. These parties may be individuals representing their own interests or representatives of larger groups. In this example, Carlson will negotiate on behalf of the audio products division. The important features of dyadic negotiation include the number of issues, the interests of the parties, and the bargaining zone as defined by the negotiators' resistance points. These fundamental elements of dyadic negotiation are also important for more complex multiparty negotiations.

Negotiations vary in terms of the number of issues involved. Single-issue negotiations are known as distributive or purely competitive negotiations in which the gain to one party comes at the direct expense of the other party. The distributive aspect is present in every negotiation and refers to how negotiators allocate scarce resources among themselves. However, when negotiations involve more than one issue, as do most negotiations, the potential for integrative agreement exists (Bazerman, 1986; Pruitt & Rubin, 1986; Raiffa, 1982).

Integrative negotiations are mixed motive in nature as they have both competitive and cooperative aspects. Negotiators are motivated to cooperate to increase the amount of available resources, which decreases the probability of impasse, but negotiators are also motivated to compete with the other party to claim most of the resources (Lewicki & Litterer, 1985; Rubin & Brown, 1975; Walton & McKersie, 1965). Integrative agreements create higher joint benefit than do simple compromises, in which parties concede along obvious dimensions to a middle ground (Walton & McKersie, 1965); a fully integrative agreement is Pareto optimal. In integrative negotiations, negotiators increase the total amount of resources to be divided through the creative search for solutions. There are several ways negotiators may expand the amount of available resources (cf. Pruitt, 1983). A common strategy used by negotiators is logrolling (Froman & Cohen, 1970). To logroll effectively, negotiators need to identify more than one bargaining issue, have divergent interests concerning the relative importance of the issues, and agree to trade off one issue for the other, such that each party concedes on issues of little importance to themselves while making large gains on issues of greater importance.

Even when negotiation situations provide opportunities for integrative agreements, negotiators often settle for compromise or distributive agreements (Bazerman, Magliozzi, & Neale, 1985; Pruitt & Rubin, 1986). In the following sections, we identify the judgments that negotiators make about the self and the other party that lead them to fail to reach integrative agreements and leave valuable resources on the table.

Rationality in Dyadic Negotiations

The rationality of negotiation behavior and outcomes may be assessed in three ways. First, negotiators should reach an agreement if their preferences define a positive bargaining zone. The bargaining zone is defined by negotiators' resistance points, or the points beyond which negotiators prefer impasse to agreement. A positive bargaining zone exists if negotiators' resistance points overlap, whereas a negative bargaining zone exists if negotiators' resistance points do not overlap. For example, Carlson may have the ability to prevent the magnetics division from producing the new material and thus restrict sales to the internal market. Based on projected internal sales, Carlson may calculate a resistance point of expected profits for audio products of $1 million. This option, however, may not maximize Carlson's gain and is likely to be challenged by the head of the magnetics division and taken to a higher level in the organization. Thus, if Carlson can arrange an agreement with the magnetics division that would benefit both parties more than if they did not have an agreement, they should reach an agreement. Many negotiators fail to reach agreement even when a positive bargaining zone exists

(Bazerman & Neale, 1982; Pruitt, 1983; Raiffa, 1982). When both negotiators have attractive resistance points, a mutually acceptable agreement
may only be found through nonobvious creative solutions, such as logrolling.
In some cases, motivational concerns, such as the fear of appearing weak by
conceding on some issues as logrolling requires, may prevent negotiators from
reaching an integrative agreement.

A second index of negotiator rationality is the extent to which an agreement takes advantage of the integrative potential of the situation, or the
efficiency of the agreement. An inefficient agreement may occur if one or
both parties falsely assume that the other party's interests are opposed to their
own and do not bother to test these assumptions. For example, Carlson may
falsely assume that the magnetics division wants to produce the product for
immediate sale, but magnetics may really want to delay external sales until
more research and development is conducted. If this common interest remains hidden, Carlson and the head of the magnetics division may reach an
agreement in which magnetics will pay audio products $1.2 million and
produce the magnetic material for immediate sale, although both parties
would have preferred to delay the date of external sales.

A third index of negotiator rationality concerns the amount of resources a
negotiator is able to claim personally. Game-theoretic analysis states that if
there exists no difference in the relative power of the two bargainers, they
should divide the resources equally (Nash, 1950). However, bargainers rarely
know the worth of an agreement to the other party and symmetric or equita-
ble outcomes are difficult or impossible to identify. Negotiators must balance
their desire to maximize their own outcomes with the need to maximize the
total or joint amount of resources. The dual tasks of creating and claiming
resources are difficult to coordinate (Lax & Sebenius, 1986; McAlister,
Bazerman, & Fader, 1986). This coordination becomes especially difficult
when negotiators bargain on behalf of larger constituencies and when concern for the overall good is critical to continued individual success. For
example, Carlson needs to expand the amount of available resource to be
divided, which benefits the company as a whole, while trying to claim as
many resources as possible for the audio products division.

Limitations on Negotiator Rationality

The task of reaching a negotiated agreement that is mutually acceptable,
efficient, and personally satisfying is a formidable one. Research and common
experience both suggest that negotiators frequently fail to reach agreements
that satisfy these three conditions of rationality. Inefficient negotiation processes may lead to a number of undesirable, costly, and sometimes disastrous
outcomes. Ineffective negotiation processes are particularly detrimental to

organizations in business settings. It is important for organizational actors to examine their negotiating behavior and identify ways to improve their performance. We believe that negotiators frequently fail to reach fully optimal agreements because of inaccurate judgments they make about themselves and the other party.

Judgments of the Self. There are several judgments that negotiators make about their own interests and behavior that may impede the effectiveness of their bargaining. The first of these concerns negotiators' preferences—negotiators may not know what their interests are. Negotiators may not know which issues are relevant to the negotiation, how to evaluate the relative importance of the issues, which alternatives they prefer for a given issue, or their resistance points.

At first glance, it may seem surprising that negotiators would not have a clear notion of their preferences, but a large literature in social psychology suggests that individuals' attitudes are often ambiguous (Bem, 1967). Individuals often infer their own attitudes and preferences from their perceptions of the environment, their own overt behavior, and the behavior of others (Chaiken & Baldwin, 1981). Individuals are more likely to have clear preferences regarding issues that are familiar, simple, and personally experienced (Fazio & Zanna, 1981; Fischhoff, Slovic, & Lichtenstein, 1980; Petty & Cacioppo, 1981). Negotiators who fail to prepare properly for a negotiation by carefully examining their interests and alternatives are especially likely not to know what their interests are. Chris Carlson needs to determine what arrangement would best serve the audio products division in terms of production, internal sales, and external sales before going to speak with the head of the magnetics division.

Negotiators who are unsure about their interests may base their judgments of their own interests on their perceptions of the interests of the other party. Such negotiators may assume that whatever the other party says is important must be the focal issue in the negotiation, especially when the adversary does not offer concessions (Stillinger & Ross, 1987); if the other party does make concessions, these will be undervalued. Thus trading off issues for integrative gains will be particularly difficult for these negotiators and they may reach unnecessary impasses.

One of the most critical judgments that negotiators make concerns the identification of their resistance points (Walton & McKersie, 1965). Before negotiation, bargainers must assess their best alternatives to negotiated agreements and translate this assessment into specific values at which they should walk away from negotiations and implement their alternatives. For example, Carlson may decide that $1 million is the least payment that the audio products division should receive for transferring the production rights of the new material to the magnetics division. At any value less than this amount,

Carlson would be willing to refuse to transfer production rights and decide to sell the product only internally.

A variety of considerations affect the identification of a negotiator's resistance point and when a negotiator will prefer to reach impasse rather than agreement. An important factor is the way negotiators frame the negotiation outcomes. For example, do negotiators frame the negotiation in terms of losses or gains? Negotiators who perceive themselves as maximizing their gains complete more transactions and earn higher payoffs than do negotiations who perceive themselves as minimizing losses (Bazerman et al., 1985; Neale & Northcraft, 1986). Within a single negotiation, bargainers may frame some issues in terms of losses and others in terms of gains. This may lead negotiators to be loss averse, or overweight the importance of the issues involving losses. When negotiators overemphasize the relative importance of the "loss" issues, they tend to earn lower payoffs (Thompson & Hastie, 1988a).

Another framing effect occurs because of the salience of negotiation related costs (Neale, 1984). When the costs related to agreement are salient, negotiators tend to be less willing to concede and more likely to reach a stalemate. When the costs related to impasse are salient, however, negotiators tend to be more willing to concede and more likely to form an agreement.

A major limitation on the quality of negotiated agreements concerns the relationship between judgment and behavior. Negotiators may have clear interests, but fail to transform their interests into actions and behaviors that serve their interests. Thus, it is possible that negotiators may be in partial or complete agreement, but perceive conflict because of behavior that is inconsistent with that agreement (Hammond, Stewart, Brehmer, & Steinman, 1975). Negotiators may not know how to achieve their interests, or they may fall victim to situational circumstances that lead them to disregard or readjust their priorities temporarily in a manner that is inconsistent with their long-term goals (Schelling, 1984). Inconsistency between judgment and behavior may result in failure to achieve one's negotiation goals; further, integrative agreements will be difficult to create because negotiators are inappropriately "signalling" the other party (Thompson, 1988).

A final judgment that negotiators make that influences the quality of their outcomes is the confidence level negotiators implicitly or explicitly attach to their judgments of the likely outcomes. A general conclusion is that individuals display overconfidence in these judgments (Einhorn & Hogarth, 1978). For example, negotiators tend to be overly confident that they will attain their aspiration value, and they are overconfident in their estimations of winning a favorable agreement from arbitration (Bazerman & Neale, 1982). Overconfidence may lead to a number of ineffective negotiation decisions. For example, negotiators may escalate their commitment to a course of action that may result in mutually disastrous consequences (Bazerman, 1986).

Judgments of the Other Party.   There are a variety of judgments that negotiators make about the other party during negotiation (cf. Thompson &
Hastie, 1988a). Probably the most important influence on judgment and
behavior in negotiation is the negotiator's perception of the interests of the
other party. There are three key judgments that negotiators make about the
other party's interests. First, negotiators must determine the other party's
evaluation of the relative importance of the issues. This judgment is important because if the two parties have different perceptions of the importance of
the negotiation issues, then an integrative solution is possible through
logrolling.

Bazerman and Neale (1983) suggested that negotiations often assume that
the amount of resources is a fixed sum that must be divided in a win–lose
manner rather than assume that integrative potential exists. A key question
concerns whether these judgments affect negotiators' performance and outcomes. Thompson and Hastie (1988b) examined the relationship between
the accuracy of negotiators' judgments of the other party's interests and
negotiation payoffs and found that judgment accuracy determined negotiation success. Although most negotiators initially expected that the other
party's interests were directly opposed to their own, many negotiators learned
about the potential for joint gain during negotiation. Further, the time at
which negotiators learn about the other party's interests affects negotiation
success. Negotiators who actively seek information from the other party
about their interests in the early phases of negotiation are more likely to earn
higher payoffs than are those who learn about the other party's interests
during the later stages of bargaining (Thompson & Hastie, 1988b).

A second judgment that negotiators make about the other party concerns
their perception of the presence or absence of conflict on the various issues
being negotiated. Negotiators may assume that the other party's interests are
totally incompatible with their own even when their interests may be completely compatible (Thompson, 1988). For example, Carlson may want to
prohibit external sale of the magnetic material for a long time in order to
keep it from audio products' competitors. Similarly, the head of the magnetics division may also want to delay external sales because of continuing
research efforts. However, each party may erroneously assume that the other
wants to "get the product out" as soon as possible and enjoy quick returns on
the sales. Such a faulty judgment would lead to a suboptimal agreement.
Negotiators who assume their interests are incompatible with the other party
when they are perfectly compatible make an *incompatibility error.*

An incompatibility error occurs in many real-life negotiation situations
(Fisher & Ury, 1981; Lax & Sebenius, 1986). Fisher and Ury (1981) claim

that shared interests are present in every negotiation. Lax and Sebenius (1986) describe several cases in which resolutions yield simultaneous gain to two parties who prefer the identical position (e.g., one spouse of a divorcing couple desires custody of the child and the other really does not; a new agency head wants to fire some current employees and the legislative body wants to significantly cut funding). Incompatibility errors represent a serious and costly judgment error because they lead negotiators to fail to reach agreements that both would clearly prefer. A substantial number of negotiators settle for suboptimal agreements because they fail to realize that they have interests that are completely compatible with those of the other party (Thompson & Hastie, 1988b).

A third type of judgment that negotiators make about the other party concerns their perceptions of the other parties' resistance points (Raiffa, 1982). A key task in negotiation is to identify the resistance point of the other party but to conceal one's own (Raiffa, 1982). The negotiator's objective is twofold: First, negotiators should assess the other party's resistance point to determine whether a positive bargaining zone exists. If the bargaining zone is negative, the negotiator will save valuable time and effort by not engaging in a frustrating bargaining session; in this situation, time is better spent trying to improve one's alternatives. Second, negotiators who know the other party's resistance point can make an offer that is just barely acceptable to the other party. This will allow the negotiator to claim a large share of the joint resources.

Prescriptions for Dyadic Negotiation in Organizations

Our conclusion is that effective dyadic negotiation behavior is primarily limited by faulty perceptions of one's own and the other party's interests. Faulty perceptions may be reduced with more preparation prior to negotiation; negotiators should identify important issues, thoroughly evaluate alternatives, and determine their resistance points. Negotiators should do this for themselves and also for the other party. In many cases, information is available about the other party that will inform negotiators' judgments. During negotiation, bargainers should test the validity of their assumptions about the other party's interests. This is a difficult task, and there are at least three factors that may lead to inaccurate judgment during negotiation (Thompson, 1988). First, error may arise because individuals are poor at making judgments even when they are provided with information and cues. Thus, even though a substantial amount of information is available during negotiation such as the disclosures of the other party, the other party's opening offer, and their concession patterns, negotiators may fail to perceive this information or misconstrue it. In this sense, judgment error represents a perceptual, decoding error on the part of the perceiver. For example, the magnetics division may reveal information about their interests, alternatives, priorities, and even resistance points, but Carlson may fail to perceive it accurately.

A second way error may arise is from an individual's failure to provide relevant information or clues to the person making the judgment. The creation of integrative agreements requires that parties reveal information about their interests. If parties do not reveal information about their interests, their opponents may become confused and will have inaccurate perceptions. In this case, faulty judgment represents an encoding or signalling error. Thus, Carlson should make clear to the head of the magnetics division which issues the audio products division considers to be the most important. However, Carlson should be careful not to reveal the resistance point of the audio products division, unless it is extremely attractive and likely to induce the magnetics division to agree to the terms that Carlson desires.

Finally, error may arise from a more complex process resulting from the failure of individuals to seek or elicit relevant, diagnostic information to inform their judgments. Negotiators often fail to seek information because they are overconfident in their judgments of the other's interests, they may not know what to do with the information, or they fear that the other party will seek information from them in exchange that they do not want to reveal. Carlson may use explicit methods to seek information such as asking direct questions, or implicit methods such as making several offers for the head of the magnetics division to evaluate. Accurate information seeking and signalling lead to more accurate judgments and better performance (Thompson, 1988). In conclusion, the tasks necessary to reach optimal negotiation agreements are complex, and the quality of negotiation outcomes depends critically on the accuracy of negotiators' judgments of the self and the other party.

NEGOTIATOR BEHAVIOR IN GROUPS

Chris Carlson's corporation has decided that it is time to replace the computer system for five of its largest divisions. Carlson and the heads of the magnetic, lighting, automotive products, and hospital products divisions are the members of the task force assigned to this project. The new system will eventually allow the divisions to take advantage of their interdependence, and thus increase everyone's efficiency. In addition, the new system will help each division individually, allowing faster and more complex data analysis and information retrieval. However, because the conversion will be quite expensive, both in terms of hardware and in computer personnel, the conversion will be accomplished in stages. The task force is to set priorities for the installation and

allocation of the new system. The task force members must reach an agreement
that all five divisions will accept and that is consistent from an organizational
viewpoint. Carlson is most concerned that the arrangements agreed to will
benefit the audio products division.

Group negotiation is a decision-making process in which three or more
people make decisions to resolve conflicting interests (Brett & Rognes, 1986;
Thompson, Mannix, & Bazerman, 1988). Individuals in organizations engage in group negotiation as a pervasive aspect of formal as well as everyday
social interaction (Lewicki & Litterer, 1985). Organizational groups may
include entire organizations, intraorganizational task forces, department
heads, decentralized divisions, or chief executive officers and their boards of
directors. When several parties are involved in a negotiation, complexities
arise that are not present in dyadic negotiations. The opportunities to find
creative agreements and expand the pie of resources tend to be greater in
groups than in dyads, but the process by which integrative agreements are
accomplished, and the allocation of resources, may be more difficult.

Decision Making and Rationality in Groups

Social psychology has identified four methods by which decision making
occurs in small groups: superordinate goals, majority rule, coalition formation, and negotiation (Brett, 1985). Although our focus is on negotiation, a
complete discussion of small group behavior should include the impact of
various decision rules and coalition formation.

Mixed-motive groups are often characterized by the presence of a superordinate goal that conflicts to some degree with the preferences of individual
group members. In many cases a superordinate goal is not strong enough to
drive the process of group decision making (Brett, 1985). Group members
may be unable to agree on a definition of the common goal, perhaps because
they view the organization through the different lenses of their departments
or functions. A divergence of time perspectives, reward structures, intra- and
interorganizational dependencies, technologies, and different organizational
subcultures can alter the perception of organizational goals. In other instances, although group members may be able to agree on the superordinate
goal, they still may not have identical preferences regarding how to achieve
this goal. The superordinate goal may also involve several components each
of which has unique importance for various group members. The presence of
some commonality of goals is necessary for the existence of a mixed-motive
group, but is insufficient to account for the agreement process completely,
leaving majority rule, coalition formation, and negotiation as possible decision-making procedures.

Rational decision making in groups may be defined in terms of the decision-making processes and outcomes of the individual actors and in terms of the quality of the overall negotiated agreement (Kahan & Rappaport, 1984). Organizational actors involved in group negotiation should seek to improve their own gain, the gain to the group, and, in the intraorganizational case, the gain to the overall organization. By seeking integrative agreements the available pie of resources is increased, allowing group members with very high aspirations, who might otherwise be unable to reach mutually acceptable agreements, to find agreements that meet their aspirations (Pruitt & Rubin, 1986). Integrative agreements can also be good for the surrounding community in which they take place: They may strengthen the relationship between negotiators, increase commitment to the agreement, and thus increase the likelihood of implementation. However, organizational members may find it difficult to focus simultaneously on the concerns of themselves and the group, because to do so is to focus at once both on integration and distribution.

Moving From the Dyad to the Multiparty Context

One superordinate goal for Carlson's task force is to get the new computing system operating in all five divisions, beginning with the divisions that are most essential. However, it is not obvious which divisions should be given priority, and several arguments might be made in favor of any of them according to need, size, degree of interdependence, past practice, or even random assignment. In addition, as each representative attempts to fulfill his or her own agenda, the definition of the task may vary. Whereas it may be obvious to the group members that they are in conflict, it may be difficult for them to recognize that each division must reveal its interests and make concessions on issues of lower priority in order to receive concessions from other divisions in return.

Although the potential to expand the pie may increase as the number of people and issues increase, there are many reasons to expect that three or more individuals will have more difficulty integrating their interests than dyads. Factors that distinguish group negotiation from two-party negotiation include increased information processing demands, more complex interpersonal dynamics, and the need for management and structure of the negotiating process (Bazerman, Mannix, & Thompson, 1988).

Information Processing. Although having additional individuals in a group provides greater creative opportunity and problem-solving capabilities, group decision-making processes place greater information-processing demands on negotiations than do dyadic processes. The group context requires an understanding of multiple parties, each with different interests, goals, and strategies. Feedback about group members' preferences and priorities is critical to group problem solving, but the amount of feedback regarding each group member decreases as the number of parties increases (Shaw, 1981).

An example of the increased cognitive complexity that occurs in groups is the assessment of the bargaining zone. The members of Carlson's task force may not have the time or resources necessary to obtain information about each members' interests and alternatives to a negotiated agreement. As such, they may falsely conclude that the other members' interests are more similar than they really are because the known interests of one member may be used to anchor judgments of the interests of others.

Translating individual preferences to a group preference is an important but problematic group decision-making process. According to Arrow's Theorem, there is no guarantee that a group preference order, arrived at either formally or informally, will be transitive, even if transitivity exists for the individual preferences of the group members (Arrow, 1963; Ordeshook, 1986). In the Carlson example, assume that each member of the task force is able to rank each of the five divisions in a transitive manner in terms of when they should be converted (transitivity implies that A > B > C, therefore A > C). This does not ensure that a group ranking will also be transitive. For example, the group ranking may result in an ordering such that; A > B > C > A. Therefore, even if group members are able to discover and clearly rank their preferences, a rational decision may not result. Indeed, group members may neither be able to determine whether an optimal solution exists nor how to achieve it.

Interpersonal Dynamics.   In addition to the complex cognitive demands placed on individuals in group negotiations, interpersonal dynamics become more complex as the number of parties increases. For example, if in a dyadic negotiation one party makes what is perceived by the other party to be an unreasonable demand, the other party may feel free to challenge this behavior directly. However, in the multiparty case, the same negotiator may feel uncertain whether to respond directly. Social psychological research suggests that as the number of individuals in a group increases, individuals tend to look to the group to determine appropriate behavior and to conform more to the behavior of other group members (Asch, 1946; Janis, 1982; Milgram, Backman, & Berkowitz, 1969). As the number of individuals increases in a negotiation, negotiators are more likely to be victims of *groupthink* (Janis, 1982), and less likely to promote their own views. This effect may be stronger in certain types of groups, such as groups with directive leadership or those that are highly cohesive, although empirical findings have been inconclusive (Cartwright, 1978; Flowers, 1978). Related to groupthink is the phenomenon of *pluralistic ignorance*. This problem occurs when group members fall victim to the illusion of unanimity, becoming afraid to voice their interests because they erroneously believe themselves to be the sole dissenter (Schank, 1932). As a result, it may be more likely for individual preferences and priorities to remain hidden in groups than in dyads, making trade-offs and therefore integrative agreements less likely.

Power or bargaining strength is an important factor in group negotiations; Bacharach and Lawler (1980) call power the essence of bargaining. In exchange relationships, power can be represented by the contributions an individual makes to the group. The power structure in dyads is less complex than the power structure in groups because fewer relationships are possible. In groups, however, the power structure can be quite complex, affecting coalition formation and the distribution of group resources.

Power in social exchange relationships may be broadly defined as the inverse of dependence; the more dependent A is on B for his or her outcomes, and the more A values those outcomes, the more power B has over A (Emerson, 1964). Although various researchers and theorists have defined power differently (Emerson, 1964; French, 1956; Lewin, 1951; Thibaut & Kelley, 1959), there is a common focus on interaction. In groups, power as dependence cannot be examined simply in terms of one relationship, but as the network of relationships that encompass each particular dyadic relationship (Bacharach & Lawler, 1980; McAlister et al., 1986).

Power alone is not solely responsible for outcomes, however. Another important factor that affects the nature of outcomes in group negotiation is the impact of justice norms (Komorita & Hamilton, 1984). In attempting to maximize one's own outcome, or to reach a mutually acceptable agreement, negotiators such as the members of Carlson's task force must be aware of the various norms of distribution. This is more difficult as the number of negotiators increases, because several different norms may apply to the same situation; the greater the number of members in a group, the greater the number of potential operative norms. Distribution based on equality (Ashenfelder & Bloom, 1984), formalized egalitarianism (Rawls, 1971), equity (Adams, 1963; Homans, 1961), need, or effort are common norms of resource allocation. Researchers have also suggested that past practice is a critical way that people make judgments about the fairness of distribution in conflict situations (Bazerman, 1985; Kahneman, Knetsch, & Thaler, 1986).

Norms interact with the negotiator's power to affect the ability of a group member to maximize his or her outcome (Komorita & Hamilton, 1984). For example, if the members of Carlson's task force have clearly unequal power levels, those in positions of higher power (with high levels of inputs) are likely to demand distribution based on equity, whereas those in low power positions are likely to prefer equal distribution (Komorita & Chertkoff, 1973; Shaw, 1981).

The power structure in groups is likely to influence the formation of coalitions and result in the opportunity for moderate and low power players to improve their bargaining position with strategic tactics. Under conditions of majority rule, when more than one dichotomous issue is being considered, forming coalitions is a likely method by which group members gain power and increase their share of the pie of resources, because seemingly low power group members are able to unite and exclude the apparently powerful individuals from the final group decision (Thompson et al., 1988). The possibility of forming coalitions forces group members to be aware of the preference compatibility on every issue among all members of the group. Group members who seem to have completely incompatible preferences may in fact have similar preferences on an isolated issue, leading them to form single-issue coalitions (Murnighan, 1986).

Coalition members must manage issues internal to the coalition, such as the distribution of gains, balancing the size of the coalition with the size of the payoffs, and continually negotiating side payments to keep members satisfied. Group members must also manage issues external to the coalition, such as recruiting new members, fending off attempts by outsiders to disrupt the inherently unstable coalition, assessing the strength of other coalitions, and looking for related issues that might need coalitional support. Group members must also be aware that by attempting to initiate coalitions they communicate dependence, whereas group members who have several coalition alternatives have less dependence and therefore increased power.

A difficulty with coalition formation in some groups is that it may lead to suboptimal agreements. Negotiation theorists have argued that decision makers will use the easiest decision-making procedure available to them that will result in an agreement (Pruitt, 1981). The process by which coalitions actually form may involve negotiation, but once a coalition is in the majority, the decision-making process has no need for negotiation, and may rely solely on majority rule. Coalition behavior may decrease the likelihood that group members will engage in problem solving and instead focus on distributional concerns. Bacharach and Lawler (1980) have argued that intercoalition negotiation stresses the distributive rather than the integrative aspects of negotiations. An unequal power balance leads groups members to focus on the norms of distribution, rather than on ways in which joint outcome might be increased, overwhelming the search for an integrative agreement.

Management and Structure. When more than two individuals attempt to reach a mutually acceptable decision, there is the need for coordination and management of the group. In the group decision-making literature there are several structural techniques used to promote group management that may lead to biased judgment and nonrational group decisions. In some instances these techniques limit the negotiators' ability to recognize or identify that a bargaining space exists and result in unnecessary impasses. More often they tend to limit the ability of the group to reach integrative agreements. We discuss here the implications of social decision rules, issue agendas, and formalized group decision-making techniques.

Carlson's task force, as a group with more than two members, must adopt a social decision rule to combine the individual preferences of the group members. This process may be either implicit or explicit. The most common methods of social choice are majority and unanimity rule (Hare, 1976). Decision rules are not a concern in dyads, which have an implicit unanimous decision rule. Groups often use majority rule because of its ease and efficiency in reaching decisions (cf. Harnett, 1967; Hastie, Penrod, & Pennington, 1983; Ordeshook, 1986). Many researchers argue that majority rule is preferable to unanimity rule because it is less time consuming and allows groups to avoid impasses that may be undesirable for some groups.

When there are more than two issues to be negotiated, majority rule is subject to numerous methods of strategic manipulation and paradoxes of voting that decrease the likelihood of an integrative outcome (Chechile, 1984; Plott, 1976). Many of these stem from Arrow's rule that makes the translation of individual to group preferences problematic. One example of a voting paradox associated with majority rule is the cyclical majority problem (May, 1982). When alternatives are voted on sequentially in pairs, the alternatives voted upon later are more likely to win. The alternative finally chosen may not actually be the solution most preferred by the majority and might lose if matched pairwise against a previously defeated alternative. Indeed, it has been argued that under some preference structures, one can manipulate a majority rule system to yield any outcome (Ordeshook, 1986).

Majority rule systems also fail to recognize the strengths of individual preferences (Kaplan & Miller, 1983) and may exclude the desires of some group members completely (Castore & Murnighan, 1978). Deviants from the majority opinion are more easily excluded under majority rule and efforts to include their concerns in the final decision are less likely. There are certainly exceptions to this outcome, as exhibited by the work on minority influence done by Moscovici and his colleagues who treat behavioral style, rather than social dependence, as the fundamental social influence mechanism (Moscovici, 1980).

Majority rule leads group members to compromise rather than to create integrative agreements (Thompson et al., 1988). When majority rule is in effect, it is not necessary to satisfy all group members. As a result, *satisficing* occurs (Simon, 1957), in which group members stop when they reach an agreement that is acceptable to a majority of the group members, rather than continuing the often difficult search for an optimal agreement.

Organizing agendas are a second factor that the task force might implement to structure their decision making. Agendas are procedures that determine the order in which negotiation issues will be raised, discussed, and decided upon in the decision-making process, and are likely to affect the decision making of negotiators in groups (Fishburn, 1974; Levine & Plott, 1977; Plott & Levine, 1978). When agendas are followed strictly, issues are considered individually and not reintroduced once the next topic has been raised. Agendas are often viewed as an aid to rational and effective decision making. Many researchers argue that groups function best under agendas that set the boundaries, timing, and order of their discussions (Phillips, 1965).

Research on dyads and groups has shown that agendas, which force issues to be discussed sequentially, result in decisions that are not fully integrative (Erickson, Holmes, Frey, Walker, & Thibaut, 1974; Kelley, 1966; Mannix, Thompson, & Bazerman, in press; Pruitt, 1981; Yukl, Malone, Hayslip, & Pamin, 1976). Whereas dyads may use agendas when they are confronted with multiple issues, their detrimental effect is likely to be enhanced in groups. Because groups have more difficulty coordinating interests and priorities than do pairs of negotiators, agendas make it extremely difficult for group members to trade-off issues or suggest other creative approaches to problems, reducing the likelihood of an integrative agreement (Mannix et al., in press). Additionally, individuals in groups may manipulate agendas to exploit the interests of other parties, and reap exorbitant and possibly inappropriate personal gains, thereby limiting integrative potential (Chechile, 1984; Ordeshook, 1986; Plott & Levine, 1978).

Several techniques have been developed that are available to the task force, with the aim of managing and coordinating the group decision-making process. These include *brainstorming* (Osborn, 1957), the *Delphi technique* (Linstone & Turoff, 1975), *nominal group technique* (Delbecq, Van de Ven, & Gustafson, 1975), and PERT (Phillips, 1970). The goal of most of these procedures is to help groups make rational decisions by reducing or eliminating common biases that occur in group decision making. Each of these techniques provides structure by defining the problem and describing a method to generate, discuss, and evaluate solutions. Group techniques often reduce the hostilities and pressures toward conformity that commonly occur in group negotiation. The problem with these formalized group decision-making techniques is that they may function as substitutes for negotiation. Unfortunately, they tend to limit the exchange of opinion and information (cf. Bazerman et al., 1988). Many of these techniques limit or eliminate face-to-face communication among group members, preventing the discovery of the preference orders and priorities of others. The simultaneous discussion and logrolling of issues is hindered and the problem-solving discussions necessary for mutually beneficial agreements are discouraged. Potential trade-offs are never revealed, opportunities to expand the pie of resources are lost, and rational outcomes are less likely to occur.

Prescriptions for Group Negotiations in Organizations

We can make several suggestions to Carlson to increase the potential for an integrative agreement that also maximizes the gain to Carlson's division. In this intraorganizational task force a superordinate goal can be applied which will help define the issues. This common goal serves to focus the group on the importance of collective as well as individual gains, but is unlikely by itself to resolve the conflict. To move beyond this point, Carlson should begin with extensive preparation; Carlson is likely to spend more time preparing for the negotiation than actually negotiating. Preparation will include assessing and possibly diagramming the power structure of the group, as well as what justice norms might be operative. This information may be based on past interactions with the task force members, or by probing group members or knowledgeable others prior to the actual meeting. Carlson should also gather information before the meeting regarding the interests and priorities of the other group members in order to identify all the priorities of the other group members in order to identify all the relevant issues, possible trade-offs, and potential coalition partners. This information is crucial, for without it Carlson may falsely conclude that other parties' interests are more narrow or more similar than they actually are, thus reducing the likelihood of beneficial trade-offs.

For example, Carlson may have information that the head of the lighting division is willing to relax demands for immediate conversion if allowed an increase in the eventual allotment of computer hardware. Based on this information, Carlson may assume that the head of automotive products will also be willing to make this trade-off. In reality, automotive products is not at all interested in more hardware. This may impede Carlson's strategy unless Carlson is aware of other issues that might be important to automotive products. For example, automotive products would be willing to trade the time of conversion for additional computer training personnel during the conversion. Carlson's power in the negotiation will be improved if these other issues and priorities are known prior to the negotiation. Carlson's assumptions will affect the development of an agreement that recognizes trade-offs and that takes advantage of the potential gains available to the group.

In the actual negotiation, Carlson should be aware of the implications of the decision rule invoked and the agenda that is used. The group should avoid the use of issue agendas, especially if Carlson's firm tends to follow a majority decision rule. An issue agenda could easily ignore automotive products' desire for more training personnel, thus reducing integrative potential. If the group needs some structure, Carlson might suggest replacing issue agendas with a problem-solving agenda where group members may structure the decision-making process by identifying priorities, revealing individual interests, and suggesting creative approaches to problems (Bazerman et al., 1988). Before making prescriptions regarding group problem-solving processes, the nature of the group task must be identified. That is, is the task competitive, cooperative, or mixed-motive? Will an impasse be unacceptable and is time pressure particularly strong? These and the other issues discussed in this section will help negotiators prepare for and structure group negotiations that will lead to rational agreements.

NEGOTIATOR BEHAVIOR IN MARKETS

> This year Chris Carlson is serving as a member of the audio products division's recruiting committee. The division has several entry level management positions and is recruiting MBA's from several prominent universities. Carlson's electronics firm is one of several in a large midwestern city and the division's recruiters are competing with other firms who are hiring this year. The recruiting committee hopes that the new managers will fit well with their firm's culture and will remain with the firm.

In addition to dyadic and small group contexts, negotiators often are in situations that involve many people. In trying to achieve their interests, negotiators may need to select among various people in order to find the best fit. Carlson's firm is about to enter the job market for graduating MBA students, hoping to find the best individuals to fill their open positions.

Many market contexts allow participants little opportunity for repeated transactions and little performance feedback. Markets where participants have distinctive attributes and enter the market infrequently are particularly likely to offer little opportunity for learning. In these *quasi-markets* participants prefer to transact with specific individuals on the other side of the market. We limit our discussion in this section to this particular kind of market. Job markets, like the one Carlson's division is entering, are quasi-markets because most individuals enter them infrequently and because participants in these markets must not only negotiate terms of agreement, but also decide with whom, out of many possible parties, to negotiate.

Rationality in Quasi-Markets

In order to maximize their gain, actors in quasi-markets must simultaneously find the best match available in the market and negotiate an advantageous contract. The negotiation aspect of quasi-markets is essentially the same as that for any pair of negotiators: Each pair of negotiators in a market should devise and adopt fully integrative agreements. Matching becomes an issue for negotiators, however, in some market contexts. The matching aspect of job markets can be illustrated by considering that who is hired by whom is often as important an issue as the terms of the particular agreements.

Along with the individual and dyadic levels of rationality that are important in quasi-markets, market-level rationality can also be specified. Markets should reach equilibrium, such that the matches between agents on different sides of the market represent a stable solution. Matching solutions are stable when no two parties on opposite sides of the market prefer each other to the parties with whom they have been matched (Roth, 1982). An unstable market solution results in a disequilibrium because pairs of dissatisfied parties would be able to form mutually preferred matches by abandoning previous commitments after the market had closed.

Individual Rationality in Quasi-Markets. There are several parts to Carlson's task of maximizing expected utility in a quasi-market. First, Carlson must identify the available parties on the opposite side of the market with whom an agreement might increase his welfare. Second, Carlson must evaluate these various alternatives by assessing the benefit to be gained from each of the possible agreements. Finally, Carlson must secure his preferred alternatives from among the possible agreements.

When a negotiator enters a market, he or she should begin by assessing the importance of the decision, the time available to make the decision, and the amount of effort to expend in making the decision. If the decision warrants a fair amount of time and effort, the negotiator should ideally identify all of the parties in the market that are potential matches. Decisions of high quality are often characterized by a thorough canvassing of alternatives (Janis & Mann, 1977). However, information-processing limitations may constrain the search for alternatives, and negotiators can be expected to overlook many relevant options (cf. Alexander, 1979). The greater the number of alternatives, the smaller the proportion of available information that is searched (cf. Abelson & Levi, 1985). Individuals also tend to reduce the comprehensiveness of their information search as the number of attributes to be considered increases, and shift to elimination strategies (Johnson & Payne, 1986; Payne, 1976). The larger the market and the more numerous the issues to be negotiated, therefore, the less complete will be the participants' consideration of alternatives, leading them to eliminate alternatives too quickly.

Negotiators, such as Carlson, who enter quasi-markets must assess the acceptability of a contract with a given opponent and compare the expected utility of that agreement with the utility expected from reaching agreements with other parties in the market (subject to search costs). Finding the best possible agreement in a market depends on how completely a negotiator has identified all possible alternatives. A proposed agreement with one party may exceed a negotiator's best known alternative and may even be fully integrative given that particular opponent, but there may be a better, as yet unrecognized, agreement possible with someone else in the market. As long as alternative agreements remain unknown to a negotiator, as when the negotiator is at the beginning of the search for an agreement, the negotiator is faced with a risky decision. The negotiator must choose between accepting the known settlement with the current party or the uncertain option of rejecting the present offer and continuing the search for a better match and agreement in the market.

Several biases may impair a negotiator's evaluation of this choice. First, individuals are overconfident in their judgments (Einhorn & Hogarth, 1978). Overconfidence may lead negotiators to reject good alternatives with the expectation of finding a better match that may not in fact exist in the market. Negotiators who are overconfident will be less receptive to possibly useful feedback from the environment. Second, individual choice behavior is often influenced by irrelevant factors, such as the order in which alternatives are presented. People tend to overemphasize the evidence encountered first in the set of evidence relevant to a judgment and to underadjust judgments from an original value (Anderson, 1981; Asch, 1946; Einhorn & Hogarth, 1985; Tversky & Kahneman, 1974). Additionally, as a decision maker begins to establish preferences among alternatives, information acquisition and processing may become directed toward confirming a preferred alternative, undervaluing disconfirming information (Nisbett & Ross, 1980; Soelberg, 1967).

The difficulty in finding and securing one's best agreement in quasi-markets reflects the inherent characteristic of these markets that what one person does depends on what everyone else is doing. Negotiators must mutually find and form agreements with the actors on the other side of the market who have particular value to them. Negotiators should therefore conduct an organized effort at contacting their most preferred matches. An agreement with a preferred party is more likely if the negotiator has idiosyncratic value to that party, and negotiators in quasi-markets should be prepared to offer more for an agreement with a preferred party. The greater the mutual benefit brought to the agreement through the quality of the match, the more likely the agreement is to last.

Game-theoretic market solutions indicate what would result in a given market if each individual behaved in a perfectly utility maximizing way throughout the course of the market. Because behavior in quasi-markets is so complex, however, it is difficult to specify these game-theoretic solutions. However, fully rational solutions at the market level, as distinct from that of individuals, can be defined.

Market Rationality.   Rational market-level solutions are those that produce a stable set of matches. There are, however, several solutions for a given quasi-market that meet this criterion. Roth (1985) has shown that when the set of possible matching solutions is restricted to stable solutions, two sets of matches can be generated such that one solution is preferred by all members of one side of the market, while the other solution is preferred by all members of the other side of the market. Indeed, the best stable solution from the point of view of one side of the market is the worst stable solution from the point of view of the other side. Because no matching solution exists that is equally well liked by both sides of a market, when instituting matching systems for real markets it is necessary to decide to which side of the market preference should be given. For some markets there will be one solution that produces greater collective benefit than the others, however in other markets no single solution will produce the greatest collective benefit.

As a company recruiter, Carlson is faced with the mixed-motive dilemma of competing to further the company's own interests while cooperating to reach a mutually acceptable solution. In market contexts this dilemma is extended in that each actor has the incentive to secure his or her best possible individual match regardless of the preferences of other negotiators on either side of the market, thus making it difficult for the set of matches to be stable. To the extent that each participant acts in accordance with self interests, all parties may be worse off than if they were to behave in a more cooperative manner, thus creating a social dilemma (cf. Dawes, 1980). Formal decision procedures and algorithms have been instituted in some real markets to ensure stable matches. The matching process for graduating medical students and hiring hospitals, for example, employs such an algorithm (Roth, 1982, 1984). Before the matching algorithm was adopted, hospitals competed for students by continually advancing the date when they extended offers for their residency positions. Eventually hospitals were making offers to students early in their second year of medical school and pressuring students to accept these offers immediately. This practice effectively hindered search strategies, decreased the ability of hospitals and students to judge each other's quality, and disrupted the educational process. The result was a large number of unstable matches. This result was duplicated in a laboratory simulation of a job market (Sondak & Bazerman, in press).

Our current research of an actual MBA job market has found that industries differ in terms of their competitive and cooperative behavior. Hiring firms must balance the need to create more efficient recruiting systems that will decrease recruiting expenses and establish better matches with the conflicting need to gain a competitive advantage over the other firms in their industry. Marketing firms that hire assistant brand managers tend to engage in cooperative recruiting practices, but investment banking firms tend to engage in competitive recruiting behaviors, such as extending offers very early. Early evidence suggest that these different recruiting patterns reflect broader patterns of competition that exist in these industries.

Unstable matches produce negative consequences for both individuals and society. The decision maker who makes a nonoptimal choice and at a later point learn that a better choice did or still does exist in the market will probably experience decision regret (Walster, 1964). Decision regret experienced by Carlson, as well as by newly hired managers, may lead to unfulfilled contracts, high rates of employee turnover, and increased costs associated with attempts to prevent these occurrences.

Matching algorithms that result in stable solutions maximize the aggregate utility for the market participants. Most negotiators will achieve greater expected payoffs under a matching algorithm than under a natural solution. However, some negotiators may achieve greater utility under a natural matching system by aggressively pursuing their own interests. Despite the societal benefits and greater expected utility associated with a matching algorithm, negotiators in many markets do not prefer the institutionalization of formal matching structures. Our current research has found that students and firms in the market for graduating management students oppose the adoption of matching algorithms. Dislike for these algorithms may be explained by individuals' overconfidence in their own abilities (Einhorn & Hogarth, 1978), distrust of a "dehumanized system" (Dawes, 1979), or lack of perceived control over important job-related choices (Bazerman, 1982; Seligman, 1975).

Prescriptions for Negotiators in Quasi-Markets

Participation in quasi-markets places complicated and somewhat conflicting demands on negotiators. Negotiators must at once engage in a search of the market that is thorough enough to provide good information, but must seek to secure agreements early. Negotiators should consider as many alternatives as possible before eliminating potential matches, and alternatives should be eliminated not by a single attribute but in terms of their overall quality. Good preparation is essential in these contexts—a negotiator should know what he or she is looking for—so that the quality of the various alternatives can be assessed quickly. Conversely, a negotiator must strive to determine for whom he or she has particular value. Assessing the benefits that market participants bring to selected individuals on the other side of the market can allow those in quasi-markets to focus their efforts more effectively.

Competing participants in quasi-markets have the common interest of maintaining a market that provides adequate opportunity for the emergence of a stable matching solution. Although early matches reduce risk to the individuals who match and create inefficiencies that primarily affect those left unmatched, the effectiveness of the market will suffer if participants compete by continually advancing the time when offers are extended. Thus, negotiators need to act early enough to secure their best alternatives, but not so early that the recruiting period is advanced for the whole market.

Carlson, therefore, has a difficult task in seeking new managers for the audio products division. The resources of the search committee should be used to gather good information about as many graduating students as possible; the thoroughness of the information about each candidate must be balanced with the number of candidates investigated. Before eliminating any candidates from consideration, Carlson's committee should try to determine their most preferred candidates, perhaps rank ordering all of them according to several attributes. In addition, the committee must quickly identify those candidates who find audio products an attractive employer; information-gathering and recruitment efforts should be concentrated on these individuals even if they are not initially at the top of the committee's list. Because employer—employee fit is of central concern, Carlson and the other committee members should not place too much effort in trying to get the "best" students, rather they should go after the right ones. However, there is always a tension between hiring the "stars" of that year's job market, and hiring the candidates with the best fit. Audio products, however, should not be overly competitive in their search for candidates, for example by contacting students months before the conventional recruiting season. This kind of non-cooperative behavior would likely be matched by the other firms in the job market, to everyone's detriment. Thus, Carlson wants to move fast once the recruiting season has begun, but not advance the season itself.

SUMMARY AND CONCLUSIONS

The research in social cognition and behavioral decision theory over the last two decades offers important insights into human behavior. We extend the decision-making perspective to the analysis of negotiations in dyadic, group, and market interactions. In each social context we reviewed current empirical research, examined the constraints on negotiator rationality, and suggested ways that negotiators might improve their decision making and performance in these contexts.

Negotiation is a pervasive form of social interaction. The consequences of inefficient negotiations and unnecessary impasses may be disastrous in many circumstances. The judgment tasks facing the negotiator are complex, and the complexity increases as the number of parties in the negotiation increases. Prescriptions for rational individual behavior are complicated by the introduction of social contexts and other parties. Negotiators should act in accordance with the basic principles of rationality outlined and temper this with an understanding of the mixed-motive nature of negotiation: Negotiators need to cooperate with other parties in order to expand the pie of available resources, but also compete with them in order to claim a large share of the resources. In market contexts that have a matching problem, negotiators should seek to reach agreements with their most preferred matches, but also realize that the unstable matches that may maximize individual utility might also lead to market disequilibrium.

First, it is clear that negotiators need to prepare thoroughly for negotiation. Negotiators need to assess their own and the other party's best alternative to a negotiated agreement, the issues in the negotiation, and the relative importance of these issues. Negotiators who fail to prepare for negotiation will make inaccurate judgments of the bargaining zone that may lead them to walk away from potentially integrative agreements or, in some cases, lead them to accept agreements that result in a lower utility than their alternative to negotiation. Negotiators are likely to be dissatisfied with inefficient agreements. As a result, implementation will be difficult, and in the case of market situations disequilibrium will result. In addition to the careful assessment of one's own and the other parties' interests, negotiators should examine the assumptions that they hold before the negotiation. Research suggests that before negotiation, negotiators assume that the amount of resources is a fixed sum rather than a variable sum, but most negotiation situations contain some potential for integrating interests.

Second, negotiators need to seek information and accurately update their judgments during negotiation. Negotiators need to seek information from the other party in order to make an accurate judgment of the task structure and to identify ways that interests may be integrated. By seeking information that disconfirms rather than confirms their hypotheses, negotiators will learn more and make more accurate judgments (Hogarth, 1981). Participants in all negotiations face the twin tasks of integrating the interests of the parties to expand the amount of available resources and distributing the resources among the parties in the negotiation. The norms and rules of distribution become less clear as the number of parties increases. In groups of three or more parties, negotiators must structure the decision-making processes using social decision rules and problem-solving agendas.

Finally, negotiators need to make judgments following the negotiation. These judgments will influence negotiators' satisfaction with the agreement, willingness to negotiate with the other party in the future, and willingness to comply with the terms of the present agreement. In the market situation, these judgments will affect the stability of the match and the equilibrium of the market. Thus, the judgments made after the negotiation is over are likely to have an important influence on future interactions between the parties.

Behavior in business and organizations inevitably involves conflict. Conflicts occur in interpersonal, group, organizational, and market settings. Understanding rational behavior in various social contexts is critical to formulating complete models of mixed-motive situations and for teaching participants in these situations how to improve performance through mutual cooperation and the integration of interests. We suggest that judgmental bias in negotiation is pervasive, but we believe that negotiators can improve their decision making and behavior. The inefficient conflict resolution that results from irrational decision making and behavior may lead to strained relationships, profit losses, and, in more global contexts may be disastrous. Research on real-world problems in varied contexts has the potential to strengthen our theories of cognition and conflict, and therefore improve our ability to give practical advice to negotiators.

ACKNOWLEDGMENTS

This research was supported by the Dispute Resolution Research Center at Northwestern University. The authors benefited from many helpful comments from John Carroll. The chapter was completed while the fourth author was in the psychology department at Northwestern University. The authors contributed equally.

REFERENCES

Abelson, R. P., & Levi, A. (1985). Decision making and decision theory. In G. Lindsey & E. Aronson (Eds.), *Handbook of social psychology* (pp. 231–309). New York: Random House.

Adams, J. S. (1963). Toward an understanding of inequity. *Journal of Abnormal and Social Psychology, 67,* 422–436.

Alexander, E. R. (1979). The design of alternatives in organizational contexts: A pilot study. *Administrative Science Quarterly, 24,* 382–404.

Anderson, N. H. (1981). *Foundations of information integration theory.* New York: Academic Press.

Arrow, K. J. (1963). *Social choice and individual values* (2nd ed.). New York: Wiley.

Asch, S. E. (1946). Forming impressions of personality. *Journal of Abnormal and Social Psychology,* 258–290.

Ashenfelder, O., & Bloom, D. E. (1984). Models of arbitrator behavior: Theory and evidence. *American Economic Review, 74,* 111–124.

Bacharach, S. B., & Lawler, E. J. (1980). *Power and politics in organizations.* San Francisco: Jossey-Bass.

Bazerman, M. H. (1982). Impact of personal control on performance: Is added control always beneficial? *Journal of Applied Psychology, 67,* 472–479.

Bazerman, M. H. (1985). Norms of distributive justice in interest arbitration. *Industrial and Labor Relations Review, 38,* 558–570.

Bazerman, M. H. (1986). *Judgment in managerial decision making.* New York: Wiley.

Bazerman, M. H., & Carroll, J. S. (1987). Negotiator cognition. In B. Staw & L. L.

Cummings (Eds.), *Research in organizational behavior* (Vol. 9, pp. 247–288). Greenwich, CT: JAI Press.

Bazerman, M. H., Magliozzi, T., & Neale, M. A. (1985). Integrative bargaining in a competitive market. *Organizational Behavior and Human Performance, 34,* 294–313.

Bazerman, M. H., Mannix, E., & Thompson, L. (1988). Groups as mixed-motive negotiations. In E. J. Lawler & B. Markovsky (Eds.), *Advances in group processes: Theory and research* (Vol. 5, pp. 195–216). Greenwich CT: JAI Press.

Bazerman, M. H., & Neale, M. A. (1982). Improving negotiation effectiveness under final offer arbitration: The role of selection and training. *Journal of Applied Psychology, 67,* 543–548.

Bazerman, M. H., & Neale, M. A. (1983). Heuristics in negotiations: Limitations to dispute resolution effectiveness. In M. H. Bazerman & R. J. Lewicki (Eds.), *Negotiating in organizations* (pp. 51–67). Beverly Hills: Sage.

Bem, D. (1967). Self-perception; An alternative interpretation of cognitive dissonance phenomena. *Psychological Review, 74,* 183–200.

Brett, J. (1985). *Task forces in group decision making.* Dispute Resolution Research Center, Northwestern University Working paper.

Brett, J., & Rognes, J. (1986). Intergroup relations in organizations: A negotiations perspective. In P. Goodman (Ed.), *Designing effective work groups* (pp. 202–236). San Francisco: Jossey-Bass.

Carnevale, P. J. D., & Isen, A. M. (1986). The influence of positive affect and visual access on the discovery of integrative solutions in bilateral negotiation. *Organizational Behavior and Human Decision Processes, 37,* 1–13.

Cartwright, J. A. (1978). A laboratory investigation of groupthink. *Communication Monographs, 45,* 229–246.

Castore, C. H., & Murnighan, J. K. (1978). Determinants of support for group decisions, *Organizational Behavior and Human Performance, 22,* 75–92.

Chaiken, S., & Baldwin, M. W. (1981). Affective-cognitive consistency and the effect of salient behavioral information on the self-perception of attitudes. *Journal of Personality and Social Psychology, 41,* 1–12.

Chapman, L. J., & Chapman, J. P. (1967). Genesis of popular but erroneous psycho-diagnostic observations. *Journal of Abnormal Psychology, 7,* 193–204.

Chechile, R. A. (1984). Logical foundations for a fair and rational method of voting. In W. Swapp (Ed.), *Group decision making* (pp. 97–114). Beverly Hills: Sage.

Clark, M. S., & Mills, J. (1979). Interpersonal attraction in exchange and communal relationships. *Journal of Personality and Social Psychology, 37,* 12–24.

Dawes, R. (1979). The robust beauty of improper linear models in decision making. *American Psychologist, 34,* 571–582.

Dawes, R. (1980). Social dilemmas. *Annual Review of Psychology, 31,* 161–191.

Delbecq, A. L., Van de Ven, A. H., & Gustafson, D. H. (1975). *Group techniques for program planning.* Glenview, IL: Scott, Foresman.

Einhorn, H. J., & Hogarth, R. M. (1978). Confidence in judgment: Persistence in the illusion of validity. *Psychological Review, 85,* 395–416.

Einhorn, H. J., & Hogarth, R. M. (1985). Ambiguity and uncertainty in probabilistic inference. *Psychological Review, 92,* 433–461.

Emerson, R. M. (1964). Power-dependence relations: Two experiments. *Sociometry, 27,* 282–298.

Erickson, B., Holmes, J., Frey, R., Walker, L., & Thibaut, J. (1974). Functions of third party in the resolution of conflict: The role of a judge in pretrial conferences, *Journal of Personality and Social Psychology, 30,* 293–306.

Fazio, R. H., & Zanna, M. P. (1981). Direct experience and attitude-behavior consistency. In L. Berkowitz (Ed.) *Advances in experimental social psychology* (Vol. 14, pp. 161–202). New York: Academic Press.

Fischhoff, B., Slovic, P., & Lichtenstein, S. (1980). Knowing what you want: Measuring labile values. In T. S. Wallsten (Ed.), *Cognitive processes in choice and decision behavior* (pp. 117–141). Hillside, NJ: Lawrence Erlbaum Associates.

Fishburn, P. C. (1974). Paradoxes of voting. *American Political Science Review, 68,* 537–546.

Fisher, R., & Ury, W. (1981). *Getting to yes.* New York: Penguin.

Flowers, M. L. (1977). A laboratory test of some implications of Janis' groupthink hypothesis. *Journal of Personal and Social Psychology, 35,* 888–896.

French, J. R. P., Jr. (1956). A formal theory of social power, *Psychological Review, 63,* 181–194.

Froman, L. A., & Cohen, M. D. (1970). Compromise and logroll: Comparing the efficiency of two bargaining processes. *Behavioral Science, 30,* 180–183.

Greenhalgh, L., Neslin, S., & Gilkey, R. (1985). The effects of negotiator preferences, situational power, and negotiator personality on outcomes of business negotiations. *Academy of Management Journal, 28,* 9–33.

Hammond, K. R., Stewart, T. R., Brehmer, B., & Steinman, D. O. (1975). Social judgment theory. In M. F. Kaplan & S. Schwartz (Eds.), *Human judgment and decision processes* (pp. 271–312). New York: Academic Press.

Hare, A. P. (1976). *Handbook of small group research.* New York: The Free Press.

Harnett, D. L. (1967). A level of aspiration model for group decision making. *Journal of Personality and Social Psychology, 5,* 58–66.

Hastie, R., Penrod, S., & Pennington, N. (1983). *Inside the jury.* Cambridge, MA: Harvard University Press.

Hogarth, R. M. (1981). Beyond discrete biases: Functional and dysfunctional aspects of judgmental heuristics. *Psychological Bulletin, 90,* 197–217.

Homans, G. (1961). *Social behavior: Its elementary forms.* New York: Harcourt.

Janis, I. L. (1982). *Groupthink: Psychological studies of policy decisions and fiascoes.* Boston: Houghton Mifflin.

Janis, I. L., & Mann, L. (1977). *Decision making: A psychological analysis of conflict, choice, and commitment.* New York: The Free Press.

Johnson, E., & Payne, J. (1986). The decision to commit a crime: An information processing analysis. In D. Cornish & R. Clark (Eds.), *The reasoning criminal: A rational choice perspective of offending* (pp. 170–185). New York: Springer-Verlag.

Kahan, J. P., & Rappaport, A. (1984). *Theories of coalition formation.* Hillsdale, NJ: Lawrence Erlbaum Associates.

Kahneman, D., Slovic, P., & Tversky, A. (Eds.). (1982). *Judgement under uncertainty: Heuristics and biases.* New York: Cambridge University Press.

Kahneman, D., Knetsch, J. L., & Thaler, R. (1986). Fairness and the assumption of economics. *The Journal of business, 59,* 5285–5300.

Kaplan, M. F., & Miller, C. E. (1983). Group discussion and judgment. In P. B. Paulus (Ed.), *Basic group processes* (pp. 65–95). New York: Springer-Verlag.

Kelley, H. H. (1966). A classroom study of dilemmas in interpersonal negotiation. In K. Archibald (Ed.), *Strategic interaction and conflict* (pp. 49–73). Berkely, CA: Institute of International Studies, University of California.

Komorita, S. S., & Chertkoff, J. M. (1973). A bargaining theory of coalition formation. *Psychological Review, 80,* 149–162.

Komorita, S. S., & Hamilton, T. P. (1984). Power and equity in coalition bargaining. In S. Bacharach & E. Lawler (Eds.) *Research in the sociology of organizations* (Vol. 3, pp. 189–212). Greenwich, CT: JAI Press.

Lax, D. A., & Sebenius, J. K. (1986). *The manager as negotiator: Bargaining for cooperative and competitive gain.* New York: The Free Press.

Levine, M. E., & Plott, C. R. (1977). Agenda influence and its implications. *Virginia Law Review, 53,* 561–604.

Lewicki, R., & Litterer, J. A. (1985). *Negotiation.* Homewood, IL: Irwin.

Lewin, K. (1951). *Field theory in social science.* New York: Harper.

Linstone, H. A., & Turoff, M. (Eds.). (1975). *The Delphi method: Techniques and applications.* Reading, MA: Addison-Wesley.

Luce, R. D., & Raiffa, H. (1957). *Games and decision: Introduction and critical survey.* New York: Wiley.

Mannix, E. A., Thompson, L. L., & Bazerman, M. H. (in press). Negotiation in small groups. *Journal of Applied Psychology.*

March, J. G., & Simon, H. A. (1958). *Organizations.* New York: Wiley.

May, K. O. (1982). A set of independent, necessary and sufficient conditions for simple majority decisions. In B. Barry & R. Hardin (Eds.), *Rational man and irrational society* (pp. 299–303). Beverly Hills: Sage.

McAlister, L., Bazerman, M. H., & Fader, P. (1986). Power and goal setting in channel negotiations. *Journal of Marketing Research, 23,* 238–263.

Milgram, S., Backman, L., & Berkowitz, L. (1969). Note on the drawing power of crowds of different size. *Journal of Personality and Social Psychology, 13,* 79–82.

Moscovici, S. (1980). Toward a theory of conversion behavior. In L. Berkowitz (Ed.), *Advances in experimental social psychology* (Vol. 13, pp. 209–239). New York: Academic Press.

Murnighan, J. K. (1986). Organizational coalitions: Structural contingencies and the formation process. In R. J. Lewicki, B. H. Sheppard, & M. H. Bazerman (Eds.), *Research on negotiation in organizations.* Greenwich, CT: JAI Press.

Nash, J. F., Jr. (1950). The bargaining problem. *Econometrica, 18,* 155–162.

Neale, M. A. (1984). The effect of negotiation and arbitration cost salience on bargainer behavior: The role of the arbitrator and constituency on negotiator judgment. *Organizational Behavior and Human Performance, 34,* 97–111.

Neale, M. A., & Northcraft, G. B. (1986). Experts, amateurs, and refrigerators: Comparing expert and amateur decision making on a novel task. *Organizational Behavior and Human Decision Processes, 38,* 305–317.

Nisbett, R., & Ross, L. (1980). *Human inference: Strategies and shortcomings of social judgment.* Englewood Cliffs, NJ: Prentice-Hall.

Ordeshook, P. C. (1986). *Game theory and political theory: An introduction*. Cambridge: Cambridge University Press.

Osborn, A. F. (1957). *Applied imagination*. New York: Charles Schribner's Sons.

Payne, J. W. (1976). Task complexity and contingent processing in decision making: An information search and protocol analysis. *Organizational Behavior and Human Performance, 16*, 366–387.

Petty, R. E., & Cacioppo, J. T. (1981). *Attitudes and persuasion: Classic and contemporary approaches*. Dubuque, IA: Wm. C. Brown.

Phillips, G. M. (1965). PERT as a logical adjunct to the discussion process. *Journal of Communication, 15*, 89–99.

Plott, C. R. (1976). Axiomatic social choice theory: An overview and interpretation. *American Journal of Political Science, 20*, 511–596.

Plott, C., & Levine, M. (1978). A model of agenda influence on committee decisions. *American Economic Review, 68*, 146–160.

Pruitt, D. (1983). Integrative agreements: Nature and antecedents. In M. H. Bazerman & R. J. Lewicki (Eds.), *Negotiating in organizations*. Beverly Hills: Sage.

Pruitt, D. G. (1981). *Negotiation behavior*. New York: Academic Press.

Pruitt, D. G., & Rubin, J. Z. (1986). *Social conflict: Escalation, stalemate and settlement*. New York: Random House.

Raiffa, H. (1953). Arbitration schemes for generalized two-person games. *Annals of Mathematics Studies*. Princeton: Princeton University.

Raiffa, H. (1982). *The art and science of negotiation*. Cambridge, MA: Harvard University Press.

Rawls, J. (1971). *A theory of justice*. Cambridge, MA: Harvard University Press.

Ross, L. (1977). The intuitive psychologist and his shortcomings: Distortions in the attribution process. In L. Berkowitz (Ed.), *Advances in experimental social psychology* (Vol. 10, pp. 173–220). New York: Academic Press.

Ross, L., Green, D., & House, P. (1977). The "false consensus effect": An egocentric bias in social perception and attribution processes. *Journal of Experimental Social Psychology, 13*, 279–301.

Roth, A. E. (1982). The economics of matching: Stability and incentives. *Mathematics of Operations Research, 7*, 617–628.

Roth, A. E. (1984). The evolution of the labor market for medical interns and residents: A case study in game theory. *Journal of Political Economy, 92*, 991–1016.

Roth, A. E. (1985). Conflict and coincidence of interest in job matching: Some new results and open questions. *Mathematics of Operations Research, 10*, 379–389.

Roth, A. E., & Malouf, M. (1982). Scale changes and shared information in bargaining: An experimental study. *Mathematical Social Sciences 3*, 157–177.

Rubin, J., & Brown, B. (1975). *The social psychology of bargaining and negotiation*. New York: Academic Press.

Schank, R. L. (1932). A study of community and its groups and institutions conceived of as behaviors of individuals. *Psychological Monographs, 43*, (Whole No. 195).

Schelling, T. C. (1984). *Choice and consequences*. Cambridge, MA: Harvard University Press.

Seligman, M. E. (1975). *Helplessness: On depression, development, and death.* San Francisco: Freeman.

Shaw, M. E. (1981). *Group dynamics: The psychology of small group behavior.* New York: McGraw-Hill.

Simon, H. A. (1957). *Models of man.* New York: Wiley.

Snyder, M., & Uranowitz, S. W. (1978). Reconstructing the past: Some cognitive consequences of person perceptions. *Journal of Personality and Social Psychology, 36,* 941–950.

Soelberg, P. (1967). Unprogrammed decision making. *Industrial Management Review, 8,* 19–29.

Sondak, H., & Bazerman, M. H. (in press). Matching and negotiation processes in quasi-markets. *Organizational Behavior and Human Decision Processes.*

Stillinger, C., & Ross, L. (1987, August). *Reactive devaluation of concessions: A Social-cognitive barrier to conflict resolution.* Paper presented at the meetings of the American Psychological Association, New York.

Thibaut, J. W., & Kelley, H. H. (1959). *The social psychology of groups.* New York: Wiley.

Thompson, L. L. (1988). *Social perception in negotiation.* Unpublished doctoral dissertation, Northwestern University, Evanston, IL.

Thompson, L. L., & R. Hastie (1988a). Judgment tasks and biases in negotiation. In B. H. Sheppard, M. H. Bazerman, & R. J. Lewicki (Eds.), *Research in negotiation in organizations* (Vol. 2). Greenwich, CT: JAI Press.

Thompson, L., & Hastie, R. (1988b). *Social perception in negotiation.* Manuscript submitted for review.

Thompson, L. L., Mannix, E. A., & Bazerman, M. H. (1988). Group negotiation: Effects of decision rule, agenda, and aspiration. *Journal of Personality and Social Psychology, 54,* 86–95.

Tversky, A., & Kahneman, D. (1974). Judgment under uncertainty: Heuristics and biases. *Science, 185,* 1124–1131.

von Neumann, J., & Morgenstern, O. (1947) *Theory of games and economic behavior* (2nd ed.). Princeton: Princeton University Press.

Walster, E. (1964). The temporal sequence of post-decision processes. In L. Festinger (Ed.), *Conflict, decision, and dissonance* (pp. 112–127). Palo Alto: Stanford University Press.

Walton, R. E., & McKersie, R. B. (1965). *A behavioral theory of labor negotiations: An analysis of a social interaction system.* New York: McGraw Hill.

Yukl, B. A. (1974). Effects of situational variables and opponent concessions on a bargainer's perception, aspirations, and concessions. *Journal of Personality and Social Psychology, 29,* 227–236.

Yukl, G. A., Malone, M. P., Hayslip, B., & Pamin, T. A. (1976). The effects of the pressure and issue settlement order on integrative bargaining, *Sociometry, 39,* 227–281.

The Impact of Layoffs on Survivors: An Organizational Justice Perspective

Joel Brockner
Graduate School of Business, Columbia University

Jerald Greenberg
College of Business, The Ohio State University

Job layoffs have long been a matter of great concern to organizational scholars and practitioners. Most of the theoretical, empirical, and applied work on layoffs has focused on the antecedents of layoffs (i.e., factors that make certain industries, organizations within industries, and jobs within organizations likely to be associated with layoffs, see, for example, Cornfield, 1983) or the consequences of layoffs for those people who have been laid off (e.g., Eisenberg & Lazarsfeld, 1938; Jahoda, 1982). Until recently, however, there has been relatively little exploration of an aspect of work layoffs of considerable practical and theoretical significance: their impact on the job behaviors and attitudes of the individuals who are not laid off (the "survivors"). This chapter describes some of the authors' theory and research on the effects of layoffs on those who remain.

The Importance of Layoffs

Several trends in corporate America since the 1970s have made layoffs a belt-tightening procedure to which organizations frequently resort. Increased competition from abroad, mergers, and acquisitions are merely some of the stimuli for management to attempt to "do more with less," be "mean and lean," and so on. The somewhat simple-minded rationale underlying management's reliance on layoffs is that the organization will be able to reduce its labor costs, without a proportional drop in the job-relevant behaviors (e.g., performance, turnover) of the surviving workforce; as a consequence, the overall productivity of the organization should improve.

Anecdotal evidence—reported regularly in the popular press—suggests that layoffs often have a dramatic effect on survivors' work behaviors. Interestingly enough, however, the anecdotal evidence offers apparently conflicting reports about how survivors may be affected. For example, in certain instances survivors may work harder following a layoff, at other times they may become demotivated, and on still other occasions their work performance may not be affected at all. If layoffs can affect numerous survivor behaviors and attitudes, and differentially so under various conditions, then it is necessary to formulate a conceptual analysis that can predict and explain the effects of layoffs on the workers who remain.

Justice and Survivors

This chapter presents such an analysis, a conceptualization derived from the theory and research on justice in interpersonal relationships (e.g., Deutsch, 1975, 1985; Leventhal, 1976; Walster, Walster, & Berscheid, 1978), especially as they apply to organizational settings (e.g., Greenberg, 1982, 1987a). The justice literature seems particularly germane because the layoff process consists of a series of events in which survivors are likely to evaluate the fairness of the organization's actions.

For example, survivors may question the legitimacy of the layoff in the first place. Was it necessary to downsize at all, or was management simply being greedy? Moreover, given that downsizing was perceived to be necessary, survivors may question whether layoffs were the most appropriate method; could the organization have cut costs in other ways (e.g., through a hiring freeze, attrition, reduced working hours, job sharing) without having to eliminate individuals' actual jobs (see Greenhalgh, Lawrence, & Sutton, 1988)? Did management provide ample forewarning to those who were laid off, thereby enabling them to be better prepared for the layoff? In the summer of 1988 both houses of Congress passed a bill into law requiring relatively large organizations to give its workforce at least 60 days notice of impending layoffs; more specifically, notice is required only if 500 workers or one third of the workforce—which ever is lower—are targeted to be laid off. Proponents of the law cited justice concerns in supporting the measure. For example, as Democratic Senator Howard M. Metzenbaum of Ohio, the bill's chief sponsor, put it, the bill "should be the law of the land. It's the fair and humane thing to do" ("Senate, by 72-23, approves. . .", 1988, p. A-1). Republican Senator John Chafee of Rhode Island noted that "it is fair and right for companies to inform workers when their jobs are to be eliminated . . . Workers will be able to plan, to utilize job training and placement services and to make financial arrangements. Corporate executives often get fabulous deals and benefits when they lose their jobs. Why shouldn't workers get fair treatment?" ("President decides. . .", 1988b, p. B5).

Management's ways of imparting the news to those laid off also may influence survivors' perceptions of justice. In conveying the news to employees that they are about to be laid off, managers need to attend to the details of how people should be told, who should tell them, and where and when they should be told. It has been suggested, for example, that those laid off should not be given the news at the end of the work week, such as at 4:30 on a Friday afternoon (Walker & Newborg, 1986). Among the reasons cited was that it would be particularly unfair to make those laid off suffer by ending their week on such a downbeat note.

Other potential determinants of survivors' perceptions of justice are factors associated with the rule(s) used to decide which employees are to remain and which are to be laid off. Some of the decisional bases that organizations employ are: (a) seniority, in which the employees having the shortest length of tenure are the first to be laid off; (b) merit, in which the poorest performers are the first to go; (c) skill, in which the individuals whose talents and capabilities do not coincide with those needed in the future are laid off first; and (d) true randomness, in which the organization *intentionally* seeks to assure that all employees have an equal chance of being laid off. Some organizations may employ a combination of these or other decisional bases. Whatever the bases, however, they are likely to be seen as less fair to the extent that they are: (a) not easily verifiable, (b) unrelated to past job performance, and (c) irrelevant to the future mission of the organization (Leventhal, 1980; Lind & Tyler, 1988).

Another set of factors that could influence survivors' justice judgments are the "caretaking activities" (or lack thereof) that the organization provides for those laid off. Such caretaking may take the form of helping individuals to find employment elsewhere, either outside the organization or at another location within the same parent organization. In addition, many organizations offer early retirement "windows," or other forms of severance pay; some even may continue the health insurance and other kinds of benefits of those laid off for a certain period of time. In general, we suspect that the less the organization takes care of those laid off, the more likely it is that survivors will perceive the layoff as unfair.

In summary, the layoff process includes many events during which survivors are likely to evaluate the extent to which the downsizing organization has acted fairly. The examples cited here map onto three interrelated foci in the justice literature that provide the theoretical grounding for the study of survivors' reactions: the *distributive justice* perspective (e.g., Deutsch, 1985;

Homans, 1961), focusing on *what* outcomes result from social interaction; the *procedural justice* perspective (e.g., Thibaut & Walker, 1975), focusing on *how* those outcomes were determined; and the *interactional justice* perspective (e.g., Bies, 1987), focusing on how fairly the organization acted during the actual implementation of its resource allocation decisions (e.g., whether the organization explained the reasons underlying its decisions).

A selective review of the literature in each of these three areas is presented in the next section. Because the presentation is intended primarily to provide relevant background, only those aspects of the literature most relevant to understanding survivors' reactions to layoffs are presented (for more thorough presentations, see Bierhoff, Cohen, and Greenberg (1986); Cohen (1986); Greenberg and Cohen (1982); Lind and Tyler (1988). Then, drawing from the literature on reactions to victims of injustice, we offer predictions about how and why survivors may respond to layoffs. After that, we summarize a series of studies of survivors' reactions to layoffs. This review highlights some applications of justice-based research and theory. Our closing section discusses additional applications of justice research to layoff situations, and potential implications of findings of the research on layoffs for expanded theoretical work on justice.

FORMS OF JUSTICE IN THE LAYOFF PROCESS

Distributive Justice

Traditionally, theorists interested in *distributive justice* (cf. Homans, 1961) have concerned themselves with questions about the normative rules people use to make decisions about the distribution of resources (for a review, see Leventhal, 1976). The most popularly studied distributive norms are *equity*—receipt of resources in proportion to contributions made, *equality*—equal receipt of resources by all parties, and *need*—receipt of resources according to the extent to which they are required by the recipients (Deutsch, 1975; Lerner, 1977). In situations in which employees are being laid off from jobs, the jobs themselves may be considered resources. What principle will be applied when decisions are made concerning who will remain employed and who will be laid off?

Although previous research has not focused on this question directly, extrapolations from related research allow us to offer some informed speculations. The job in jeopardy may be considered to be a scarce resource; when decisions are made about the allocation of scarce resources, considerations of justice take on a special character. Under such circumstances, scarce resources tend to be distributed with particular emphasis placed on considerations of need and efficiency (Greenberg, 1981).

Need, for example, has been found to be the preferred criterion used in the allocation of scarce hemodialysis machines to kidney patients (Calabresi & Bobbitt, 1978). Other studies (e.g., Greenberg, 1981; Karuza & Leventhal, 1976; Leventhal & Weiss, 1975) also support the notion that "under conditions of scarcity, considerations of need predominate in making allocation decisions" (Greenberg, 1981, p. 296).

Another important consideration in allocating scarce resources is efficiency—distributions that minimize waste and make the best use of available resources. When supplies of resources are abundant, people making distributive decisions are less likely to focus on efficiency than when resources are scarce. This generalization is supported by several sociohistorical observations. For example, providers of special and highly valued services (e.g., physicians) command longer waits, as those desiring to see them must queue up, thereby minimizing the time wasted by these providers (Greenberg, 1989; Schwartz, 1975). Additional evidence has shown that the pricing schemes believed to be fairest for scarce resources are those that encourage efficiency and discourage waste—schemes that penalize high users of scarce resources with an increasing payment scale (Greenberg, 1981).

It is interesting to speculate about how these findings regarding need and efficiency may be applied to decisions made about which employees will be retained and which will be laid off. The findings with respect to need would imply that supervisory personnel would be inclined to retain employees who have the greatest need for the job (e.g., those who need their jobs to support large families, or those who may find it most difficult to find alternate employment). In contrast, because scarcity also heightens the perceived need for the most efficient allocation decisions, one would expect that layoff decisions would be made that retain the employees who were most productive in the past, and who were expected to be most productive in the future, regardless of their need for the job. In other words, an equity-based, rather than a need-based allocation rule would be favored.

How such conflicts between distributive rules are resolved is, of course, an empirical question. Unfortunately, the research focusing on the question of "what justice norm is followed when?" (e.g., Deutsch, 1975; Leventhal, 1976) has not dealt specifically with the layoff situation. However, based on previous research, we suspect that layoff decisions are not made primarily on the basis of workers' needs. Instead, a distributive practice favoring overall efficiency is likely to be employed. At the organization-wide level, administrators need to be concerned about maintaining the performance of all employees who remain on their jobs. As such, management may choose to lay off those employees who were least productive in the past, or who were expected to be least productive in the future. Of course, the task of choosing survivors based on their performance and/or anticipated future performance is no simple matter. Given uncertainties with respect to the metric of job performance, and the inevitable differences in perceptions of quality of job performance, organizations may rely upon a less ambiguous decision rule, such as seniority (Ichniowski, Brockner, & Davy, 1988).

To summarize, layoff conditions highlight the scarcity of jobs. Although scarce resources are often allocated according to the distributive principle of need, scarcity in the post-layoff environment primarily arouses a heightened concern for efficiency that may well conflict with the application of the need rule. Overall organizational efficiency may be sought by implementing a distributive rule that rewards workers for their perceived past and expected future contributions.

Procedural Justice

In contrast to the focus on the fair allocations of *outcomes* inherent in analyses of distributive justice, the procedural justice perspective focuses on the fairness of the *processes* used to arrive at those outcomes (Folger & Greenberg, 1985). Although the fairness of the processes may well influence people's beliefs about the fairness of outcome distributions (Greenberg, 1987c), there is considerable evidence attesting to their independence (e.g., Alexander & Ruderman, 1987; Greenberg, 1986a; Tyler & Caine, 1981).

In the context of employee layoffs, workers' concerns about fairness may well be expected to revolve around procedural issues—among them, how was the layoff accomplished? Was it a legitimate response to an economic downturn, or a greed-motivated reaction? Insight into these questions is provided by Leventhal's (1980; Leventhal, Karuza, & Fry, 1980) theory of procedural justice. Specifically, Leventhal hypothesizes that fair procedures are ones that are made: (a) following consistent procedures, (b) without self-interest, (c) on the basis of accurate information, (d) with opportunities to correct the decision, (e) with the interests of all concerned parties in mind, and (f) following moral and ethical standards (see Greenberg, 1986a; Sheppard & Lewicki, 1987, for supportive evidence). Although there have been no previous attempts to apply these guidelines to layoff situations, their potential applicability is apparent. For example, workers' acceptance of layoffs may well depend on their beliefs that layoff decisions were due to environmental factors largely beyond management's control (rather than due to past mismanagement, in which case the layoff victims might be viewed as unjustly "paying" for the mismanagement).

One especially active line of investigation among procedural justice researchers concerns the importance of workers' input into decision-making processes. Here, the pioneering research of Thibaut and Walker (1975) on comparative legal systems is most relevant. In a series of studies it was found that dispute-resolution practices that give disputing parties control over the process by which their disputes are resolved (e.g., opportunities to select attorneys, to offer evidence) are believed to be more fair than those procedures that do not offer any such opportunities for "process control" (see also Greenberg & Folger, 1983). Similarly, laboratory studies of reward distribution behavior also have found that outcomes—even negative ones—are better accepted when people have a voice in determining those outcomes than when no such "voice" is provided (e.g., Folger, 1977; Tyler, Rasinski, & Spodick, 1985). Applications of this so-called fair process effect to organizational settings have been particularly prevalent in the context of performance appraisals (for reviews, see Folger & Greenberg, 1985; Greenberg, 1986b), where several investigations have shown that workers' input into the appraisal process is a critical determinant of their acceptance of the appraisals as fair (e.g., Greenberg, 1986b, 1987b; Kanfer, Sawyer, Earley, & Lind, 1987; Lissak, 1983).

These conclusions hold particular relevance for the study of lay-offs. If, in fact, negative outcomes are better accepted by workers who have had a voice in the decision-making process than those who remain mute, it may be advisable for supervisory personnel to involve employees in the process of deciding about layoffs. For example, survivors of layoffs may be reminded of the fact that their representatives negotiated with management the decision rule to be used (e.g., merit, seniority) if layoffs were necessary. Such a prompt may highlight the fact that survivors—through their representatives—had some input into the layoff procedures, thereby enhancing the perceived fairness of the procedures.

Interactional Justice

The administration of layoffs presents a challenge for supervisors to confront workers—both those who are laid off, and survivors—with negative information in a manner that they will find acceptable (i.e., without "adding insult to injury"). Relevant to such concerns is the work on *interactional justice*— the fairness of the interpersonal treatment people receive *during* the implementation of resource allocations (Bies, 1987). As Bies (1987; Bies & Moag, 1986) and Greenberg (1988, in press) have recently noted, workers' reactions to procedures greatly depend on how information is presented to them— information such as *why* certain selection decisions were made (Bies, 1986), *why* certain proposals were accepted or rejected (Bies & Shapiro, 1987), and *why* certain performance ratings were given (Greenberg, 1987d). To date, this research has shown that offering explanations of administrative actions greatly ameliorates workers' reactions to the negative impact of those actions; they promote the belief that the decision makers' actions were fair, the result of a considered judgment (Greenberg, 1987d, 1987e, 1988, in press).

Bies (1986), for example, has shown that in the administration of bad news, the use of various types of social accounts enhanced feelings of fairness and acceptance of the resulting outcomes. Certainly, a layoff may be seen as a bad news situation. Based on Bies' (1987) theorizing, it follows that administrators of layoffs might offer various types of social accounts, such as:

- *causal accounts:* for example, "We were forced to lay off workers because of the poor economy."
- *ideological accounts:* for example, "We had to lay off workers to ensure the company's financial survival."
- *referential accounts:* for example, "Things surely will improve, and then we'll hire back workers we laid off."
- *penetential accounts:* for example, "I'm really very sorry to have to lay you off."

Although existing research does not yet enable us to specify which type of social account may be most ameliorative in the case of layoffs, research in performance appraisal situations has shown that most types of social accounts enhance the perceived fairness of decisions, relative to no social accounts at all (Greenberg, 1987d).

Given this background of distributive, procedural, and interactional justice, we are in a better position to appreciate the potential contributions of the justice literature to layoff situations. That is, survivors are likely to attend to the various issues of distributive, procedural, and interactional justice inherent in management's handling of the layoff. But, the relevance of the justice literature to the analysis of survivors' reactions does not stop here. More specifically, the survivor situation closely resembles one that has received much attention from interpersonal justice theorists: how individuals react to victims of injustice.

REACTIONS TO VICTIMS OF INJUSTICE

Some insight into survivors' reactions to layoffs is provided by the more general literature on observers' reactions to injustice (for a review, see Walster et al., 1987). In this analogy, survivors may be cast in the role of observers who witness a harmdoer (the downsizing organization) injure victims (the laid-off workers). Previous research has shown that observers may exhibit two different types of behavioral and/or psychological reactions to the injustice. On the one hand, they may respond in a seemingly "unsympathetic" manner toward the victim. Such unsympathetic reactions could take the form of denying that any injustice was done in the first place, blaming the victim of the injustice for his or her own plight, distancing oneself from the victim, and/or aligning oneself with the perpetrator of the injustice.

On the other hand, observers may react in a more "sympathetic" fashion towards the victims. Sympathetic reactions include acknowledging (rather than denying) the injustice, blaming the perpetrator rather than the victim, taking action on behalf of the victimized party to restore justice, and distancing oneself from (rather than aligning with) the perpetrator.

It is easy to translate these general principles from the justice literature to the layoff situation. "Unsympathetic" reactions by survivors may include believing that the layoff is not so unfair after all, blaming the victims for being laid off ("they deserved it anyway"), breaking any ties that they might have had with the victims (e.g., not socializing with them any longer outside of the workplace), and working harder, which may serve the dual purpose of distancing themselves from the victims and aligning themselves with the downsizing organization. "Sympathetic" responses could include the belief that the victims were treated unfairly, feeling angry towards the organization, being willing to work fewer hours so that the layoff victims may be recalled, and looking for a job elsewhere (i.e., becoming less committed to the organization).

Interestingly, all of the possible survivors' reactions—whether sympathetic or unsympathetic—seem designed to protect them from the belief that they will be laid off unjustly, too. For example, the unsympathetic reaction of believing that the victims brought the unjust treatment upon themselves—either through their actions or attributes—may be survivors' way of perceiving that they are so different from the victims that they will not suffer a similar fate. The unsympathetic reaction of working harder may be survivors' way of demonstrating that they "deserve" to remain in the organization. The sympathetic reaction of job sharing (i.e., helping to take care of those laid off) may allow survivors to believe that they too will be provided for, were the organization to treat them as unjustly as it treated the laid-off employees. The sympathetic reaction of becoming less committed (e.g., looking for employment elsewhere) may be a way of distancing oneself from the perpetrator of the injustice, thereby enabling survivors to believe that they will not become victims themselves of unjust treatment by the organization.

Causes of Survivors' Reactions

Although both the sympathetic and unsympathetic types of survivors' reactions may stem from the same underlying motivation, the *consequences* of such reactions obviously are quite different for the survivors, the organization, and the laid-off workers. Therefore, it becomes crucial to delineate the conditions under which survivors respond sympathetically rather than unsympathetically toward the victims. Heider's (1958) balance theory may offer some insight into this matter. Consider the survivors (Party A), the organization (Party B), and the layoff victims (Party C) as representing three points of a balance triangle. Heider (1958), Festinger (1957), and other consistency theorists state that people strive to reduce imbalance between their behaviors and beliefs. Behaviors and beliefs are organized into "unit relationships," which refer to the presence of a sense of affiliation, liking for, or "connectedness" between the individual and his/her various beliefs; a plus sign (+) refers to the presence of a unit relationship, whereas a minus sign (−) refers to its absence. Belief systems in a Heiderian balance triangle are said to be consistent or balanced when the product of the three signs is positive, and imbalanced—and thus in need of further work to reduce the imbalance— when the product is negative. Survivors probably take as their starting point the absence of a unit relationship between the organization and the layoff victims (i.e., a minus sign between Party B and Party C), and then somehow must bring about consistency among all three elements of the balance triangle.

This analysis suggests that whether survivors respond sympathetically (unsympathetically) toward those laid off—in which case a plus (minus) sign exists between survivors and victims—depends on the nature of their previous relationships with the layoff victims as well as the organization. If a unit relationship already exists between themselves and the layoff victims—or, if the unit relationship between themselves and the victims is stronger than the one that exists between themselves and the organization—then survivors are likely to manifest some type of sympathetic response. If, however, there is a strong unit relationship between the survivors and the organization (or at least stronger than the one between the survivors and the layoff victims), then survivors may be more apt to react unsympathetically.

Numerous factors may affect the strength of survivors' prior attachment to (or unit relationship with) the layoff victims. They include: (a) the extent to which the survivors had worked closely (e.g., interdependently) with the layoff victims, (b) the degree of personal and/or attitudinal similarity between the survivors and layoff victims, (c) whether the survivors ever have been layoff victims themselves, and (d) whether the survivors believe that they might be layoff victims in the not-too-distant future. In short, survivors may identify with the layoff victims either on a *personal* basis (e.g., see Factor b) or on a *role* basis (e.g., see Factor c); if, for whatever reason, survivors feel a strong sense of identification or "connectedness" to the victims, then they are likely to react sympathetically.

Many factors may influence survivors' prior degree of attachment to, or unit relationship with, the organization, including: (a) their current (or aspired) level of formal authority, with higher level managers more strongly identified with the organization's goals and values; (b) their length of tenure in the organization, with those working in the organization for a relatively long period of time regarding it as a second (or maybe even first) family; and (c) their personal work ethic. Workaholics, for example, are particularly devoted to their jobs, and, by extension, may feel a strong sense of allegiance to their organizations.

To summarize this chapter to this point, we suggest that two rather broad categories of factors moderate the impact of layoffs on survivors: (a) the perceived degree of unfairness in the management of the layoff process, based on the various aspects of distributive, procedural, and interactional justice mentioned earlier; and (b) the relative strength of survivors' prior attachment to, or identification with, the layoff victims versus the organization. Layoffs perceived as fair (a rare event, in our observations) are likely to have minimal impact on survivors. However, layoffs perceived as unfair are likely to elicit: (a) sympathetic reactions in survivors to the extent that they previously felt strongly attached to the layoff victims, and (b) unsympathetic reactions to the extent that they previously felt strongly attached to the organization.

EMPIRICAL EVIDENCE

Some of the empirical evidence that is consistent with the reasoning just given is described. Four studies are reported; the first three were performed under controlled laboratory conditions, in which student subjects observed another subject being "laid off" from a paid task (see Brockner, Davy, & Carter, 1985, for further details). The fourth study was conducted in a naturalistic setting in which actual layoffs occurred in branches of a retail company.

The Laboratory Procedure

Most subjects were college students who took part voluntarily in order to receive extra course credit or a $5 payment. Upon arriving at the laboratory for a "test validation" experiment, subjects were brought into a common waiting area with a confederate (posing as another subject). They were told that they would be performing several proofreading tasks, presumably to help the researchers validate the tests. At this point they were ushered into individual cubicles to perform the initial (baseline) task. After proofreading the first task the subject and confederate were brought back into the common waiting area "in order to take a rest before going on to the next task."

The layoff manipulation took place at this time. Those in the layoff condition were told that due to an unforeseen "room scheduling" problem it was necessary to dismiss one of them. Moreover, the "really bad news" in all of this was that the dismissed person could not receive any remuneration for the time and effort that he or she had devoted already to the study. The experimenter then went on to say that "to simplify things," the subject and confederate would "draw lots" to determine who would stay and who would have to leave. Of course, the layoff always was conducted such that the confederate was dismissed and the true subject survived. The confederate protested mildly about this unfair treatment prior to departing; without much fanfare, the experimenter agreed that it was a "tough break" for the confederate. The confederate then departed and subjects were led back to their individual cubicles to perform the second proofreading task.

The no-layoff condition was relatively uneventful. The experimenters simply made busy work for themselves during the rest period to control for the mere passage of time. Subjects then were escorted back to their individual cubicles to perform the second proofreading task.

The primary behavioral measures were the quantity and quality of participants' proofreading performance; subjects previously had been instructed to strive for both. Performance quantity and quality were invariably inversely correlated across conditions, although performance quality typically was unrelated to any of the independent variables. Hence, we discuss the outcomes only on the quantity measure. Postexperimental questionnaires assessed subjects' perceptions of fairness, as well as their attitudes toward the confederate.

Study 1: Unfair Layoffs. Subjects in this experiment (Brockner et al., 1985) also completed a self-esteem scale prior to performing the proofreading task. Compared to those in the no-layoff condition, subjects in the layoff condition strongly derogated the confederate. That is, they rated the confederate as less attractive and less similar to themselves when the confederate was laid off rather than not. Subjects in the layoff condition also worked significantly harder than those in the no-layoff condition, and especially if they were low, rather than higher in self-esteem. One interpretation of the increased performance in the layoff condition is that subjects were trying to distance themselves from the laid-off person; by working harder, they may have attempted to show that they were relatively more "deserving" of being chosen to remain (than the confederate), even though the choice was apparently made at random. The fact that low self-esteem subjects (low SEs) were most likely to work harder also is consistent with this interpretation. Lacking confidence in their own sense of self-worth, low SEs may have been especially motivated to show that they "deserved" to remain.

The two categories of factors believed to moderate survivors' reactions—the injustice of the layoff and the extent to which survivors identified with those laid off (vs. the "organization")—were not manipulated. However, virtually all subjects reported on the postexperimental questionnaire that the laid-off confederate was treated rather unfairly; after all, the confederate was forced to go home empty-handed. Moreover, it seems likely that the subject did not feel especially close to the laid-off confederate; the two parties were complete strangers prior to the study, had minimal contact with one another during the study, and had no anticipation of interacting with each other later in the study or after the experiment ended. Given that the layoff was perceived as rather unfair, and if our assumption is correct that the survivors had little reason to identify with the laid-off confederate, then the layoff should have engendered "unsympathetic" reactions in the survivors. The facts that subjects reacted negatively to the laid-off person and worked harder in the layoff than no-layoff condition may have reflected survivors' attempts to distance themselves from the victims of the layoff.

Study 2: Merit-Based Layoffs. The second experiment (Brockner et al., 1986) was designed to replicate and extend the previous one. Subjects were assigned to one of three conditions: the layoff and no-layoff conditions studied previously, and a third condition in which a layoff also took place, but the basis of survival was not random. Specifically, this third group of participants were told that they were chosen to survive by virtue of having performed better than their co-participant, who, of course, was actually our confederate (merit layoff condition). As in the earlier study, the confederates were treated rather unfairly, by being "laid off" without receiving any compensation for their efforts.

The performance quantity data in the random layoff and no-layoff conditions replicated those found in Study 1: Subjects exhibited more of a proofreading boost in the former than the latter condition; moreover, this tendency was somewhat more pronounced among the low than the high self-esteem participants. The proofreading boost in performance of those in the merit layoff condition did not differ from that shown in the Control condition; moreover, subjects' self-esteem was unrelated to their performance in the merit condition.

One interpretation of the performance results in the second study is perfectly compatible with our explanation of survivors' reactions: If subjects had little reason to identify with the victims of the unjust layoff, they may have wished to distance themselves from the layoff victims. As in the layoff condition in Study 1, survivors in the random layoff condition may have sought to distance themselves by working harder on the subsequent task. Those in the merit condition, however, were provided information that already could have enabled them to feel distant from (or "better than") their laid-off "co-participant": the fact that they had outperformed their co-participant at the earlier task. Indeed, when asked to evaluate their performance at the earlier (pre-layoff) task, those in the merit layoff condition reported that they had done better than participants in the random and no-layoff conditions, whose evaluations did not differ from one another.

Taken together, the results from the first two experiments are consistent with our justice-based analysis of survivors' reactions. Empirical evidence revealed that the layoff was perceived as rather unfair. Moreover, we have assumed that survivors did not feel a strong sense of attachment or kinship with the victims of the unjust layoff. Consequently, they reacted in ways that might have enabled them to feel distant from, or more worthy than, the layoff victims. If, however, subjects in the layoff condition *already* felt distant from, or more worthy than, their laid-off co-participant—such as in the merit layoff condition in Study 2, and the high SEs in both studies, who have generally favorable views of their self-worth—then they should have less of a need to respond to the layoff in ways that would distance themselves from the layoff victim.

Study 3: Compensating the Victims.   Unlike in the previous two studies, the independent variables in both this and the subsequent study (Brockner, Grover, Reed, DeWitt, &O'Malley, 1987) were drawn from the two broad categories of factors believed to moderate the impact of layoffs on survivors: (a) the degree of injustice associated with the layoff, and (b) the extent to which survivors felt a prior sense of attachment to the layoff victims (rather than to the organization).

Study 3 was a laboratory experiment that partially replicated and extended Study 1. As in the earlier study, some subjects witnessed a layoff in which the confederate was treated rather unfairly (uncompensated layoff), and a second group constituted the no-layoff or control condition. In a third condition, subjects observed the confederate being laid off, but also were led to believe that the layoff victim had been treated relatively fairly in the process. Specifically, after the layoff occurred—as in Study 1, the confederate always was chosen to be dismissed through an ostensibly random procedure—the experimenter announced that it would seem only right for the laid-off person to receive some compensation for the time that he or she had devoted to the study. In fact, the experimenter gave a partial cash payment to the confederate, and the confederate departed saying that such treatment seemed fair (compensated layoff condition). These events were quite different from those that transpired in the uncompensated layoff condition, in which the confederate was sent home emptyhanded and seemed at least mildly upset about that fact.

We also attempted to manipulate participants' prior degree of identification with the laid-off person. Those in the high identification condition were led to believe that their attitudes were quite similar to the layoff victim's on a variety of political, economic, and social dimensions. The other half (low identification condition) were informed that the victim's attitudes were quite different from their own (Byrne, 1971).

Our justice-based analysis of survivors' reactions posits that when survivors identify with the victims of an unfair layoff they will respond not by trying to distance themselves from the victim but, rather, by acting negatively toward the perceived perpetrator of the unjust layoff. In the present context, such "acting out against the perpetrator" should take the form of working *less* hard after the layoff has occurred; after all, subjects had been instructed by the experimenter to work as quickly and as accurately as possible. If they were displeased with the experimenter (i.e., the perpetrator of the injustice) for acting unjustly toward someone with whom they identified, then they should withhold their effort at the subsequent task. Thus, subjects were expected to work least hard in the uncompensated layoff/high identification condition.

The performance data supported the predictions. Unlike the previous two experiments, under no conditions did survivors work significantly harder than the participants in the no-layoff control condition. Rather, and as can be seen in Table 3.1, those in the uncompensated layoff/high identification condition were least productive on the second proofreading task, significantly less so than in each of the other two high identification conditions and the uncompensated layoff/low identification condition. (Within the low identification condition, subjects' performances did not differ from one another across different levels of the layoff variable.)

To check on whether the layoff manipulation evoked differential perceptions of fairness, subjects rated the extent to which their "co-participant" had been treated fairly during the course of the experiment. As expected, perceived fairness was highest in the no-layoff condition, lowest in the uncompensated layoff condition, and moderate in the compensated layoff. Of even greater interest, and as can be seen in Table 3.2, this pattern was significantly

TABLE 3.1
Increase in Perfomance Quantity (Lines Proofread)
from First to Second Task (Study 3)

| | Layoff Condition | | | | | |
| | Uncompensated | | Compensated | | No-Layoff | |
Identification	M	SD	M	SD	M	SD
High	2.05	11.52	13.95	12.86	11.12	13.34
Low	12.63	17.39	6.10	16.13	7.03	11.95

Note: Each proofreading task consisted of 123 lines; higher scores reflect greater productivity on the second than the first task.

TABLE 3.2
Fairness Rating Assigned to Other (Study 3)

| | Layoff Condition | | | | | |
| | Uncompensated | | Compensated | | No-Layoff | |
Identification	M	SD	M	SD	M	SD
High	1.95	1.51	4.71	2.22	6.42	0.64
Low	3.68	2.47	4.10	2.05	5.90	1.27

Note: Scores could range from 1 to 7, with higher scores reflecting greater fairness.

more pronounced in the high than the low identification condition. Apparently, subjects were much more sensitive to the (fairness of the) way in which their co-participants had been treated when they were similar rather than dissimilar to themselves (Deutsch, 1985). Indeed, one interpretation of the results in Tables 3.1 and 3.2 is that when subjects perceived that someone *like themselves* had been laid off unfairly (i.e., in the uncompensated layoff condition), they took out their strong feelings of injustice against the perpetrator (i.e., the experimenter) by withholding their effort at the subsequent task. Of course, such an interpretation is perfectly compatible with the conceptual framework underlying this entire line of research.

Several other aspects of the results of Study 3 are worth noting. First, unlike in Study 1 (as well as in a replication of Study 1; see Brockner, Grover, O'Malley, DeWitt, Reed, & Glynn, 1988), subjects did not judge the layoff victim more negatively in the uncompensated layoff than in the control condition (or the compensated layoff condition, for that matter). Rather, the co-participant was rated more negatively in the low identification than the high identification condition. Such results not only replicate the well-established relationship between attitudinal similarity and attraction (Byrne, 1971); they suggest that information about the co-worker's attitudes is a much more important determinant of survivors' feelings about the co-worker than is whether the co-worker was laid off.

Second, although the results of cross-study comparisons must be judged tentatively, it is interesting to compare the procedures and results in the uncompensated layoff conditions in Study 3 with the random layoff condition in Studies 1 and 2. There were two main differences in methodology. First, in Study 3 subjects were led to believe that the layoff victim was attitudinally similar or dissimilar to themselves, whereas in the earlier experiments subjects were not given any information about the other's level of similarity. Second, in Study 3 subjects were told at the outset that they would work on a task with one another later in the experiment. In other words, those in this study were led to anticipate some future (and presumably cooperative) future interaction with each other, whereas no such information was conveyed to those in Studies 1 and 2.

When subjects believed that they would be interacting with a similar other who had been laid off unfairly (Study 3), they exhibited a significant *reduction* in work performance, relative to the control condition (see the uncompensated layoff/high identification and the no-layoff/high identification conditions in Table 3.1). When they anticipated future interaction with a dissimilar other who had been laid off unfairly, their performance was not significantly different from that observed in a control condition (see the uncompensated layoff/low identification and the no-layoff/low identification conditions in Table 3.1). However, when subjects were not led to expect any interaction with the victim of an unjust layoff whose level of similarity was unknown (Studies 1 and 2), they showed a significant *increase* in work performance (again, relative to a control condition).

How might the collective set of results be explained? In all of the studies subjects witnessed the layoff victim being treated unfairly. However, their level of identification with the victim may have varied across conditions. To the extent that the layoff was unfair, survivors should react sympathetically (e.g., by working less hard) when their identification with the layoff victims is high, and unsympathetically (e.g., by working harder) when their identification is low. We suspect that identification with the victim was highest in the high identification/uncompensated layoff condition in Study 3, lowest in the random layoff conditions of Studies 1 and 2, and intermediate in the low identification/uncompensated layoff condition in Study 3. In the first of these three conditions, survivors had two reasons to identify with the layoff victims: attitudinal similarity, as well as the fact that they had been previously led to expect to interact with the victim at a later point in the study. The latter fact may be relevant in that the anticipation of future interaction has been shown to enhance individuals' attachment to one another (e.g., Tyler & Sears, 1977). In the random layoff conditions of Studies 1 and 2, neither of these factors was present. In the low identification/uncompensated layoff condition one of the two factors was present: Although the victim was viewed as attitudinally dissimilar (possibly leading to low identification), subjects had been led to anticipate future interaction (possibly leading to some sense of identification). If our judgments about survivors' level of identification with layoff victims is correct, then the pattern of findings across studies is consistent with the theoretical framework upon which the research was predicated.

Study 4: Compensating the Victims (Field Study). The third experiment provided a direct test of the conceptual framework posed at the outset of the chapter. Both categories of independent variables, that is, perceived injustice and attachment to layoff victim (vs. the organization) were manipulated, and the emerging results were consistent with predictions. Nevertheless, Study 3 contained several shortcomings. First (and perhaps foremost), the laboratory methodology is far removed from the actual organizational context, making it appropriate to wonder if similar results would emerge among survivors in their natural habitat. For example, it is appropriate to ask whether the layoff compensation variable was a reasonable approximation of the naturally occurring caretaking activities that downsizing organizations often offer to their laid-off employees.

Second, the construct validity of the primary dependent variable in Study 3—performance quantity—is at least somewhat questionable. We hypothesized that when survivors feel attached to layoff victims who are perceived to have been treated unfairly, they respond by becoming more withdrawn from the organization, the apparent perpetrator of the injustice. The fact that subjects were least productive in the uncompensated layoff/high identification condition was interpreted to reflect survivors' withdrawal from the experimenter, who presumably was responsible for the injustice meted out to the layoff victim. However, it is possible that other explanations could account for subjects' tendency to be least productive in the uncompensated layoff/high identification condition.

Study 4 was designed to address these shortcomings of Study 3. We investigated survivors in an actual organization that had been undergoing layoffs for the past year. Moreover, the independent variables—survivors' prior identification with, and their perceptions of compensation provided to, the laid-off workers—were operationalized in ways very different from the procedures used in the laboratory experiment. Furthermore, the dependent variable was operationalized rather differently. If the obtained results are consistent with those previously found (i.e., if survivors respond most negatively toward the organization when they perceive that the organization failed to take care of layoff victims with whom survivors identify), then we can attach considerable internal *and* external validity to the findings across studies.

Questionnaires were sent to employees in a chain of small retail stores throughout the United States. Many stores in the chain had closed during the previous 12-month period; thus, all employees were survivors of the layoff. The questionnaire included measures of survivors': (a) retrospective change in organizational commitment, relative to before the layoffs (e.g., "I am proud to tell my friends that I work for this company," "I plan to work in this organization (rather than another one) for the foreseeable future): (b) identification with the layoff victims (e.g., "I had a close working relationship with at least some of the laid off people"); and (c) perception of the organization's compensation to the victims (e.g., "Management tried to help the laid-off people find a comparable job elsewhere in the company." "The severance pay that the company offered to the laid-off people was a generous amount"). The 504 respondents were predominantly female, White, and married. Average age was 37.06 years, and tenure in the organization was slightly over 4 years. Their occupations were either sales clerks (74%) or store managers (26%).

Multiple regression analysis revealed that the identification and compensation variables interactively combined to predict survivors' change in organizational commitment relative to the pre-layoff period. As can be seen in Table 3.3, all participants reported feeling less committed to the organization compared to prior to the layoff. However, and consistent with predictions, this was especially true when survivors identified with the layoff victims and perceived that the victims were not well compensated.

IMPLICATIONS

Taken together, the results of these four studies are consistent with the justice-based theoretical framework of survivors' reactions presented at the outset. In Studies 1 and 2 we suggested that subjects probably felt little sense of identification with, or attachment to, those who were laid off rather unfairly; therefore, the survivors appeared to react rather unsympathetically towards the layoff victim (e.g., by evaluating the victim harshly, and working harder). Studies 3 and 4 varied the two factors hypothesized to moderate the effects of layoffs on survivors: survivors' perceptions of the injustice of the layoff and their degree of identification with those laid off. As expected, survivors reacted most sympathetically toward the victim (and/or most negatively from the organization's vantage point) when they identified with laid-off parties who were perceived to have been dismissed relatively unfairly. We now consider some of the theoretical and practical implications of our con-

TABLE 3.3
Mean Level of Organizational Commitment

| Identification | Perceived Compensation | |
	Low	High
High	68.23	99.30
Low	90.47	98.93

Note: Results are based on median splits of the independent variables. Higher scores reflect greater increase (or less of a decrease) in organizational commitment relative to prior to the layoff. Scores could range from 18 to 198. Neutral point = 108. Therefore, all groups showed a decline in commitment.

ceptual and empirical analyses. Moreover, in discussing limitations, we simultaneously suggest several avenues for further investigation.

Theoretical Implications

First and most basic, the present research demonstrates that fundamental concepts from the voluminous literature on interpersonal and organizational justice (Greenberg, 1987a) may elucidate the effects of layoffs on the work behaviors and attitudes of those who remain. Indeed, the relationship between survivors' reactions as a content area in organizational psychology and justice theory as an explanatory framework is a mutually beneficial one. That is, one can begin to make sense of the highly varying and seemingly contradictory reactions of survivors by relying on basic concepts and principles of interpersonal justice theory. Moreover, the study of survivors' reactions provides a "living laboratory" in which to test and refine basic notions of interpersonal justice. Thus, justice theory helps us to understand survivors' reactions, and vice versa. Moreover, the study of survivors extends the external validity of justice theory by providing yet another domain in which the principles of interpersonal justice are relevant.

Let us elaborate on the mutually beneficial relationship between justice theory and survivors' reactions. That the former helps shed light on the latter should be self-evident by this point. In what way(s), however, might the study of survivors' reactions help to sharpen justice theory? One of the most knotty issues in research on interpersonal justice is being able to predict how individuals deal with perceived injustice. Many scholars agree that perceived injustice is distressing (for both the victims and observers), and that victims and observers therefore will be motivated to "do something" to redress the injustice-produced distress (Walster et al., 1978). From this point on, however, things become much more murky. In particular, theorists have encountered some difficulty in predicting exactly how individuals deal with perceived injustice; for example, Adams (1965) posited that individuals have no fewer than six ways of redressing perceived inequity. Moreover, it has proven even more difficult to predict the situational and dispositional factors that moderate individuals' modes of restoring or creating justice.

A key feature of the conceptualization guiding our study of survivors' reactions is that it offers some insight into: (a) *how* survivors may react to perceptions of injustice in the layoff process, and (2) *when* they will respond one way rather than another. Whether survivors respond sympathetically or unsympathetically towards the layoff victims depends on the survivors' prior (to the layoff) relationship with both the victims of the layoff and the organization (i.e., the perceived perpetrator of the injustice). From the consistency theories in social psychology (Festinger, 1957; Heider, 1958), we predicted that the closer the relationship between the survivors and the victims (rather than the organization), the more likely it is that the survivors will respond sympathetically toward the victims and/or unsympathetically toward the organization. This hypothesis was tested and confirmed in a number of empirical investigations, especially Studies 3 and 4. In short, by studying survivors' reactions, we come to better understand an important issue in basic justice research: the factors affecting individuals' preferred way of dealing with injustice.

In a similar vein, the process of studying survivors' reactions may address a number of related basic research questions. For example, justice scholars (e.g., Deutsch, 1985; Folger & Greenberg, 1985) have noted that individuals' perceptions of justice are based not only on the substantive outcomes of resource allocation decisions (i.e., distributive justice) but also on the processes used to arrive at such decisions (i.e., procedural justice). So, for example, survivors' perceptions of injustice may not only depend on the legitimacy of a given decision rule (e.g., seniority, merit), but also the procedures used to arrive at the rule. The relationship between distributive and procedural justice may be better understood through research on survivors' reactions. For example, how does one affect the other (if at all)? Which is more important in affecting survivors' justice judgments (cf. Greenberg, 1987a)? Do they combine additively or interactively to affect individuals' justice judgments and related behaviors? To reiterate the more general point: The analysis of survivors' reactions may address basic research questions of interpersonal and organizational justice.

Practical Implications

The present theory and research also may provide a number of guidelines for the management of layoffs. Many of the factors that moderate survivors' reactions may be influenced by managers' actions and attitudes associated with the handling of the layoff. In general, it is important for managers to act and think in ways that do not elicit survivor reactions that are predominantly sympathetic to the victim and/or unsympathetic (or even hostile) to the organization. Central to managers' task is creating the impression in survivors that the layoff was managed as fairly as possible (Greenberg, 1987e). Moreover, managers should pay particular attention to at least four key issues as they attempt to elicit the most positive (or least negative) survivor reactions.

1. *Perceptions of Fairness are Multiply Determined.* Managing layoffs is a *process* in which issues of fairness may arise (and must be dealt with appropriately) at many steps along the way. It is probably not sufficient, for example, for managers to "throw" a generous severance

package at the laid-off workers, and expect that survivors will perceive the layoff management as relatively fair. Perhaps just as important is how managers contend with other previously-mentioned justice issues, such as the amount of advance warning, how (where, when, and by whom) the news was imparted, and the bases for the decision rule, to name a few. In short, we would advise layoff managers to devote attention to each of the "before, during, and after" stages of downsizing (and the distributive, procedural, and interactional justice issues arising within each stage), in order to increase the likelihood that survivors view the process as maximally fair.

2. *Communication is Key.* As Peter Drucker and others have said, management *is* communication. That general credo certainly applies to the layoff management situation. Managers must provide clear and ongoing communications to survivors about how the organization has attempted, is attempting, and will attempt to be as fair as possible to the laid-off workers. One of us recently consulted to a downsizing organization who had in fact devoted considerable resources to compensating the employees it was dismissing; however, the survivors still responded quite negatively to the layoff. One possible explanation is that the organization—by its own admission—did not do a particularly effective job communicating to survivors about its compensation for those who were dismissed. More generally, if our hunch is correct that survivors will be influenced by the distributive, procedural, and interactional justice aspects of the layoff management process, then communications from the organization should address these sets of concerns. For example, management could communicate that it offered certain provisions for those laid off (e.g., outplacement counseling), *because* a survey of rank-and-file employees identified this particular provision as most valuable, relative to other possible ways of taking care of those laid off. Survivors may perceive such caretaking to be just on both distributive and procedural grounds; not only is the provision of outplacement substantively legitimate, but also workers had some say in the setting of priorities during times of scarce resources. As Greenberg (1986a) and others have demonstrated, individuals are likely to perceive that a particular course of action was fair—*independent* of its substance—to the extent that they had some input into the course of action.

Moreover, we suspect that survivors' judgments of the fairness of the layoff management process will be affected strongly by the organization's accounts for its actions. Thus, the organization not only must communicate *what* it is doing (e.g., laying off a certain percentage of employees, providing outplacement to those laid off), but also—at least under certain conditions—*why* it has taken or is taking certain actions. As Bies (1987) noted, individuals' judgments of the injustice associated with certain acts often are determined by the causal accounts provided for such acts. For example, the organization may convince survivors that the layoff was a necessary reaction to environmental pressures *beyond the organization's control.* Results from the same data base used in Study 4 suggest that survivors showed a greater decrease in organizational commitment to the extent that they felt that management did *not* offer a clear explanation of why the organization had resorted to layoffs; moreover, this was especially true when survivors felt a strong prior attachment to the layoff victims. Such results, of course, are strikingly parallel to those found in Studies 3 and 4.

To induce the perception in survivors that the layoff was the inevitable result of external factors beyond the organization's control, management may point out that other organizations within the same industry also are undergoing layoffs. Indeed, to soften the blow of the layoff (i.e., reduce survivors' perceptions of its injustice) organizations may communicate that their layoffs are not as extensive or severe as those in comparison organizations; Bies (1987) referred to this as a social referential account. Or, the organization may offer clear communications that no further layoffs are planned; Bies dubbed this a temporal referential account. In short, survivors' perceptions of the justice or injustice associated with the layoff are, to a large extent, dependent on the communications that the organization provides to account for its actions.

3. *Survivors' Identification with the Layoff Victims May Be a Moderating Factor.* Thus far in our discussion of practical implications, we have advocated downsizing in ways that survivors perceive to be fair to those laid off. At first blush, the position taken seems to be a universal one (i.e., that the management of layoffs *always* should be as fair as possible). However, such a stance may distract practitioners from the task of considering *the conditions under which* it is especially important to engender impressions of fairness in survivors. Based on the present theory and empirical research, it is particularly crucial that survivors perceive that the layoff was managed fairly when they previously felt attached to, or identified with, the victims of the layoff. In Studies 3 and 4 (see Tables 3.1 and 3.3) it was found that survivors responded rather negatively when the layoff was unfair and they identified with the dismissed workers. However, when there was little identification between the two parties, then the adverse effects of an unfair downsizing were substantially lower. We are not suggesting that management need not concern itself with the fairness of its downsizing when survivors do not identify with those laid off; rather, our position is that management

should be *especially* careful to downsize fairly when survivors do identify with the layoff victims.

4. *It's Important to Be (or Appear) Earnest.* We have equated effective layoff management with being able to create the impression in survivors that the layoff has been, is being, and will be handled fairly. Said differently, downsizing organizations have an impression management task (Goffman, 1959) on their hands. As in many impression management tasks (e.g., Jones & Wortman, 1973), it is crucial for the targets of influence not to believe that they are being "manipulated" by the influencing agent. Thus, organizations that *genuinely* wish to treat its laid-off workers as fairly as possible—and who manifest concrete expressions of that desire—probably will do an effective job of creating impressions of fairness in the eyes of survivors; in sharp contrast, organizations who resort to gimmicks intended to produce the impression (or, perhaps more accurately, illusion) of fairness probably will be recognized for their insincerity, and may exacerbate an already volatile situation.

Future Research

Although our theory and empirical investigations provide a useful start to the study of survivors' reactions, much more needs to be learned through future research. In this concluding section, we touch upon some of the many questions evoked by the present analysis that warrant further inquiry.

Generality of the Conceptual Framework. Throughout we have suggested that two broad categories of factors—survivors' perceptions of the degree of injustice meted out to the layoff victims and the extent to which survivors' identify with the victims (rather than the organization)—moderate the effects of layoffs on survivors. Moreover, each category includes numerous variables, *only a small portion of which have been investigated thus far.* Specifically, injustice was operationalized via the extent to which the layoff victim was compensated or taken care of by the downsizing organization. Identification was implemented through attitudinal similarity (Study 3) and closeness of the personal and professional and relationship between the survivors and victims (Study 4).

Further evaluations of our reasoning should explore the impact on survivors of different operationalizations of the two categories of independent variables. For example, perceptions of injustice could be influenced by the degree of legitimacy of the layoff (rather than a different cost-cutting procedure) in the first place, the amount of advance notice given to those laid off, and the details of how the news was delivered to employees. Identification with the victim (vs. the organization) could depend on such unexplored factors as: (a) whether the survivors ever have been laid off in the past themselves; (b) whether the survivors could be the victims of a future layoff; (c) whether the survivors currently maintain, or aspire to achieve, positions of formal authority that link them closely with the core mission of the organization; and (d) survivors' longevity in the organization. To the extent that survivors have been or could become layoff victims themselves, they are more likely to identify with the dismissed workers (Factors a and b). However, to the extent that survivors occupy, or aspire to occupy, positions that link them closely with the mission of the organization, and/or the greater their tenure in the organization (i.e., Factors c and d), the more likely it may be that they will feel greater allegiance to the organization.

In short, our conceptual framework allows—indeed, encourages—numerous ways of operationalizing the independent variables. By the same token, future research should explore the effects of perceived injustice and identification on a wide variety of *dependent variables,* not all of which were mentioned in Studies 1 through 4. For example, it is quite possible that survivors' turnover, absenteeism, and attitudes toward their jobs and fellow survivors also may be influenced by the two categories of factors that moderate the impact of layoffs. To repeat, then, the conceptual framework implies that many variables related to survivors' perceptions of injustice and identification with the layoff victims could affect a variety of survivors' reactions. Future research needs to expand the modes of operationalizing both independent and dependent variables, to evaluate the generality of the conceptual framework.

Further Refinement in Predicting Survivors' Reactions. We have suggested that survivors typically respond either "sympathetically" or "unsympathetically" toward the layoff victims. Moreover, both types of reactions may be manifested in a variety of ways. Unsympathetic reactions include denying or minimizing injustice, derogating the layoff victim, and working harder. Sympathetic responses include acknowledging that the injustice exists, working less hard, and looking for a job elsewhere. While the partitioning of survivors' reactions into these two categories seems useful, it also raises a number of theoretically and practically important questions. For example, are the two types of reactions mutually exclusive, or can survivors show both types of responses? In discussing the role of survivors' prior to identification (with the layoff victims *or* the organization), we have implied that survivors already have "chosen sides."

However, there may be certain conditions under which survivors have strong feelings of attachment to *both* the layoff victims and the organization. For instance, suppose that the survivors *currently* occupy a position of formal authority (in which case they may feel aligned with the organization), but *previously* worked among the ranks of those who were laid off (in which case they may identify with the plight of those who were dismissed). Or, imagine a downsizing organization that has a paternalistic or "one big family" type of corporate culture (e.g., Kodak). Such an atmosphere may encourage employees to feel a sense of commitment to the organization *as well as* to one another. Hence, when the "parent" dismisses their "siblings," survivors may feel caught in a bind between taking the role of the parent (and thus reacting unsympathetically toward the siblings) or the siblings (and therefore responding sympathetically toward them). Indeed, it just may be that the conditions that *simultaneously* promote survivors' prior allegiance to the organization and the ultimate layoff victims produce the greatest conflict in survivors about with whom to "side." These may be precisely the circumstances under which survivors react with the greatest ambivalence, exhibiting both sympathetic and unsympathetic reactions toward the dismissed workers.

Furthermore, *within* the broad categories of sympathetic and unsympathetic reactions, it is important to evaluate the relationships between the various types of responses. Do the different types of reactions form a syndrome, in which if survivors show one type of unsympathetic reaction (e.g., blaming the victim) they are likely to show another (e.g., working harder)? Or, is a "hydraulic" model more accurate, in which survivors choose one or two primary ways to "work off" their sense of injustice? This general question has not gone unnoticed by interpersonal justice theorists. Kenrick, Reich, and Cialdini (1976) reported that behavioral versus psychological modes of redressing the injustice meted out to another are asymmetrically related. Their results suggested that if the observers took action to redress the injustice, then no longer needed to restore fairness psychologically. However, restoring justice through psychological means did not eliminate observers' need to restore justice through behavioral means. Future research on the question of how the possible constellation of survivor reactions are related to one another thus may help elucidate yet another basic research question in the interpersonal justice literature.

Incompleteness of the Conceptual Model. We believe that the two-factor conceptual framework may go a long way toward explaining survivors' reactions. This is not to say, however, that the framework explains all (or nearly all) of the variation in survivors' reactions. As shown in Tables 3.1 and 3.3, survivors' responded negatively from the organization's point of view when they perceived that the organization was stingy toward the layoff victims, and especially when they identified with the victims. What would happen, however, if the layoff "victims" were treated in ways that survivors perceived to be "too" generous? Certain organizations have offered very generous caretaking activities to the employees that they laid off, in the form of lucrative severance pay or early retirement packages, or assistance in finding jobs elsewhere. Importantly, these same benefits sometimes are not offered to the survivors; instead, survivors are allowed to keep their jobs. Anecdotal evidence suggests that such downsizing procedures may leave survivors with the feeling that they were unlucky to remain (i.e., that it was not fair that they did not receive the considerable resources allotted to the laid-off employees). Thus, not only might survivors react negatively when they perceive that the laid-off workers were treated less than fairly, but also when they felt that— relative to themselves—the laid-off employees were being treated more than fairly. We have no empirical evidence on the latter hypothesis, merely anecdotal reports.

Furthermore, other factors seemingly unrelated to the fairness with which the layoff victims were treated and survivors' identification with the victims may moderate the effects of layoffs on survivors. For example, layoffs often produce changes in the quantity and quality of survivors' post-layoff job responsibilities. On the negative end (from the survivors' viewpoint), they may be asked to assume some of the work that had been performed previously by those laid off, without receiving a commensurate pay raise or promotion; if so, their motivation and/or morale might plummet. On the positive side, survivors' new duties may represent a form of job enrichment (Hackman & Oldham, 1976), in which case they might approach their work more enthusiastically than they did prior to the layoff.

Moreover, layoffs are a potential threat to the job security of survivors, which could affect their reactions (Greenhalgh & Rosenblatt, 1984). We recently discovered that very low or very high levels of layoff-induced job insecurity were associated with survivors becoming less committed to their jobs and the organization, relative to moderate amounts of job insecurity (Brochner et al., 1988). Such findings are reminiscent of the long-noted inverted-U relationship between individuals' arousal—a likely concomitant job insecurity—and task performance (Yerkes & Dodson, 1908).

In summary, our two-factor framework represents some of the driving forces underlying survivors' reactions; however, other factors and processes also are relevant. Future research needs to attend to these other determinants of survivors' reactions, and how they might combine with the variables inherent in our framework to moderate the effects of layoffs on those who stay.

Finally, our discussion of questions and topics that warrant further research is not exhaustive. For example, it would seem important to study the longitudinal reactions of survivors. Layoff survivorship may be likened to a grief process, in which individuals pass through a number of qualitatively different psychological stages (e.g., Kubler-Ross, 1969). If so, then survivors' reactions to co-worker layoffs might depend on the point in time at which such reactions are assessed. Furthermore, the psychological nature of survivors' identification with layoff victims deserves further attention. When survivors see workers with whom they identified laid off unfairly, do they feel that they have been treated unfairly themselves? If so, is it because their identification with the victims makes it more easy to imagine being treated unfairly, as Folger's (1986) referent cognitions model would suggest? Our hope is that the pursuit of these and other questions (Brockner, 1988) evoked by the present theory and research will deepen our understanding not only of survivors' reactions, but more generally social psychology, organizational psychology, and the relationship between the two.

ACKNOWLEDGMENTS

The authors thank John Carroll and Denise Rousseau for their constructive comments on an earlier version of the chapter.

REFERENCES

Adams, J. S. (1965). Inequity in social exchange. In L. Berkowitz (Ed.), *Advances in experimental social psychology* (Vol. 2, pp. 267–299). New York: Academic Press.

Alexander, S., & Ruderman, M. (1987). The role of procedural and distributive justice in organizational behavior. *Social Justice Research, 1,* 177–198.

Bierhoff, H. W., Cohen, R. L., & Greenberg, J. (1986). *Justice in social relations.* New York: Plenum.

Bies, R. J. (1986). *Individual reactions to corporate recruiting procedures: The importance of fairness.* Unpublished manuscript, Northwestern University, Evanston, IL.

Bies, R. J. (1987). The predicament of injustice: The management of moral outrage. In L. L. Cummings & B. M. Staw (Eds.), *Research in organizational behavior* (Vol. 9, pp. 289–319). Greenwich, CT: JAI Press.

Bies, R. L., & Moag, J. S. (1986). Interactional justice: The management of moral outrage. In R. J. Lewicki, B. H. Sheppard, & M. Bazerman (Eds.), *Research on negotiation in organizations* (pp. 43–55). Greenwich, CT: JAI Press.

Bies, R. J., & Shapiro, D. L. (1987). Interactional fairness judgments: The influence of causal accounts. *Social Justice Research, 1,* 199–218.

Brockner, J. (1988). The effects of work layoffs on survivors: Research, theory, and practice. In B. M. Staw & L. L. Cummings (Eds.), *Research in organizational behavior* (Vol. 10, pp. 213–255). Greenwich, CT: JAI Press.

Brockner, J., Davy, J., & Carter, C. (1985). Layoffs, self-esteem, and survivor guilt: Motivational, affective, and attitudinal consequences. *Organizational Behavior and Human Decision Processes, 36,* 229–244.

Brockner, J., Greenberg, J., Brockner, A., Bortz, J., Davy, J., & Carter, C. (1986). Layoffs, equity theory, and work performance: Further evidence on the impact of survivor guilt. *Academy of Management Journal, 29,* 373–384.

Brockner, J., Grover, S., O'Malley, M., DeWitt, R., Reed, T., & Glynn, M. A. (1988). *The effects of layoffs, job insecurity, and self-esteem on survivors' work effort and attitudes: Evidence from the laboratory and the field.* Manuscript submitted for review.

Brockner, J., Grover, S., Reed, T., DeWitt, R., & O'Malley, M. (1987). Survivors' reactions to layoffs: We get by with a little help for our friends. *Administrative Science Quarterly, 32,* 526–541.

Byrne, D. (1971). *The attraction paradigm.* New York: Academic Press.

Calabresi, G., & Bobbitt, P. (1978). *Tragic choices.* New York: W. W. Norton.

Cohen, R. L. (1986). *Justice: Views from the social sciences.* New York: Plenum.

Cornfield, D. B. (1983). Chances of layoff in a corporation: A case study. *Administrative Science Quarterly, 28,* 503–520.

Deutsch, M. (1975). Equity, equality, and need: What determines which value will be used as the basis for distributive justice? *Journal of Social Issues, 31*(3), 137–149.

Deutsch, M. (1985). *Distributive justice: A social-psychological perspective.* New Haven, CT: Yale University Press.

Eisenberg, P., & Lazarsfeld, P. F. (1938). The psychological effects of unemployment. *Psychological Bulletin, 35,* 358–390.

Festinger, L. (1957). *A theory of cognitive dissonance,* Stanford: Stanford University Press.

Folger, R. (1977). Distributive and procedural justice: Combined impact of "voice" and improvement on experienced inequity. *Journal of Personality and Social Psychology, 35,* 108–119.

Folger, R. (1986). Rethinking equity theory: A referent cognitions model. In H. W. Bierhoff, R. L. Cohen, & J. Greenberg (Eds.), *Justice in social relations* (pp. 145–162). New York: Plenum.

Folger, R., & Greenberg, J. (1985). Procedural justice: An interpretive analysis of personnel systems. In K. Rowland & G. Ferris (Eds.), *Research in personnel and human resources management* (Vol. 3, pp. 141–183). Greenwich, CT: JAI Press.

Goffman, E. (1959). *The presentation of self in everyday life.* Garden City, NY: Doubleday, Anchor Books.

Greenberg, J. (1981). The scarcity of distributing scarce and abundant resources. In M. J. Lerner & S. C. Lerner (Eds.), *The justice motive in social behavior* (pp. 289–315). New York: Plenum.

Greenberg, J. (1982). Approaching equity and avoiding inequity in groups and organizations. In J. Greenberg & R. L. Cohen (Eds.), *Equity and justice in social behavior* (pp. 389–435). New York: Academic Press.

Greenberg, J. (1986a). Determinants of perceived fairness of performance evaluations. *Journal of Applied Psychology, 71,* 340–342.

Greenberg, J. (1986b). Organizational performance appraisal procedures: What makes them fair? In R. J. Lewicki, B. H. Sheppard & M. Bazerman (Eds.), *Research on negotiation in organizations* (pp. 25–41). Greenwich, CT: JAI Press.

Greenberg, J. (1987a). A taxonomy of organizational justice theories. *Academy of Management Review, 12,* 9–22.

Greenberg, J. (1987b). Using diaries to promote procedural justice in performance appraisals. *Social Justice Research, 1,* 219–234.

Greenberg, J. (1987c). Reactions to procedural injustice in payment distributions: Do the ends justify the means? *Journal of Applied Psychology, 72,* 55–61.

Greenberg, J. (1987d). *Justice in organizations: An impression management perspective.* Paper presented at the meeting of the Society for Organizational Behavior, Columbus, OH.

Greenberg, J. (1987e). *Managing impressions of organizational justice.* Paper presented at the Academy of Management Conference, New Orleans, LA.

Greenberg, J. (1988). Cultivating an image of justice: Looking fair on the job. *Academy of Management Executive, 2,* 155–158.

Greenberg, J. (1989). The organizational waiting game: Delay as a status-asserting and status-neutralizing tactic. *Basic and Applied Social Psychology, 10,* 13–26.

Greenberg, J. (in press). Looking fair: Managing impressions of organizational justice. In B. M. Staw & L. L. Cummings (Eds.), *Research in organizational behavior.* Greenwich, CT: JAI Press.

Greenberg, J., & Cohen, R. L. (Eds.). (1982). *Equity and justice in social behavior.* New York: Academic Press.

Greenberg, J., & Folger, R. (1983). Procedural justice, participation, and the fair process effect in groups and organizations. In P. B. Paulus (Ed.), *Basic group processes* (pp. 235–256). New York: Springer-Verlag.

Greenhalgh, L., Lawrence, A. T., & Sutton, R. I. (1988). Determinants of work force reduction strategies in declining organizations. *Academy of Management Review, 13,* 241–254.

Greenhalgh, L., & Rosenblatt, Z. (1984). Job insecurity: Toward conceptual clarity. *Academy of Management Review, 9,* 438–448.

Hackman, J. R., & Oldham, G. R. (1976). Motivation through the design of work: Test of a theory. *Organizational Behavior and Human Performance, 16,* 250–279.

Heider, F. (1958). *The psychology of interpersonal relations.* New York: Wiley.

Homans, G. C. (1961). *Social behavior: Its elementary forms.* New York: Harcourt, Brace, & World.

Ichniowski, C., Brockner, J., & Davy, J. (1988). *Performance of survivors after seniority-based layoffs: A multi-method approach.* Manuscript submitted for review.

Jahoda, M. (1982). *Employment and unemployment: A social psychological analysis.* New York: Academic Press.

Jones, E. E., & Wortman, C. B. (1973). *Ingratiation: An attributional approach.* Morristown, NJ: General Learning Press.

Kanfer, R., Sawyer, J., Earley, P. C., & Lind, E. A. (1987). Fairness and participation in evaluation procedures: Effects of task attitudes and performance. *Social Justice Research, 1,* 235–249.

Karuza, J., & Leventhal, G. S. (1976). *Justice judgments: Role demands and perceptions of fairness.* Paper presented at the meeting of the American Psychological Association, Washington, DC.

Kenrick, D. T., Reich, J. W., & Cialdini, R. B. (1976). Justification and compensation: Rosier skies for the devalued victim. *Journal of Personality and Social Psychology, 34,* 654–657.

Kubler-Ross, E. (1969). *On death and dying.* New York: MacMillan.

Lerner, M. J. (1977). The justice motive: Some hypotheses as to its origins and forms. *Journal of Personality, 45,* 1–52.

Leventhal, G. S. (1976). The distribution of rewards and resources in groups and organizations. In L. Berkowitz & E. Walster (Eds.), *Advances in experimental social psychology* (Vol. 9, pp. 91–131). New York: Academic Press.

Leventhal, G. S. (1980). What should be done with equity theory? In K. J. Gergen, M. S. Greenberg & R. H. Willis (Eds.), *Social exchange: Advances in theory and research* (pp. 27–55). New York: Plenum.

Leventhal, G. S., Karuza, J., & Fry, W. R. (1980). Beyond fairness: A theory of allocation preferences. In G. Mikula (Ed.), *Justice and social interaction* (pp. 167–218). New York: Springer-Verlag.

Leventhal, G. S., & Weiss, T. (1975). *Perceived need and the response to inequitable distributions of reward.* Unpublished manuscript, Wayne State University, Detroit, MI.

Lind, E. A., & Tyler, T. R. (1988). *The social psychology of procedural justice.* New York: Plenum.

Lissak, R. I. (1983). *Procedural fairness: How employees evaluate procedures.* Unpublished doctoral dissertation, University of Illinois, Champaign, IL.

President decides not to veto bill requiring notice of plant closings. (1988, August 3). *The New York Times.* pp. A1, B5.

Schwartz, B. (1975). *Queueing and waiting.* Chicago: University of Chicago Press.

Senate, by 72-23, approves notice of plant closings. (1988, July 6). *The New York Times,* pp. A1, D13.

Sheppard, B. H., & Lewicki, R. J. (1987). Toward general principles of managerial fairness. *Social Justice Research, 1,* 161–176.

Thibaut, J., & Walker, L. (1975). *Procedural justice: A psychological analysis.* Hillsdale, NJ: Lawrence Erlbaum Associates.

Tyler, T. R., & Caine, A. (1981). The role of distributional and procedural fairness in the endorsement of formal leaders. *Journal of Personality and Social Psychology, 41,* 642–655.

Tyler, T. R., Rasinski, K., & Spodick, N. (1985). Influence of voice on satisfaction with leaders: Exploring the meaning of process control. *Journal of Personality and Social Psychology, 48,* 72–81.

Tyler, T. R., & Sears, D. O. (1977). Coming to like obnoxious people when we must live with them. *Journal of Personality and Social Psychology, 35,* 200–211.

Walker, S. O., & Newborg, M. N. (1986). Termination: A manager's toughest job. In J. L. DiGaetani (Ed.), *Handbook of executive communication* (pp. 699–709), Homewood, IL: Dow Jones-Irwin.

Walster, E., Walster, G. W., & Berscheid, E. (1978). *Equity: Theory and research.* Boston: Allyn & Bacon.

Yerkes, R. M., & Dodson, J. D. (1908). The relation of strength of stimulus to rapidity of habit formation. *Journal of Comparative Neurological Psychology, 18,* 459–482.

4

Beyond Formal Procedures: The Interpersonal Context of Procedural Justice

Tom R. Tyler
Robert J. Bies
Northwestern University

Do people care about justice on the job? If you ask any manager or worker that question, you would hear such answers as "of course," and "you'd better believe it." There is no doubt that people care very much whether they get what they feel they deserve in terms of performance evaluations, raises, promotions, budget allocations, and so forth. Indeed, fairness is a central concern to people in any allocation of resources or dispute resolution process in the workplace.

Over the past two decades, psychologists have increasingly recognized the importance of people's judgments about the fairness of their dealings with authorities and organizations. This recognition first centered on the fairness of the outcomes people received—that is, a concern for *distributive justice* (Deutsch, 1985; Homans, 1961). The dominant framework of distributive justice, equity theory (Adams, 1965; Walster, Berscheid, & Walster, 1973), inspired research on (a) how a decision maker attempts to create a fair outcome distribution such as giving raises to employees who perform the best or have been employed the longest (e.g., see Leventhal, 1976, for a review), and (b) how people react to unfair outcome distributions (e.g., see Greenberg, 1982, for a review). A similar focus on distributive justice is also found in the research on relative deprivation (Crosby, 1984; Martin, 1981).

More recently, psychologists have recognized that people have a concern with the fairness of the process by which outcomes are allocated and disputes are resolved that is independent of their concerns with the fairness of those outcomes. By process we mean such issues as the way performance appraisals are carried out, the kind of information used in performance appraisals, the rules for determining who gets a raise, among others. This concern with *procedural justice* was initially established by Thibaut and Walker (1975) in a series of studies comparing the adversarial and inquisitorial courtroom procedures for dispute resolution. In an adversary procedure, a third party resolves disputes by binding judgment but only after the disputants have had a chance to explain their positions. In an inquisitorial procedure, the third party resolves the dispute by binding judgment without explicit provision for information input by the disputants. Thibaut and Walker found that people viewed the adversary procedure as a fairer way of resolving legal disputes, and, in addition, were more satisfied with the outcomes of their trials in the adversary procedure, irrespective of what those outcomes were.

Since the publication of *Procedural Justice* by Thibaut and Walker (1975), an increasing amount of research has been conducted on issues of procedural justice (see Lind & Tyler, 1988, for a comprehensive review). The findings of Thibaut and Walker's initial research have been widely confirmed in subsequent studies of trials (e.g., Lind, Kurtz, Musante, Walker, & Thibaut, 1980), in studies of other nontrial procedures used in resolving legal disputes, such as plea bargaining (Casper, Tyler, & Fisher, 1988; Houldon, 1980), and mediation (Adler, Hensler, & Nelson, 1983), as well as police officer dealings with citizens (Tyler, 1988, in press; Tyler & Folger, 1980). In addition, researchers have found that concerns about procedural justice extend to business (Folger & Greenberg, 1985; Greenberg & Folger, 1983; Sheppard, 1984), political (Tyler & Caine, 1981), interpersonal (Barrett-Howard & Tyler, 1986), and educational (Tyler & Caine, 1981) settings. In fact, wherever procedural issues have been studied they have emerged as an important concern.

As research on procedural justice has broadened in scope there has been an increasing recognition that the idea of procedural justice means much more to those involved in disputes or allocations than the formal properties of procedures used in making decisions. In addition, people focus on how decision makers conduct themselves during the enactment of the decision-making procedure. For example, is the decision maker attentive, considerate, and respectful? Such decision-maker conduct and people's assessment of it are part of the *interpersonal context* of formal decision-making procedures (Bies & Moag, 1986). In this chapter, we outline some of the aspects of the interpersonal context that have emerged as important in research subsequent to that of Thibaut and Walker. Our intention is not to reject the basic procedural justice paradigm, which has been strongly supported both by the work of Thibaut and Walker and by subsequent studies on procedural justice. Instead, we intend to elaborate the concept of procedural justice beyond that defining the initial efforts of Thibaut and Walker.

Our chapter is divided into three sections. First, we analyze the Thibaut and Walker paradigm and explain why it has excluded the interpersonal context of formal decision-making procedures. Second, we review the empirical research on the interpersonal context of formal decision-making procedures and identify factors that influence employees' judgments of procedural justice. Third, we propose a broader concept of procedural justice and explore its implications for theory, research, and application to business settings.

THE THIBAUT AND WALKER PARADIGM: INTENDED AND UNINTENDED EFFECTS

Thibaut and Walker's view of procedural justice has dominated the conceptualization of procedural justice issues and research (Lind & Tyler, 1988). Indeed, Thibaut and Walker have created a "paradigm" for the study of procedural justice (Lind & Tyler, 1988). This paradigm has guided subsequent research in particular directions with two dominant effects.

One effect of the Thibaut and Walker paradigm is a focus on the decision-making function of procedures. By defining procedural variations in formal structural terms, Thibaut and Walker directed attention toward those aspects of procedure that were related to the decision (i.e, decision quality and accuracy). This emphasis was not an accident: In their theory of procedural preference (Thibaut & Walker, 1975, chapter 12) and their normative theory of procedure (Thibaut & Walker, 1978), Thibaut and Walker focused on the ability of procedures to produce accuracy and distributive justice—two key attributes of the decision.

A second effect of Thibaut and Walker's approach to procedural justice has been an emphasis on the formal and structural properties of procedures. In their original work on legal procedures Thibaut and Walker focused on abstract representations of the adversarial and inquisitorial procedures, rather than on the operationalizations of those procedures in various actual courtrooms. This emphasis on formal, structurally defined, decision-making procedures, rather than on the conduct of decision makers during the enactment of those procedures, has continued to dominate the study of procedures.

This is not to suggest that decision-maker conduct has been completely overlooked in analysis of procedural justice. For example, in an alternative model of procedural justice, Leventhal (1980) identified six procedural justice rules: consistency, bias suppression, accuracy, correctability, representativeness, and ethicality. The consistency rule says that allocative procedures should be applied consistently across people and over time. The bias suppression rule says that personal self-interest and blind allegiance to narrow preconceptions should be prevented. The accuracy rule says that decisions must be based on as much good information and informed opinion as possible. The correctability rule says that opportunities must exist to modify and reverse decisions. The representativeness rule says that the allocation process must represent the concerns of all important subgroups and individuals. Finally, the ethicality rule says that the allocation process must be compatible with prevailing moral and ethical standards.

Leventhal's model suggests that a broad range of issues about decision-maker conduct may be important to judgments about procedural justice. Leventhal's model has immense heuristic value (Lind & Tyler, 1988). It is, however, the Thibaut and Walker model that has guided procedural justice researchers.

The Thibaut and Walker paradigm has markedly advanced our understanding of procedural justice, particularly with respect to business settings (Greenberg, 1987). A comparison of that paradigm to the larger set of issues articulated by Leventhal (1980) suggests, however, that the Thibaut and Walker approach to procedural justice may have too narrow a focus. In particular, Leventhal's discussion of procedural justice suggests that the interpersonal aspects of procedures may also be important elements in judgments about procedural fairness.

More recently, Bies and Moag (1986) argued that viewing a decision-making procedure as an abstract set of formal decision-making rules is inadequate. People are also influenced by the decision maker's conduct during the enactment of the procedure. Bies and Moag identify two critical aspects of decision-maker conduct that are salient to people in forming their judgments of procedural justice. First, people focus on the interpersonal treatment that they received from the decision maker. Not only can such behavior be an independent criterion in evaluations of procedural justice (Leventhal, 1980), but the quality of interpersonal treatment helps people make attributions about the decision maker's motives which may generalize to judgments about the procedure itself.

Second, people focus on whether the formal procedure was enacted properly (Lind & Lissak, 1985). For example, decision makers typically have considerable discretionary authority and can enact the formal decision-making procedure in a variety of ways. The courtroom trial procedure is a case in point. If we were to sit in different courtrooms and watch different judges, we would see that trial judges run their courtrooms in different ways. In work settings, in which standardization of procedures may not exist or necessarily be valued, variation in the enactment of procedures such as performance appraisal can be as great, if not greater. As proposed by Leventhal (1980), the fairness of such actions will be evaluated by the prevailing norms of appropriate decision-maker conduct.

THE INTERPERSONAL CONTEXT OF PROCEDURAL JUSTICE

A Review of the Empirical Evidence

Our basic argument is that once a decision maker enacts a procedure, it is an interpersonal process that employees evaluate in terms of procedural justice. Recent research has found that people's procedural fairness judgments are influenced by (a) interpersonal treatment they receive from the decision maker, which may have little or nothing to do with the formal procedure, and (b) whether the formal decision-making procedure is properly enacted by the decision maker.

Interpersonal Treatment

Recent studies have suggested that people react quite strongly to the quality of interpersonal treatment they receive during the enactment of a decision-making procedure (Bies & Moag, 1986; Tyler, 1988). Bies (1986) conducted two studies of MBA job candidate reactions to corporate recruiting procedures. His results identify important aspects of interpersonal treatment in people's judgments of procedural justice. In the first study, MBA students were asked to list the criteria they would use to evaluate the fairness of corporate recruiting procedures. They did the rating prior to their job search. In addition to procedural considerations (e.g., opportunity to present their point of view), the job candidates identified four aspects of interpersonal treatment that would be important to them: honesty, courteous treatment, timely feedback, and respect for their "rights" (e.g., no statements or questions regarding race, sex, or marital status).

In the second study, Bies asked MBA students to describe situations in which they felt fairly or unfairly treated during the course of the recruitment process. They did their evaluation after their job search. Bies found that job candidates distinguished procedural considerations from those dealing with interpersonal treatment in their judgments of procedural fairness. Consistent with Thibaut and Walker's (1975) hypothesis, job candidates felt fairly treated when they had the opportunity to fully present their "case" to the interviewers (i.e., "voice"), but felt unfairly treated when they were denied that opportunity. In addition, Bies found that job candidates focused on the interpersonal treatment they received during the job interview. Corroborating the findings of the first study, job candidates were concerned about the honesty of the recruiter, courteous treatment, timely feedback, and respect for their "rights" (e.g., no statements or questions regarding race, sex, or marital status). Moreover, Bies found the job candidates were concerned about the quality of interpersonal treatment irrespective of whether or not they were ultimately offered a job. In other words, judgments about the inappropriateness of interpersonal treatment were not simply the "rationalizations" of those unwilling to accept that they performed poorly during the job interview. Both "winners" and "losers" reacted negatively to poor interpersonal treatment.

Concerns about interpersonal treatment extend beyond corporate recruitment to other organizational domains. For example, a series of studies have shown that interpersonal treatment can influence "survivor" judgments of the procedural fairness of how employees were laid off (Brockner & Greenberg, this volume). Glass and Singer (1972) reported the results of a laboratory study in which people felt unfairly treated when they were unduly embarrassed or humiliated by a "bureaucratic administrator" who acted in an arrogant manner. Similarly, in a study of service agency clients, Katz, Gutek, Kahn, and Barton (1975) found that clients were angry and resentful of bureaucratic officials who were unresponsive to their needs and acted irresponsibly.

The suggestion that interpersonal aspects of process matter to those dealing with authorities have also been supported in several studies of citizen dealings with the police and the courts. Tyler and Folger (1980) examined the influence of citizen dealings with the police on satisfaction with police performance. They found that citizens focused on how appropriately the police handled their interactions in evaluating police performance. In particular, people expected the police to show concern for their rights, to be courteous, and to otherwise conform to their conception of the appropriate behavior of public servants when dealing with citizens.

The suggestion that the public is concerned with interpersonal issues in encounters with legal authorities is also supported by the results of Tyler's (1988) study of citizen dealings with the police and the courts. That study found that honesty and ethical appropriateness (e.g., politeness and respect for their rights) were the second and third most important independent factors people used in assessing the fairness of their treatment. The only factor that was more important were assessments of the degree to which the authorities tried to be fair to the citizen. The independent nature of the contributions of the honesty and ethical appropriateness factors suggest that people's concern with interpersonal treatment was distinct from their concern with the more traditional aspects of procedural justice that are linked to the nature and quality of the authority's decisions (Tyler, 1988).

Although studies of the effects of interpersonal treatment on procedural justice have been conducted in business, government, and legal organizations, there is additional evidence that such concerns may be universal in scope. Barrett-Howard and Tyler (1986) explored the importance of different criteria of procedural fairness across allocation situations varying in the four basic dimensions of social relationships outlined by Deutsch (1982): formal–informal, cooperative–competitive, social–task, and equal or unequal power. These four dimensions result in 16 possible combinations of situations high or low on those four basic dimensions. Subjects were asked to rate, among other things, how important procedural justice was in each situation, and then rate the importance of each of Leventhal's six rules of procedural justice in that situation. Across all 16 settings, the ethicality rule, which encompasses the interpersonal issues we have described, was the second most important dimension. In addition, it was generally an important issue irrespective of the nature of the allocation setting.

In summary, findings from empirical studies in a variety of settings provide converging evidence that the interpersonal treatment that people receive from decision makers is an important consideration in people's evaluation of procedural justice. The next section extends this interpersonal focus to an analysis of the way that formal procedures are enacted by decision makers. In particular, we focus on the propriety of the decision maker's conduct during the enactment of the formal decision-making procedure.

Proper Enactment of the Formal Decision-Making Procedure

Formal procedures typically give the decision maker discretionary authority in enacting the procedure. Indeed, a manager may have a great deal of latitude in "interpreting" and enacting organizational procedures (McCall & Kaplan, 1985). Such freedom is not without restraints as decision makers do have responsibilities in enacting the decision-making procedure (Folger & Bies, in press). These responsibilities are defined by the prevailing norms that define proper and socially acceptable decision maker behavior (Leventhal, 1980).

A review of the empirical evidence identifies five norms with respect to a proper decision-maker conduct in enacting formal decision-making procedures in business settings. Adapting from a framework suggested by Folger and Bies (in press), these norms include: (a) adequately considering employees' viewpoints, (b) suppressing personal biases, (c) applying decision-making criteria consistently across employees, (d) providing timely feedback to employees after a decision, and (e) providing an account of (or explanation for) the decision. Each of these norms, and the empirical evidence, is discussed here.

Adequately Considering Employees' Viewpoints.   When decision makers ask employees for their viewpoints on a particular decision, employees expect such views to be considered as important and evaluated carefully (Tyler, 1987). Such consideration is important because employees hope to influence the decision maker when they voice their opinion (Thibaut & Walker, 1975). If, after asking for employee viewpoints, decision makers ignore such views, employees will not only judge the decision-making process to be "corrupt" (Cohen, 1985), but they will likely feel manipulated (cf. Bies & Shapiro, 1988). Thus, decision-maker consideration should be an important factor in employees' assessments of procedural fairness (Tyler, 1987).

Several studies support this claim. In a series of laboratory experiments, Folger and his colleagues (Folger, 1977; Folger, Rosenfield, Grove, & Corkran, 1979) found that when decision makers invited the viewpoints of employees, but then ignored or "failed to consider" such information, employees judged the decision-making process as more unfair than did those employees who had never been given the chance to present their points of view. In a survey of worker suggestion systems, Reuter (1977) found that if employees felt that their suggestions have been adequately considered by upper management, it enhanced the perceived procedural fairness of the suggestion system. Similarly, in the legal arena, Tyler and Folger (1980) found that citizens focused on whether police took their complaints seriously in assessing the fairness of the process.

Suppressing Personal Biases.   Cohen (1985) suggested that concerns about decision-maker bias are especially likely to occur in business settings, in contrast to legal settings in which judges are widely viewed as neutral and disinterested decision makers. In work settings employees recognize that the decision maker may have a vested interested in the allocation and thus may not be neutral. Yet, employees expect decision makers to be neutral and suppress their personal biases as a criterion of procedural justice (Leventhal, 1980). Thus, any appearance of decision-maker bias should render the procedure suspect, even though the procedure itself is ostensibly a fair one (Lind & Lissak, 1985).

The effects of decision-maker bias have been found to be very clear in judgments of procedural justice. Lind and Lissak (1985) studied an adversary trial procedure in which there was sometimes evidence suggesting that the judge had an improper interpersonal relationship with the other party to the case, that is, she or he was biased. When there was no evidence of such a relationship the authors found, as is typically true, that the outcome of the case had no influence on whether the person involved thought that the adversary system is a fair trial procedure. On the other hand, if there was evidence that the judge might be biased, people's judgments of the fairness of the procedure were connected to the outcome. If they lost their case they lost respect for the trial procedure and reduced their evaluation of procedural justice; if they won their case they gained greater respect for the trial procedure. These findings suggest that those involved evaluated the fairness of the procedure in terms of its robustness in combatting that potential bias. In fact, the ability of the procedure to overcome the apparent bias involved in the personal relationship led those affected by the third parties' decision to be even more impressed by the procedure than when there was no suggestion of impropriety.

Two studies corroborate the Lind and Lissak findings. Barrett-Howard and Tyler (1986) found that, in business-like situations, bias suppression by the decision maker was significantly associated with people's judgments of procedural justice. Similarly, in a survey of managers, Sheppard and Lewicki (1987) found that bias suppression was one of the most frequently cited characteristics of procedural justice.

Applying Decision-Making Criteria Consistently Across Employees. On the job, most of us expect that a decision maker will treat each person or "case" the same. That is, we view the consistent application of decision-making rules and criteria as an essential feature of procedural fairness (Leventhal, 1980). Indeed, to act arbitrarily or inconsistently should undermine perceptions of procedural fairness (Fry & Cheney, 1981; Fry & Leventhal, 1979; Leventhal, 1980).

Several studies support this claim. In a survey of middle managers, Greenberg (1986) found that the consistent application of standards across people was identified as a key determinant of procedural fairness in performance evaluations. That finding has been corroborated by Barrett-Howard and Tyler (1986) who found that, in business-like situations, decision-maker consistency across people was an important characteristic of procedural fairness. Similarly, Sheppard and Lewicki (1987) found that managers perceive decision-maker consistency in applying rules across people and settings as a key criterion in assessing procedural fairness in the workplace. Interestingly, however, the managers in that study also expected their bosses to be flexible as another characteristic of a procedural fairness. The possible paradoxical implications of being consistent and flexible are examined later in the chapter.

Timely Feedback After a Decision. Aram and Salipante (1981) identified timely feedback as one standard to evaluate fairness in the workplace. Indeed, most of us want to hear the outcome of a decision in a timely fashion rather than experiencing unreasonable delays in receiving such information. Thus, we should expect timely feedback to enhance perceptions of procedural fairness, while unduly late feedback should reduce the perceived fairness of the decision-making process.

Two studies support this claim. In a survey of MBA job candidates, Bies (1986) found that timely feedback about the outcome of an interview was a frequently cited characteristic of "fair" corporate recruiting procedures, while lengthy delays in receiving feedback was a frequently cited characteristic of "unfair" corporate recruiting procedures. Moreover, the job candidates' assessments of procedural fairness were independent of whether they received a job offer. Reuter (1977) found that employees' perceptions of the procedural fairness of employee suggestion systems were influenced by the timeliness of feedback from management on their suggestions.

Providing an Account of the Decision. Employees expect a decision maker to provide an account (Bies, 1987b) for a decision, particularly when the outcome is unfavorable. An account is an explanation with a reason for the decision. Because many decisions in business settings are made in private, the decision maker's account may be the primary basis of employee evaluations of whether the decision maker acted properly in making the decision (Bies, 1988a, 1988b).

Interestingly, current theories of procedural justice (e.g., Leventhal, 1980; Thibaut & Walker, 1975) have ignored the role of decision-maker accounts. This omission is somewhat surprising because in the courtroom setting, the primary focus of procedural justice research, judges frequently provide an account of their decision. Indeed, by doing so, judges are providing "evidence" to people that they acted in an impartial and unbiased manner, and which signals to people that the decision maker has *considered* their point of view before rejecting it (Tyler, 1987). Thus, a decision-maker account will be associated with employees' judgments of procedural justice.

Several studies support this claim. In a series of laboratory and field studies, Bies and Shapiro (1987) found that the presence of a causal account claiming mitigating circumstances (i.e., an excuse) for an unfavorable allocation (e.g., budget cutback, no job offer) reduced people's feelings of procedural injustice and their disapproval of the decision maker relative to a similar situation without a causal account. In a laboratory experiment in a job recruitment context, Bies and Shapiro (1988) found that variations in the type of formal procedure (e.g., voice, no voice) and the presence or absence of an account for an unfavorable outcome had independent effects on procedural fairness judgments. In a later field survey, Bies and Shapiro (1988) asked employees to evaluate the procedural fairness of an unfavorable budget decision, to assess the amount of opportunity they had to persuade the decision maker (i.e., voice), and the presence of an account. As in the laboratory experiment both the voice procedure and the account had independent effects on procedural fairness judgments. Taken together, these studies not only suggest that an account can influence procedural fairness judgments, but they provide the first empirical evidence that an account acts independently of the formal procedure in influencing such judgments.

As a replication and extension of these studies, Bies (1987a) surveyed employees regarding their opportunity to persuade the decision maker (voice), the presence of an account, and the sincerity of the decision maker in giving the account for an unfavorable budget decision. Bies (1987a) again found that the formal procedure and the presence of an account had independent effects on procedural fairness judgments. In addition, decision-maker sincerity had an independent effect. Bies, Shapiro, and Cummings (1988) surveyed currently employed subordinates about situations in which a boss provides a causal account for refusing a subordinate's request for resources. They found that the mere claim of mitigating circumstances does not explain the influence of a causal account in enhancing perceptions of procedural fairness; rather, it is the adequacy of reasoning in support of the claim and the boss' sincerity in communicating the causal account that explain the variance in that perception. In other words, a managerial account can influence procedural fairness judgments as long as it is perceived to be adequate and sincere.

In a related research program, Folger and his colleagues (Folger & Martin, 1986; Folger, Rosenfield, & Robinson, 1983) have found that when managers provide an adequate justification (mitigating circumstances) for apparently "arbitrary" changes in the rules for distributing rewards, it reduces employees' feelings of procedural injustice. In one study (Folger, Rosenfield, & Robinson, 1983) information about what would have happened under the old rules did not influence feelings of resentment over losing as long as subjects were given a good reason for the rule change. Without a good account for the rule change, however, subjects who would have won under the old rules, but lost under the new rules, were more resentful than were other subjects. In a second study (Folger & Martin, 1986) subjects were denied a favorable outcome as the result of an experimenter's actions, and either good reasons (mitigating circumstances) or poor reasons (an arbitrary decision) were provided for such inequitable actions. Folger and Martin (1986) found that subjects were more willing to recommend the experimenter when the explanation of the experimenter's action suggested it was due to mitigating circumstances as opposed to an arbitrary decision.

Further support for the importance of accounts is found in Tyler's (1988) study of people's encounters with legal authorities. Tyler found that the most important judgment about an experience influencing people's assessments concerning its procedural fairness was their inference that the authority involved was trying to be fair to them. In other words, people made a judgment about the intentions of the third-party decision maker. Accounts are an opportunity for the third party to communicate information about his or her intentions and, hence, are key to how an experience is interpreted (Bies, 1987a).

In summary, there is growing evidence that the proper enactment of formal procedures is another aspect of what employees evaluate when judging the fairness of a process. In particular, employees focus on whether the decision maker (a) adequately considered their viewpoints, (b) suppressed their personal biases, (c) applied decision-making criteria consistently, (d) provided timely feedback, and (e) provided an account with adequate reasoning and sincerely. We propose that this evidence, along with findings on interpersonal treatment, suggest a broader view of procedural justice. In the next section, we explore the implications of this more comprehensive perspective.

TOWARD A BROADER VIEW OF PROCEDURAL JUSTICE

Implications and Applications in Business Settings

The review of empirical evidence has supported the argument for a broader concept of procedural justice—one that integrates formal procedure and decision-maker conduct considerations. This broader view of procedural justice suggests four major implications for theory, research, and application. Our discussion focuses on: (a) decision-maker conduct, or the "missing link" in procedural justice; (b) the attribution and social construction of procedural justice, (c) the "human" side of procedural justice, and (d) conduct, community, and procedural justice.

Decision-Maker Conduct, or the "Missing Link" in Procedural Justice

The empirical evidence we reviewed in this chapter suggests the need to elaborate the Thibaut and Walker paradigm. An increasing number of studies provide converging evidence that, in most people's minds, procedural justice means more than the formal procedures used to allocate resources or resolve disputes. In particular, people's judgments of procedural fairness are influenced by the quality of interpersonal treatment they receive from decision makers and whether the decision maker enacted the formal procedure properly. These findings occurred in a variety of business situations including corporate recruitment (Bies, 1986), budget decision making (Bies & Shapiro, 1987), performance appraisal (Greenberg, 1986), and employee termination (Brockner & Greenberg, this volume). Moreover, a similar pattern of results were found in legal (Tyler, 1988) and government (Katz et al., 1975) settings. Thus, although the Thibaut and Walker paradigm has overlooked the role of decision-maker conduct and the interpersonal context of formal procedures, the evidence suggests that employees, themselves, do not neglect these considerations.

One reason for this omission in previous studies may be found in the original Thibaut and Walker (1975) formulation of the research problem. That is, the Thibaut and Walker focus is on the formal decision-making procedure as the "figural" element of their analysis, while the influence of the decision maker's conduct was controlled, making the decision maker the "ground" element of the analysis (cf. Lind & Lissak, 1985). Based on the evidence we reviewed in this chapter, it is clear that the decision maker's conduct during the enactment of the procedure can be a "figural" element. As such, to assess procedural justice without incorporating the role and influence of decision-maker conduct results in an inadequate model of procedural justice.

The evidence strongly suggests that employees evaluate decision-maker conduct according to the prevailing norms in the situation. Although some researchers argue that norms are merely standards to evaluate decision-maker conduct (Sheppard, Lewicki, & Minton, 1986), recent research suggests that norms can possess procedural qualities in the minds of employees. Norms learned from the corporate culture (Martin, Feldman, Hatch, & Sitkin, 1983), or those that emerge in an on-going relationship between parties in organizations, take on the status of an implied contract with procedural properties (Rousseau, 1988). For example, if a manager consistently consults a subordinate in making decisions, such consultation may be perceived as a *quasi-procedure*, which is analogous to a standard operating procedure (Cyert & March, 1963), but without its formal properties. If, at some point, the boss does not consult the subordinate on a decision, then the subordinate may feel unfairly treated. As such, decision-maker behavior that is consistent across time emerges as a quasi-procedure and the manager has a responsibility to enact this quasi-procedure properly. Thus, we argue for a broader interpretation of what constitutes a procedure, one that includes both formal procedure and social norms as bases for evaluating procedural justice in business settings.

The Attribution and Social Construction
of Procedural Justice

We argue that once a procedure is enacted, people may make inferences about the fairness of the procedure from the actions of the decision makers. For example, from decision-maker actions, people's judgments about how they have been treated during the decision-making process (Bies & Moag, 1986; Tyler, 1988) and their attributions regarding the motives underlying the decision maker's actions (Bies & Shapiro, 1987; Tyler, 1988) could influence reactions to the experience, the outcome, the decision maker, and the institution within which the decision occurs (Lane, 1985; Leventhal, 1980).

The importance of attributions about decision maker's intentions is illustrated in Tyler's (1987) finding that decision-maker consideration, which involves a causal inference, is a precondition of value-expressive effects of voice procedures. In a series of studies, Bies and his colleagues (Bies, 1987a; Bies & Shapiro, 1987, 1988; Bies et al., 1988) found that providing a sincere, credible account, which contains attributional information, can strongly influence procedural fairness judgments—even apart from formal procedure considerations. Similarly, Tyler (1988) found that information influencing attributions about the dispositions of legal authorities (e.g., police, courts) was key to people's assessments of procedural fairness.

Because attributional information can influence procedural fairness judgments, decision-makers often attempt to "manage" other people's attributions with the intent of influencing employees' judgments of procedural justice (Bies, 1988a). For example, a boss may say it was a "top management decision" that forced budget cutbacks or salary freezes rather than a deliberate action on his or her part. The use of such impression management in organizations has been proposed by Bies (1987b) and has been extended by Greenberg (in press). According to an impression management perspective, decision makers will provide an account to minimize the appearance of impropriety (Bies, 1988b), and thus enhance the perception of procedural fairness (Bies & Shapiro, 1987). In other words, procedural justice judgments are socially constructed (Bies, 1987b, 1988b; Greenberg, in press).

The social construction of procedural justice can include formal procedure and interpersonal elements. For example, a boss who asks subordinates for their opinions (a "voice" procedure) may be using a management strategy to maintain the subordinates' support for an unfavorable decision (Tyler & Caine, 1981). Similarly, a decision-maker account may minimize the appearance of decision-maker impropriety (Bies & Shapiro, 1987), which may provide the necessary "cushion of support" when bad news occurs (Lind & Tyler, 1988). As such, researchers might explore the influence of impression management tactics such as the publicity of the procedure (Greenberg, in press) and the timing of the account (Bies, 1989), or whether it is given before or after the unfavorable decision.

Although evaluations of procedural justice are socially constructed, it does not follow that subordinates have passive roles in that process (Bies, 1988b). Indeed, the data suggest a more active role for subordinates in the social construction of procedural fairness. For example, Tyler (1987) suggested that employees must *believe* their viewpoints were considered as a precondition of procedural justice. Similarly, Bies and his colleagues (Bies, 1987a; Bies et al., 1988) found that although a boss's account was influential in shaping a subordinate's perception of procedural justice, it was also clear that the subordinate's attributions of adequacy and sincerity were critical in evaluating procedural fairness. As such, these findings are consistent with the premise that an account must meet certain "requirements" before it is *honored* or accepted by an "offended" party (Blumstein, 1974). Following from this premise, we argue that the subordinate, too, can play an active role in the social construction of procedural fairness, not just the boss.

It must be noted that we are not advocating or endorsing the view that one should manipulate impressions or deceive others. We are only arguing that people use procedures and accounts to communicate fairness in the context of an injustice (Greenberg, in press). Indeed, our analysis may have liberating consequences for employees. For example, as a result of this analysis, employees may become more sensitive to the possible manipulation by procedures and accounts. They are then in a better position to protect themselves.

The "Human" Side of Procedural Justice

Focusing on the interpersonal aspects of procedural justice also highlights the affective consequences of procedural injustice (Bies, 1987b). Procedural justice is not just a cognitive judgment, as suggested by the Thibaut and Walker (1975) paradigm. It is also a "human" experience that is heavily affective in nature, particularly when there is an injustice (Bies, 1987b). In the case of procedural injustice employees may experience the "sympathetic reaction of outrage, horror, shock, resentment, and anger, those affections of the viscera and abnormal secretions of the adrenals that prepare the human animal to resist attack" (Cahn, 1949, p. 24). For example, Bies and Moag (1986) cite evidence that job candidates feel that "stress" interviews are unfair because such encounters lead to strong feelings of discomfort among job candidates. As a result, they felt angry and bitter, which corroborates research that the experience of being unjustly treated is psychologically aversive (Mikula, 1986; Steil, Tuchman, & Duetsch, 1978).

Lane (1985) raised a similar point in identifying procedural pain as a criterion of procedural justice. By procedural pain, Lane referred to harmful psychological or physiological states such as embarrassment, humiliation, and stress, which might be caused by participating in certain types of procedures such as performance appraisal or the employment interview. Research supports Lane's suggestion that experiencing some procedures can cause psychological pain. For example, a series of studies have shown that people can

become upset, frustrated, and angry when dealing with bureaucratic administrators who are unresponsive to their needs or act in an arrogant manner
(Glass & Singer, 1972; Katz et al., 1975). Thus, future theory and research
should incorporate the affective aspects of procedural injustice.

Procedural pain can also be threatening because it is perceived as an attack
on the person's dignity as a human being (Lane, 1985). That is, people
believe they have intrinsic value, the violation of which is a fundamental
threat that arouses the "sense of injustice." One direction for future research
is to examine the influence of violations of dignity in people's procedural
fairness judgments. For example, feeling "manipulated" or being the target of
gratuitous rudeness may be central to the experience of procedural injustice
(Bies, 1986). As such, it suggests a view of procedures as instruments of
authority that can harm employees, not just instruments of decision making
(Thibaut & Walker, 1975).

The Sheppard and Lewicki (1987) study suggests a paradoxical element to
the human side of procedural justice. Sheppard and Lewicki found that
managers wanted their bosses to be both "consistent" and "flexible" as indi-
cators of procedural justice. Because flexibility can be perceived as making
exceptions to the rules, or a form of inconsistency, this finding suggests that
strict consistency may not necessarily be what employees really want. In
other words, employees may want both consistency and inconsistency from
decision makers, which is paradoxical. The nature of this paradox, and how
decision makers deal with it, represent a new direction for theory and
research.

Conduct, Community, and Procedural Justice

In their group value model of procedural justice, Lind and Tyler (1988)
proposed that people value identification with social groups such as business
organizations. Social groups both provide a source of self-knowledge and self-
identification and offer an arena within which people can cooperate to their
own and others' mutual benefit. For both of these reasons, people seek group
membership and actively participate in business organizations.

In order to participate in these organizations, individuals must be willing
to supplant their motivation to maximize their personal gain with a cooperative motivation in which all organizational members receive some of the
rewards they desire. And, at times, employees must forsake potential short-
term personal gains for the greater long-term gains that flow from group
membership.

Because individuals are forsaking their own most desired outcomes out of a
desire for long-term personal gain, there is an inherent tension in the relationship between the individual and the group. Individuals must be sensitive

to the possibility that their sacrifices are not being returned by the group and must be able to reevaluate their loyalty to that group when they feel that they are receiving inadequate returns for their loyalty. When a person does not win on some organizational decision and sees rewards and opportunities going to others, why do they continue to remain loyal to that organization?

Lind and Tyler (1988; Tyler, in press) propose that loyalty to social groups is rooted in a willingness to focus on procedures of allocation and decision making, rather than on the outcomes one is receiving in any given social situation. This focus stems from a belief that, even if one is not always successful in achieving one's desired outcomes, over time one's well-being can still be served by loyalty to the group if there is a mechanism to assure that outcomes are distributed fairly. Hence, in the face of negative decisions, evidence that allocation procedures (e.g., salary, budget) are fair provides a basis for a continued belief in the value of organizational loyalty. As such, procedural justice can promote a sense of "community" in organizations.

If decision makers fail to conduct themselves properly, and the procedures are perceived as unfair, employees will not feel part of this community and therefore may attempt to subvert the organization in the service of their personal gain. For example, Friedland, Thibaut, and Walker (1973) found less compliance by subjects with the rules when the rule-making authority was actively exploiting the subjects. Similarly, Lissak (1983) found that enlisted personnel in the Canadian Air Forces reported greater use of improper influence (e.g., circumventing organizational procedures) when promotion and transfer procedures were improperly enacted by decision makers.

Evidence that procedures are being inappropriately implemented should be particularly important in undermining people's support for the authorities with whom they are dealing (Folger & Bies, in press). What is unclear is the extent to which support for the procedures themselves is also undermined. The results of the studies we have discussed certainly suggest that dealing with authorities who inappropriately implement procedures out of a desire for personal gain has the potential to threaten support for the procedures themselves. Whether such a generalization actually occurs depends on the attributions of responsibility that people make for the unfair procedures that they experience. If they attribute responsibility to the ineptness of particular authorities, generalization is muted. If they attribute responsibility to characteristics of the system itself, generalization is strengthened.

In summary, employee loyalty to an organization is an essential feature of community in that setting. In deciding whether to be loyal, employees consider the fairness of the decision-making procedures and whether the particular authority with whom they have dealt has enacted those procedures in a responsible way. Unfair procedures or improper decision-maker conduct can reduce employee loyalty, which will undermine the sense of community in the organization (Lind & Tyler, 1988; Tyler, in press).

CONCLUSION

In this chapter, we argue that the Thibaut and Walker focus on formal procedures is limited, and that one must consider the interpersonal context within which the decision-making procedure exists. In particular, people's experiences during the enactment of formal procedures are an important aspect of what they mean by a "fair process." This finding raises questions that are above and beyond the traditionally studied questions of fair procedures for decision making. For example, we have identified the importance of normative expectations regarding interpersonal treatment and decision-maker conduct. In so doing, issues concerning attributions, human dignity, and organizational community were raised, which identify potential areas for future research on procedural justice.

In conclusion, the evidence is clear and consistent in suggesting the need to elaborate the concept of procedural justice, which is the purpose of this chapter. At the same time it should be clear, however, that by this broadening and questioning, we are not rejecting the basic Thibaut and Walker procedural justice paradigm. Rather, we believe such inquiry is necessary to elaborate the complexities implicit in that paradigm. As a result, this inquiry will hopefully provide a better understanding of procedural justice in organizations, which is consistent with the theoretical aims and goals of Thibaut and Walker and others in justice research, and with the practical needs of managers and workers in business organizations.

ACKNOWLEDGMENTS

Our thanks to the following people for their constructive comments and suggestions on earlier versions of this chapter: Susan Bies, Becky Beggs, Avi Kay, Uschi Backes-Gellner, Susan Scott, and John Carroll. Our thanks also to the Dispute Resolution Research Center at the Kellogg Graduate School of Management at Northwestern University for providing support in writing this chapter.

REFERENCES

Adams, J. S. (1965). Inequity in social exchange. In L. Berkowitz (Ed.), *Advances in experimental social psychology* (Vol. 2, pp. 267–299). New York: Academic Press.

Adler, J. W., Hensler, D., & Nelson, C. E. (1983). *Simple justice: How litigants fare in the Pittsburgh Court arbitration program.* Santa Monica, CA: RAND.

Aram, J. D., & Salipante, P. F., Jr. (1981). An evaluation of organizational due process in the resolution of employee/employer conflict. *Academy of Management Review, 6,* 197–204.

Barrett-Howard, E., & Tyler, T. R. (1986). Procedural justice as a criterion in allocation decisions. *Journal of Personality and Social Psychology, 50,* 296–304.

Bies, R. J. (1986, August). Identifying principles of interactional justice: The case of corporate recruiting. In R. J. Bies (Chair), *Moving beyond equity theory: New directions in research on justice in organizations.* Symposium conducted at the meeting of the Academy of Management, Chicago, IL.

Bies, R. J. (1987a). Beyond "voice": The influence of decision-maker justification and sincerity in procedural fairness judgments. *Representative Research in Social Psychology, 17,* 3–14.

Bies, R. J. (1987b). The predicament of injustice: The management of moral outrage. In L. L. Cummings & B. M. Staw (Eds.,), *Research in organizational Behavior* (Vol. 9, pp. 289–319). Greenwich, CT: JAI Press.

Bies, R. J. (1988a). *The delivery of bad news in organizations: Managerial strategies and tactics.* Unpublished manuscript.

Bies, R. J. (1988b, August). Saying no: Communicating fairness in rejection. In J. Greenberg & R. J. Bies (Co-chairs), *Communicating fairness in organizations.* Symposium conducted at the meeting of the Academy of Management, Anaheim, CA.

Bies, R. J. (1989). Managing conflict before it happens: The role of accounts. In M. A. Rahim (Ed.), *Managing conflict: An interdisciplinary approach* (pp. 83–91). New York: Praeger.

Bies, R. J., & Moag, J. S. (1986). Interactional justice: Communication criteria of fairness. In R. J. Lewicki, B. H. Sheppard, & M. H. Bazerman (Eds.), *Research on negotiations in organizations* (Vol. 1, pp. 43–55). Greenwich, CT: JAI Press.

Bies, R. J., & Shapiro, D. L. (1987). Interactional fairness judgments: The influence of causal accounts. *Social Justice Research, 1,* 199–218.

Bies, R. J., & Shapiro, D. L. (1988). Voice and justification: Their influence on procedural fairness judgments. *Academy of Management Journal, 31,* 676–685.

Bies, R. J., Shapiro, D. L., & Cummings, L. L. (1988). Causal accounts and managing organizational conflict: Is it enough to say it's not my fault? *Communication Research, 15,* 381–399.

Blumstein, P. W. (1974). The honoring of accounts. *American Sociological Review, 39,* 551–566.

Cahn, E. (1949). *The sense of injustice.* New York: New York University Press.

Casper, J. D., Tyler, T. R., & Fisher, B. (1988). Procedural justice in felony cases. *Law and Society Review, 22,* 483–507.

Cohen, R. L. (1985). Procedural justice and participation. *Human Relations, 38,* 643–663.

Crosby, F. (1984). A relative deprivation in organizational settings. In B. M. Staw & L. L. Cummings (Eds.), *Research in organizational behavior* (Vol. 6, pp. 51–93). Greenwich, CT: JAI Press.

Cyert, R. M., & March, J. G. (1963). A behavioral theory of the firm. Englewood Cliffs, NJ: Prentice-Hall.

Deutsch, M. (1982). Interdependence and psychological orientation. In V. J. Derlager & J. Grzelak (Eds.), *Cooperation and helping behaviors: Theory and research* (pp. 15–42). New York.

Deutsch, M. (1985). *Distributive justice.* New Haven, CT: Yale University Press.

Folger, R. (1977). Distributive and procedural justice: Combined impact of "voice" and improvement on experienced inequity. *Journal of Personality and Social Psychology, 35,* 108–119.

Folger, R., & Bies, R. J. (in press). Managerial responsibilities and procedural justice. *The Employee Responsibilities and Rights Journal.*

Folger, R., & Greenberg, J. (1985). Procedural justice: An interpretive analysis of personnel systems. In K. Rowland & G. Ferris (Eds.). *Research in personnel and human resources management* (Vol. 3, pp. 141–183). Greenwich, CT: JAI Press.

Folger, R., & Martin, J. (1986). Relative deprivation and referent cognitions: Distributive and procedural justice effects. *Journal of Experimental Social Psychology, 22,* 531–546.

Folger, R., Rosenfield, D., Grove, J., & Corkran, L. (1979). Effects of "voice" and peer opinions on responses to inequity. *Journal of Personality and Social Psychology, 37,* 2253–2261.

Folger, R., Rosenfield, D., & Robinson, T. (1983). Relative deprivation and procedural justifications. *Journal of Personality and Social Psychology, 45,* 268–27.

Friedland, N., Thibaut, J., & Walker, L. (1973). Some determinants of the violation of rules. *Journal of Applied Social Psychology, 3,* 103–118.

Fry, W. R., & Cheney, G. (1981, May). *Perceptions of procedural fairness as a function of distributive preferences.* Paper presented at the annual meeting of the Midwestern Psychological Association, Detroit, MI.

Fry, W. R., & Leventhal, G. S. (1979, March). *Cross-situational preferences: A comparison of allocation preferences and equity across different social settings.* Paper presented at the annual meeting of the Southeastern Psychological Association, Washington, DC.

Glass, D. C., & Singer, J. E. (1972). *Urban stress.* New York: Academic Press.

Greenberg, J. (1982). Approaching equity and avoiding inequity in groups and organizations. In J. Greenberg & R. L. Cohen (Eds.), *Equity and justice in social behavior* (pp. 389–435). New York: Academic Press.

Greenberg, J. (1986). Determinants of perceived fairness of performance evaluations. *Journal of Applied Psychology, 71,* 340–342.

Greenberg, J. (1987). A taxonomy of organizational justice theories. *Academy of Management Review, 12,* 9–22.

Greenberg, J. (in press). Looking fair: Managing impressions of organizational justice. In B. M. Staw & L. L. Cummings (Eds.) *Research in organizational behavior.* Greenwich, CT: JAI Press.

Greenberg, J., & Folger, R. (1983). Procedural justice, participation, and the fair process effect in groups and organizations. In P. B. Paulus (Ed.), *Basic group processes* (pp. 235–256). New York: Springer-Verlag.

Homans, G. C. (1961). *Social behavior: Its elementary forms.* New York: Harcourt Brace Jovanovich.

Houlden, P. (1980). Plea bargaining. *Law and Society Review, 15,* 267–291.

Katz, D., Gutek, B. A., Kahn, R. L., & Barton, E. (1975). *Bureaucratic encounters.* Ann Arbor, MI: Institute for Social Research.

Lane, R. (1985). *Procedural justice: How one is treated vs. what one gets.* Unpublished manuscript, Yale University, New Haven, CT.

Leventhal, G. S. (1976). The distribution of rewards and resources in groups and organizations. In L. Berkowitz & E. Walster (Eds.), *Advances in experimental social psychology* (Vol. 9, pp. 91–131). New York: Academic Press.

Leventhal, G. S. (1980). What should be done with equity theory? New approaches to the study of fairness in social relationships. In K. Gergen, M. Greenberg, & R. Willis (Eds.), *Social exchange: Advances in theory and research* (pp. 27–55). New York: Plenum.

Lind, E. A., Kurtz, S., Musante, L., Walker, L., & Thibaut, J. W. (1980). Procedure and outcome effects on reactions to adjudicated resolution of conflicts of interest. *Journal of Personality and Social Psychology, 39,* 643–653.

Lind, E. A., & Lissak, R. I. (1985). Apparent impropriety and procedural fairness judgments. *Journal of Experimental Social Psychology, 21,* 19–29.

Lind, E. A., & Tyler, T. R. (1988). *The social psychology of procedural justice.* New York: Plenum.

Lissak, R. I. (1983). *Procedural fairness: How employees evaluate procedures.* Unpublished doctoral dissertation, University of Illinois, Champaign, IL.

McCall, M. W., Jr., & Kaplan, R. E. (1985). *Whatever it takes: Decision-makers at work.* Englewood Cliffs, NJ: Prentice-Hall.

Martin, J. (1981). Relative deprivation: A theory of distributive injustice for an era of shrinking resources. In L. L. Cummings & B. M. Staw (Eds.) *Research in organizational behavior* (Vol. 3, pp. 53–107). Greenwich, CT: JAI Press.

Martin, J., Feldman, M. S., Hatch, M. J., & Sitkin, S. B. (1983). The uniqueness paradox in organizational stories. *Administrative Science Quarterly, 28,* 438–453.

Mikula, G. (1986). The experience of injustice: Toward a better understanding of its phenomenology. In H. W. Bierhoff, R. L. Cohen, & J. Greenberg (Eds.), *Justice in social relations.* New York: Plenum, pp. 103–124.

Reuter, V. G. (1977). Suggestion systems: Utilization, evaluation, and implementation. *California Management Review, 19,* 78–89.

Rousseau, D. M. (1988). Human resources planning for the future. In J. Hage (Ed.), *Futures of organizations: Innovating to adapt strategy and human resources to rapid technological change* (pp. 245–266). Lexington, MA: Lexington Books.

Sheppard, B. H. (1984). Third-party conflict intervention: A procedural framework. In B. M. Staw & L. L. Cummings (Eds.), *Research in organizational behavior* (Vol. 6, pp. 141–190). Greenwich, CT: JAI Press.

Sheppard, B. H., & Lewicki, R. J. (1987). Toward general principles of managerial fairness. *Social Justice Research, 1,* 161–176.

Sheppard, B. H., Lewicki, R. J., & Minton, J. W. (1986). A "new" view of organizations: Some retrospective comments and integrative themes. In R. J. Lewicki, B. H. Sheppard, & M. H. Bazerman (Eds.), *Research on negotiation in organization* (Vol. 1, pp. 311–321). Greenwich, CT: JAI Press.

Steil, J., Tuchman, B., & Deutsch, M. (1978). An exploratory study of the meanings of injustice and frustration. *Personality and Social Psychology Bulletin, 4,* 393–398.

Thibaut, J., & Walker, L. (1975). *Procedural justice.* Hillsdale, NJ: Lawrence Erlbaum Associates.

Thibaut, J., & Walker, L. (1978). A theory of procedure. *California Law Review, 66,* 541–566.

Tyler, T. R. (1987). Conditions leading to value expressive effects in judgments of procedural justice: A test of four models. *Journal of Personality and Social Psychology, 52,* 333–344.

Tyler, T. R. (1988). What is procedural justice? *Law and Society Review, 22,* 301–335.

Tyler, T. R. (in press). *Why people obey the law: Procedural justice, legitimacy and compliance.* New Haven, CT: Yale University Press.

Tyler, T. R., & Caine, A. (1981). The influence of outcomes and procedures on satisfaction with formal leaders. *Journal of Personality and Social Psychology, 41,* 642–655.

Tyler, T. R., & Folger, R. (1980). Distributional and procedural aspects of satisfaction with citizen-police encounters. *Basic and Applied Social Psychology, 1,* 281–292.

Walster, E., Berscheid, E., & Walster, E. (1973). New directions in equity research. *Journal of Personality and Social Psychology, 25,* 151–176.

Top-Management Teams:
Preparing for the Revolution

Deborah Gladstein Ancona
Alfred P. Sloan School of Management
Massachusetts Institute of Technology

This is the competitive age. Today, global economies and rapid technological change pose the major challenges to corporations. To meet these challenges most people look to the top echelons of their corporations to map the route to a promising economic future. It is the top-management team whose primary task is to align the organization with its external environment in order to assure survival, profit, and growth. It is the top-management team that is held accountable for the strategy and performance of the firm (Virany & Tushman, 1986). Consequently, as competitive pressures mount and business failures increase, industry becomes more and more interested in management-team processes that will lead to success. This chapter focuses on the process by which top-management team members go about their task, and the link between this process and performance.

The push for the study of top-management teams comes from academe as well as industry. There has been a demand for research to model the role of the top team in organizational evolution (Tushman & Virany, 1986), in mediating the relationship between team composition and firm performance (Hambrick & Mason, 1984), and in the collection and dissemination of strategic information (Dutton & Duncan, 1987). Although much of the research on top teams concentrates on the link between group demography and performance, diverse sources have called for more exploration of executive team processes.

Social psychology with its long tradition of analyzing the interactions among group members provides a partial framework for examining these processes (cf. Cartwright & Zander, 1968; Kiesler, 1978; Lott & Lott, 1965). This perspective is limited, however, by its concentration on behavior within the group. An additional focus is from the group boundary outward. Such an external perspective (Ancona, 1987) seems particularly applicable in the case of a top-management team that must not only manage its internal dynamics but also monitor the external competitive environment, get input from other parts of the organization, and react to external sources of threat.

This chapter posits that at any point in time the CEO and top team face a task with complex internal and external demands. Differentiation between these two sets of demands are perhaps most clearly seen in government, which must both determine foreign policy and run the country. These demands determine the degree and kind of group processes that will lead to firm success; moreover, the demands change over time. The question addressed here is: How can the CEO and top team manage the corporation so that it is efficient in its current operations, while simultaneously, and without undue cost, exploring ways to transform the organization to a form appropriate to meet future demands? How can the team be set up to meet demands during both evolutionary and revolutionary change? How can the top team become, and remain, a learning, adaptive system?

DOES TOP MANAGEMENT MAKE A DIFFERENCE?

Implicit in this chapter is a model relating group process to team effectiveness, with task as a moderator variable. That is, given a particular task, I assume there is a way to design group process so as to improve or increase effectiveness. I assume, furthermore, that the effectiveness of the team will influence organizational effectiveness. In essence, the most basic assumption is that top-management teams matter. In fact, there is mixed evidence on the subject.

Researchers have defined top teams in a variety of ways. Some refer to top-level managers who are also board members (Boeker, 1988), whereas others include all those people who are corporate officers (Wagner, Pfeffer, & O'Reilly, 1984). Here I refer to the CEO and his or her direct reports. Although numerous researchers have concentrated solely on the CEO, the importance of the top team has been amply demonstrated. Michel and Hambrick (1968) found that in a sample of 133 firms top-team characteristics and behaviors were more predictive of company performance than CEO behavior alone. Virany and Tushman (1986) found that under conditions of CEO change alone, firms were not able to successfully accomplish reorientations, whereas CEO change coupled with top-team change did represent a successful strategy. Finally, Bourgeois and Eisenhardt (1988) found that high-performing firms involved the top team in strategic decision making, whereas low-performing firms had more autocratic CEOs who made these decisions. There is still much debate, however, on whether the top team influences firm performance.

Top Management Has Little Impact

On one side are those who believe that the top-management team has little impact on organizational outcomes. One argument is that top executives are constrained by bureaucratic rules and organizational customs (Hall, 1976). That is, the organization has habitual ways of dealing with employees, tasks, or competitors that are determined by standard operating procedures that are inertial and thus inhibit the team's ability to affect the organization (Nelson & Winter, 1981). Another rationale given for limited impact comes from the population ecology perspective (Aldrich, 1979; Astley & Van de Ven, 1983), which asserts that environmental selection determines whether firms succeed or fail; firms that are ill-suited to the demands of their environment will be selected out. Proponents of this view assert that most organizations have limited control over their complex and often uncertain environment and a limited ability to adapt, at least in the short run.

Others argue that the top team has limited control in that it manages symbolically not substantively (Cohen & March, 1974; Pfeffer & Salancik, 1978). That is, the team controls the symbols that influence organization norms and values, and these in turn have an impact on performance in the long term. Here, the team is viewed as the source of the organizational culture or shared basic assumptions about the environment, work, people, and relationships (Schein, 1985). Because these assumptions are deeply embedded in the organization, change is difficult, and much time is required for substantive attitude and behavior change.

Top Management Matters

On the opposite side of the argument are those who posit that top management can make a difference. A number of studies indicate that performance can improve, particularly when a new leader comes in during a period of low performance (Helmich & Brown, 1972; Pfeffer, 1981). Case studies often present industrial giants who, with a selected top team, have brought a new organizational gestalt and reversed an organization's performance (Miller & Friesen, 1980; Samuelson, Galbraith, & McGuire, 1985). Certainly, it is difficult to reconcile the view that top management has little impact with the stories of miraculous organizational transformations brought about by Alfred

Sloan at General Motors (Chandler, 1962) or Steve Jobs and later John Scully at Apple Computer.

In a study of both contextual and leadership variables, Lieberson and O'Connor (1972) concluded that organizational and environmental factors exert a much greater influence on organizational success than executive leadership. Weiner and Mahoney (1981) criticized this work, however, because of the order of entry of variables in the regression equations. In a reanalysis of the data, they argue that 45% of the variance in profitability can be attributed to stewardship.

In an attempt to reconcile these two divergent views, Romanelli and Tushman (1986) argue that the top-management group exerts influence over organizational outcomes differentially over the life of the firm. Specifically, organizations evolve in a pattern of punctuated disequilibrium. For long periods they exist with slight changes in people, processes, structures, or culture. Interrupting these periods of slow evolutionary change are brief periods of more radical change when environmental shifts, technological discontinuities, or marginal organizational performance push for quick, substantive change (Tushman & Anderson, 1986; Tushman & Romanelli, 1985).

The evolutionary part of the cycle has been referred to as "muddling through" (Lindblom, 1959), and strategic incrementalism (Quinn, 1982). During these periods, top management is basically in control of symbolic outcomes, as it influences values and beliefs throughout the corporation. In evolutionary periods, when the organization has a set direction and vision, top management works at convergence, that is, getting the organizational components to work more efficiently together to realize the vision.

During revolutionary periods, top management makes both symbolic and substantive changes in people, processes, structure, strategy, and, in some extreme cases, culture. These discontinuous periods are seen as reorientations as the executive team redirects the firm. During reorientations it is the strategy and vision itself that becomes the focus of change, and consequently the organizational components needed to change to support the new direction.

Tushman and Romanelli (1985) predict a pattern of slow convergent change intersected by brief periods of fast, revolutionary change. Differing from Greiner's (1972) model of evolution as ordered stages, Tushman and Romanelli simply report a pattern of punctuated disequilibrium. There has been evidence of this pattern in the minicomputer, cement, and airline industries (Tushman & Anderson, 1986). Changes at Prime Computer are one example:

> Prime Computer was founded in 1971 by a group of individuals who left
> Honeywell. Prime's initial strategy was to produce a high-quality/high-price

minicomputer based on semiconductor memory. These founders built an engineering-dominated, loosely structured firm which sold to OEMs and through distributors. This configuration of strategy, structure, people, and processes was very successful. By 1974, Prime turned its first profit; by 1975, its sales were more than $11 million.

In the midst of this success, Prime's board of directors brought Ken Fisher to reorient the organization. Fisher and a whole new group of executives hired from Honeywell initiated a set of discontinuous changes throughout Prime during 1975–1976. Prime now sold a full range of minicomputers and computer systems to OEMs and end-users. To accomplish this shift in strategy, Prime adopted a more complex functional structure, with a marked increase in resources to sales and marketing. The shift in resources away from engineering was so great that Bill Poduska, Prime's head of engineering, left to form Apollo Computer. Between 1975–1981, Fisher and his colleagues consolidated and incrementally adapted structure, systems and processes to better accomplish the new strategy. During this convergent period, Prime grew dramatically to over $260 million by 1981.

In 1981, again in the midst of this continuing sequence of increased volume and profits, Prime's board again initiated an upheaval. Fisher and his direct reports left Prime (some of whom founded Encore Computer), while Joe Henson and a set of executives from IBM initiated wholesale changes throughout the organization. The firm diversified into robotics, CAD/CAM, and office systems; adopted a divisional structure; developed a more market driven orientation; and increased controls and systems. It remains to be seen how this "new" Prime will fare. Prime must be seen, then, not as a 14-year-old firm, but as three very different organizations, each of which was managed by a different set of objectives. . . . Prime initiated these discontinuities during periods of great success. (Tushman, Newman, & Romanelli, 1986, pp. 2–3)

Executive-team behavior has been shown to be vital to effective organizational evolution in a study of the minicomputer industry (Virany & Tushman, 1986). Under conditions of environmental change, such as technological discontinuities or shake-outs in the industry, firms that failed showed one of two patterns: no CEO or top-management team change (and no reorientation in response to the environment), or desperate action repeated successively. Moderate-performing organizations responded to declining performance by changing both the CEO and executive team while simultaneously undergoing a reorientation. Corporate success in these circumstances was greater for internal than for external managers who had no knowledge of history, precedent, and informal linkages. Note that for these firms both CEO and top-team change were required; either one alone was less effective.

A few high-performing organizations were able to successfully initiate reorientations just prior to environmental changes, but before performance declined. Somehow these high-performing firms managed reorientation without massive executive-team change. Virany and Tushman (1986) speculate that group-process variables determine whether teams are able to be visionary in predicting the need for change and flexible enough to carry it out. This chapter explores what those process variables may be.

THE TASK OF THE TOP-MANAGEMENT TEAM

As numerous researchers have noted, it is impossible to understand how group members should interact without understanding what they do (Goodman, 1986; Herold, 1979). Task definition in this case is admittedly difficult because a top-management team has a great deal of leeway in defining its own task. Nonetheless some general characteristics seem to be common across teams.

The task is extremely complex. Top management makes major strategic decisions for the firm about products to produce, markets to serve, technologies and structures to employ, and stance toward the competition. These decisions each may be made in a different timeframe, require huge amounts of information processing, yet often demand conclusions based on scarce information. These decisions are technically complex in that they involve multiple acceptable solutions, unpredictable changes across decisions and during decision making, a high degree of difficulty, and knowledge and skill dispersed across many individuals rather than centralized in one person (Herold, 1979).

The top-management team's task is also highly uncertain, rather than routine. Issues that are nonroutine and fall outside the realm of prior decisions get sent up the hierarchy. Only the most difficult and unusual get sent all the way to the top team (Galbraith, 1982; Quinn, 1982).

The top team's task is also socially complex (Herold, 1979). Tasks high in complexity of social demands require extensive and potentially problematic social interaction, with the group's product shaped and determined by the nature of that interaction process. The task attributes of ego involvement, agreement on means, and agreement on ends determine the social complexity of a task.

Ego involvement is exceptionally high because the team's decisions often can involve deeply rooted values (for example, do we lay off people), affect important aspects of participants' lives (such as whether you will get the desired budget for your group), and engage highly valued skills where performance reflects individual self-concepts (such as the ability to negotiate and win). Top teams may also experience considerable disagreement on means and ends because participants often come from different parts of the organization, each with different priorities, languages, values, and desired outcomes (Bourgeois, 1980). Despite the best of intentions, team members may have difficulty shedding their perspectives and biases when thinking about firm-level decisions (Kets de Vries, 1988).

Adding to the social complexity of the task is the fact that the top-management team is very visible. Inside the organization, lower level managers constantly monitor the top team to glean clues about the future direction of the company and the appropriate behaviors and values (Peters, 1978). Externally, the news media, competitive firms, interdependent firms, financial analysts, headhunters, and stockholders watch top-team progress and behavior, analyzing and evaluating it through their own sets of lenses and priorities. Therefore, the team must not only do its work, but must also think about how its work is portrayed to the outside world.

Finally, the task of the top-management team is very politically complex. There is a lot at stake in the decision made by the top team. Limited resources are allocated, making winners and losers, and creating inevitable conflict (Brett & Rognes, 1986). By definition, strategic decisions involve influence and power inside and outside the firm. Shifting the status quo involves shifting that power balance among multiple stakeholders.

Careers are at stake, for this is the top of the organizational pyramid; if a manager does not succeed here, there are not many lateral positions to turn to. Perhaps most important, everyone on the team knows that the next CEO and chairman of the company might be sitting at the meeting table (Vancil & Green, 1984). The uncertainty and the high stakes make the top team's process one where power acquisition and maintenance become dominant forces (Kets de Vries, 1988). Here we may see shifts of coalitions and attempts to take control that have little to do with the particular decision being made (Pfeffer, 1981).

In summary, the top-management team's task is fraught with technical, social, and political difficulties that have to be resolved. The task requires specialized skills and knowledge, along with effective ways of allocating work. Even with the best process there is often no one best alternative; major disagreements over the desirability of various alternatives, goals, beliefs, or traditions may stand in the way of task accomplishment. The question becomes how the team can meet this complex set of demands. We look to both the internal perspective of social psychology and the external perspective of resource dependence to answer the question.

THE INTERNAL PERSPECTIVE

Traditional social psychology takes an internal perspective, in that the group is seen as a setting that shapes individual attitudes, attributions, and decisions (Stephan, 1984). The lens of inquiry is positioned on the group boundary looking in toward the members, and not toward the external environment. Group research in the internal tradition can be mapped according to a framework showing how individual, group, and organizational inputs influence group process, which in turn influences group and individual outputs (see Fig. 5.1) (Gladstein, 1984; Hackman & Morris, 1975). For example, group-member homogeneity in values, attitudes, age, and organizational tenure have been shown to result in low levels of intragroup conflict, high levels of communication and conformity, and subsequently to low turnover and high performance (see McGrath, 1984; Shaw, 1971; Wagner et al., 1984).

Input Variables

Numerous input variables influence a group's internal processes. One important input is group composition. Group-member similarity, for example, is associated with interpersonal attraction and low conflict. The low level of conflict in the Ford and Eisenhower cabinets, in contrast to the Nixon and Carter cabinets, has been attributed to the homogeneity of membership (Wrightsman, 1985). Recent work looking at the demography of top-management teams postulates a relationship between the diversity of the top-management team and social integration or cohesiveness, and then between cohesiveness and performance. Financial performance is positively related to the coefficient of variation in terms of date of entry to the firm. In other words, companies with top-team members who joined the organization at intervals that are not too far apart do better than those without cohorts. At the individual level, those managers who were more dissimilar in terms of age were more likely to leave (Wagner et al., 1984).

In top-management teams, both age patterns and time of entry distribu-

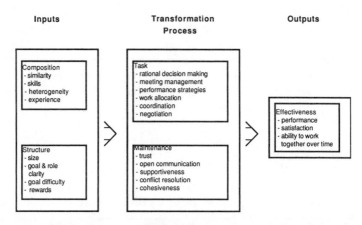

FIG. 5.1. An internal perspective of group behavior.

tions will tend to predict similarity of attitudes and values, as well as interconnected communication patterns (Wagner et al., 1984). Similarity of individual characteristics promotes low conflict, an ability to work together, and positive group feelings. In turn, the group process somehow selects out individuals who are different, thereby increasing homogeneity and smooth processes.

The interplay between group composition and process is seen in Song's (1982) study of 53 U.S. firms that had diversified and grown between 1965 and 1980. He found that the background and prior experience of the CEO was associated with the firm's diversification strategy. Those who were from production and marketing tended to be internal diversifiers, whereas those from finance, accounting, and law tended to diversify through acquisition. These strategies, in turn, were associated with top-team composition. Internal diversifiers had more people in the top levels from R&D, marketing, and manufacturing, whereas those following the acquisition strategy had more representatives from finance and law.

Other aspects of group composition that are believed to affect process and effectiveness are: skills needed to perform the task; enough group heterogeneity to assure that the team has the requisite knowledge and adequate diversity to match the environmental complexity, but not so much that conflict overwhelms the group's ability to act; and enough experience with the organization to assure a group's knowledge of standard operating procedures, organizational culture, and knowledge sources (McGrath, 1984; Shaw, 1971; Sutton & Rousseau, 1979).

Group structure also influences group process and productivity. Increases in group size expand the pool of potential resources, while making internal processes more difficult (Steiner, 1972; Thomas & Fink, 1963). Goal and role clarity and specific norms about work determine the degree to which member behavior is specified by routines, procedures, and prescribed roles. Specificity clarifies the task of each member, but tasks fixed for too long may limit the group's ability to remold itself in response to changed conditions (Cartwright & Zander, 1968; Cummings, 1978). The degree of goal difficulty also has an impact on group process. Difficult goals can inspire high levels of motivation and commitment, whereas goals that are viewed as impossible to reach are seen as threats that lead to rigidity in the group and possible failure (Staw, Sandelands, & Dutton, 1981).

Process Variables

Numerous theoretical schools hypothesize relationships between group process and effectiveness. The humanistic school has concentrated on maintenance functions that act to regulate group life and smooth interpersonal interactions (Bales, 1958; Likert, 1981; Philip & Dunphy, 1959). Important variables for organizational groups would include the establishment of trust among members (Gabarro, 1978), free and open communication, effective conflict management (Bettenhausen & Murnighan, 1985; Filley, 1975), and supportiveness (Bourgeois & Eisenhardt, 1988; Kiesler, 1978). A study of eight top teams showed that in low-performing teams information was often withheld or distorted in meetings, and there was a low level of trust. Outside of meetings, team members met in small subgroups where they complained about how meetings were run, and new side deals were made (Eisenhardt & Bourgeois, 1988).

Other theorists have concentrated on task functions that enable the group to solve the objective problem it has been assigned. Variables that would be important to groups in the organizational environment include rational decision making (Bourgeois & Eisenhardt, 1988; Janis, 1982; Schein, 1988), participative decision making if commitment is needed and information about the decision is dispersed (Hatvany & Gladstein, 1982; Vroom & Jago, 1974), effective meeting and agenda management (Jay, 1976), discussing performance strategies so that processes can be changed if the task warrants it (Hackman, 1983), and a process to distribute work to match capabilities with task priorities (Hackman & Walton, 1986). Smooth coordination of member effort is also an important process dimension.

The inadequacies in basic skills that have been shown to hinder performance in laboratory groups cause even more damage to top teams that require interaction for complex task accomplishment. For example, the need to have a group discuss performance strategies so as to be able to alter its work patterns when task demands shift is more important for highly complex tasks than for simple ones (Hackman & Morris, 1975). These internal processes are linked to the performance of the top team to the extent that the team task has high coordination demands.

THE EXTERNAL PERSPECTIVE

Traditional social psychology focuses on activities within the group's boundaries. Task and context variables are often controlled under laboratory conditions, in order to obtain more fine-grained analyses of internal processes (Hackman & Morris, 1975). Group members in organizations, however, view group process as including a separate set of activities beyond intragroup activities: cross-boundary activities aimed at interaction with those outside the group (Gladstein, 1984). The external perspective concentrates on this second set of activities and examines the relationship between a group or team and its environment. The environment includes the organization in which the group is situated and the external task environment outside the organizational boundaries that either provides input to or receives output from the group (Ancona, 1987).

The external perspective expands our model of group behavior (see Fig. 5.2). Added to group composition are immigrants, emigrants, and captives from other parts of the organization. Now heterogeneity reflects not only the mixture of skills, abilities, and personality dimensions, but also the degree of representation of external views, ideas, and expertise. Structure expands beyond the degree of clarity of group member boundaries vis-à-vis the group, to the degree of permeability or clarity of group boundaries vis-à-vis the organization. Added to task and maintenance processes are external, boundary activities aimed at modeling, influencing, and coordinating the activities of the team with the external environment. In the same vein, performance is extended beyond internal efficiency and satisfaction, to effective interaction and evaluation from external agents.

Central to the external perspective is the notion that the group is not a passive entity; it initiates activities toward those outside its borders in order to influence those outsiders and to deal with external dependence (Nadler & Tushman, 1988; Pfeffer, 1986). For example, research on boundary spanning indicates that research and development teams evolve specialized roles to import needed technical information from other parts of R & D, other

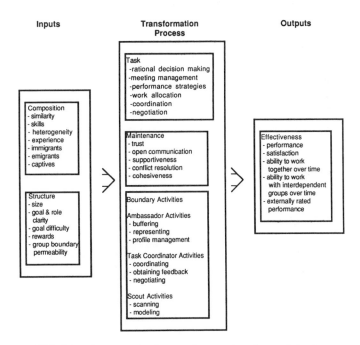

FIG. 5.2. An internal and external perspective of group behavior.

functions, and those outside the organization such as university experts and customers (Allen, 1984; Katz & Tushman, 1981; Roberts & Fusfeld, 1983; Tushman, 1977, 1979; Von Hippel, 1977). A recent study of new product teams (Ancona & Caldwell, 1988) has examined not only the importation of technical information but also the external communications aimed at coordination, influence, and mapping of the external environment. Ancona and Caldwell (1987) found that groups use three strategies to manage their external environment: cross-boundary transactions, boundary permeability, and/or boundary definition.

Cross-Boundary Transactions

Cross-boundary transactions cluster into activity sets (Ancona & Caldwell, 1988). *Ambassadorial activities* include buffering activities aimed at protecting the team and representational functions aimed at presenting a positive view of the team to outsiders and soliciting support for the team's activities. These activities attempt to influence powerful outsiders to support the team and provide it with resources while keeping other members free for other types of work. *Task coordinator activities* are aimed at getting specific technical information and coordinating work interdependence with outsiders. These activities include negotiating for delivery deadlines with external groups and getting feedback on the technical work of the group. They serve to improve coordination among organizational units and to improve the product via external inputs. *Scout activities* involve scanning the external task environment for ideas and trends that might have significance to the team. Scout activities, unlike task coordinator activities, do not include focused search for a particular piece of information or settlement, but rather more general search aimed at modeling the environment or detecting early signs of trouble or changes in external demands that may be important to the group. These activities help the group to monitor external trends and to collect data about changes that do not coincide with the group's model of the external world.

Boundary Permeability

Although the group depends on certain external initiatives, sometimes the group needs to decrease its permeability, or cut itself off from the outside, in order to protect its internal process from interruption, excess information, and pressure. Several studies offer evidence that over the lifecycle of a group there are periods of openness to external communication and a frenzy of external initiatives followed by periods of internal focus with only small amounts of guarded external interaction; this cycle may repeat itself (Ancona

& Caldwell, 1988; Gersick, 1988). The extreme of protection is to separate the group physically from the organization.

Decreasing the permeability of the group's boundary may be adaptive or maladaptive. It is adaptive to the extent that it is used as a short-term tactic to prevent overload and/or buy time for the group to get its internal functions running more efficiently (Adams, 1980). For example, skunkworks are a mechanism to improve product development by removing team members from organizational pressures and habitual approaches to product design (Galbraith, 1982). Isolation is maladaptive, however, if it is a long-term and sole response to external threat (Janis, 1972; Staw et al., 1981). Long-term isolation, for example, can lead groups to become more and more out of touch with new environmental contingencies (Katz, 1982). Isolation allows the group to move more quickly and efficiently, but perhaps in the wrong direction. Groups need to find ways to both buffer themselves from excess information and pressure, while simultaneously monitoring changes in external constraints and demands (Adams, 1980).

Boundary Definition

An important tool for defining the nature of the interactions of the team with other groups is deciding who is included in the team. The immigrant, captive, and emigrant are individuals whose presence suggests that external dependence has been brought into the group (Ancona & Caldwell, 1988). The immigrant is an outsider who voluntarily joins the group, whereas the captive is an assigned member. The emigrant leaves the focal team in order to manage linkages with other groups (Adams, 1980; Ancona & Caldwell, 1987). These individuals transfer information and resources, link the focal team to other groups by communicating or holding joint membership, and co-opt outsiders.

Through the use of boundary transactions and boundary definition, the group manages its external dependence. By bringing members of interdependent groups inside the group boundary with the addition of immigrants and captives, the team at least partially moderates its external dependence. Through boundary transactions, a group is able to model and shape external demands, constraints, and opportunities so that it actually can decrease dependence or at least know the parameters of that dependence. Through changes in the permeability of its boundary, a group can protect its internal process, or conversely open itself up to external information and influence.

Applying the External Perspective to Top Teams

Although these descriptions of external processes have come from a sample of new product teams, top-management teams can also pursue external initiatives. Some examples follow.

External Influence.   Ambassadorial activities are aimed at influencing the external environment. Given its visibility, the top team automatically sends signals to both external and internal constituencies (Peters, 1978). Through careful monitoring of those signals, the team can mold the views of those outsiders, market the image it wishes to create, and hence lessen external dependence and the need to adapt. For example, top-management team members can regularly meet with the press, stockholders, and government officials to tell them how the firm is doing and how particular strategies are working. By providing a view of the organization to these outsiders, the team is shaping outside opinion, not merely reacting to a vision shaped by competitors or news taken out of context. For example, by presenting its cars as the best designed and built in North America, Ford identifies itself as the best among a group of its own choosing rather than leaving itself open to comparison to other groups where it might not fare so well, such as imports.

This view of the team and the organization is consistent with the strategic management view of organizations (Astley & Van de Ven, 1983), which suggests that environments are partially enacted, and that top teams can shape and influence those environments. Unfortunately there are distinct limits to enactment, and adaptation is necessary.

Specialized Committees.   One mechanism by which to increase scout, ambassador, and task-coordinator activities, and hence increase external initiatives, is through involvement of the next level of management. People at this level do not have to be made members of the top team, but they can serve on committees to assist the top team (Vancil & Green, 1984). Committees are a temporary structure that provides flexibility to the top team. New committees can be formed for new problems thereby reducing rigidity in problem solving.

Specialized committees afford the group an opportunity for increased scout or scanning activity to deal with environmental diversity, while not increasing the size of the actual team. The mechanism maintains internal communication and coordination and provides the contribution of alternative external views. Committees can also take on the ambassadorial role of protecting the team from excess information and undue pressure. They can work through the complexities of a problem and provide the top team with organized data and options from which to choose. Information from these lower levels also is closer to the actual source of uncertainty, and hence presumably more accurate.

Specialized committees made up of both top team and lower level executives expand the task-coordinator activities of the team by involving those who actually must implement the decisions (Quinn, 1982). The various factions that have to commit to deadlines can be brought together to negotiate delivery deadlines, whereas the top team can be sure that new initiatives and agreements fit strategic objectives. Finally, committees serve the function of exposing senior executives to the top team, allowing them access to privileged information and the views of the top team, while providing the team with new perspectives and language.

Vancil and Green (1984), in a study of several top management teams, showed widespread use of executive committees. An example is at Texas Instruments, where one committee advises on current operations and another works in the area of new product development. This allows the company to separate decisions on long-term versus short-term product planning, facilitating decision making. Other top-level committees are more focused, formed to deal with CEO agendas such as diagnosing the severity of a competitive threat and outlining possible next steps for the corporation (Vancil & Green, 1984).

Interlocking Directorates. Interlocking directorates—the CEO or other top-level executives from another company serve on your board, while your company executives serve on other boards—are a means for achieving immigrant and emigrant benefits. Interlocking directorates allow team members to collect information about related and interdependent firms and industries, and also to influence the directions and perceptions of those at the top of these industries (Pfeffer, 1986). The top-team member who observes decision making at other firms is forced to compare and contrast the style and external models of his or her firm to those of others. This allows for questioning and updating of the model and alternative processes. Interlocking directorates also provide opportunities for executives to communicate and explore specific linkages such as joint ventures and development agreements (Pennings, 1980). The opportunity for co-optation is also present. Thus, this link to other companies helps to manage external dependence through scanning, influence, and coordination at the interorganizational level.

MATCHING GROUP PROCESS TO TASK DEMANDS DURING CONVERGENT PERIODS

Having described evolutionary changes in the firm, the team task, and both internal and external processes, it is time to combine these perspectives and to make some predictions about organizational performance. In essence, I argue that during convergent periods the top team faces some combination of coordination and environmental demands that determine appropriate group composition and process. Although a certain composition and process may optimize performance under current conditions, the combination actually may sow the seeds of failure under changed conditions. The task facing the

CEO is how to organize the team for current functioning while preparing for the revolution.

At any one time, a top-management team is faced with both coordination demands and environmental demands (see Fig. 5.3). Coordination demands relate to the degree of interdependence among top-team members. The higher the technical, social, and political complexity, the greater the need for top members to work together, and therefore the higher the interdependence. Teams with low coordination demands can be loosely coupled, whereas those with high demands must integrate their work very closely. This integration can be met through sophisticated internal group processes (Shaw, 1971).

Using Rumelt's (1974) typology, Michel and Hambrick (1988) argue that interdependence, and therefore the need for coordination, is related to a firm's diversification strategy. Firms lowest in interdependence are those following a strategy of unrelated diversification. This is followed by related-linked businesses, related-constrained, and finally, vertically integrated firms. The latter show the highest coordination requirements and therefore the highest need for task and maintenance skills. Only in teams with high coordination requirements is cohesiveness related to performance. Similar results were obtained by Song (1982), who found that cohesion and performance were related for internal diversifiers (high coordination demands), whereas they were not related for firms following an acquisition strategy.

Environmental demands have to do with the complexity occasioned by the rate of environmental and performance changes (Aldrich, 1979; Galbraith, 1982; Nadler & Tushman, 1986). In order to meet high environmental demands, teams need to engage in high levels of external scanning,

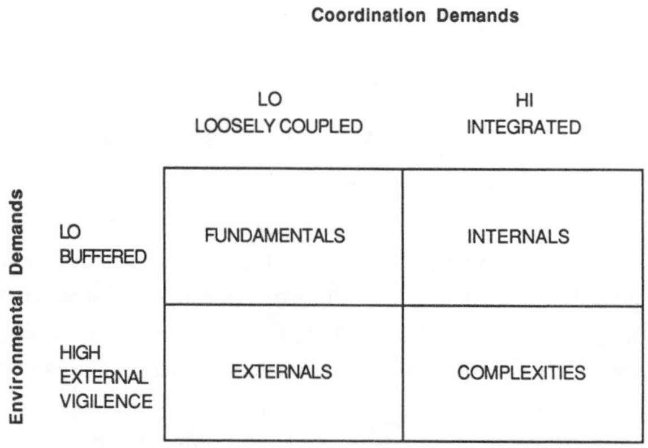

Coordination Demands

	LO LOOSELY COUPLED	HI INTEGRATED
Environmental Demands — LO BUFFERED	FUNDAMENTALS	INTERNALS
HIGH EXTERNAL VIGILANCE	EXTERNALS	COMPLEXITIES

FIG. 5.3. Group processes needed to meet coordination and environment demands.

modeling, and influence. There needs to be coordination and information exchange with outsiders. The faster the rate of change in the environment the more the team has to find mechanisms to determine how fast it is changing, how others are adapting to those changes, and what the potential implications of those changes are on group and organizational behavior.

Similarly, a dynamic environment accentuates complexity. Terreberry (1968) posited that a complex, or heterogeneous, environment will reward organizations that engage in effective scanning and mapping of the environment. With a number of dissimilar elements in the environment, more external activity is needed to effectively map and track environmental change. Finally, declining performance poses environmental demands. When a firm's performance suffers, stockholders, the press, suppliers, customers, and competitors all increase their demands. Pressure to turn performance around results in the need to both buffer the organization from undue impact, and the need to respond to and mold external opinion. Thus, under conditions of high environmental demands, external behaviors are essential for improved performance.

Low Coordination and Low Environmental Demands—The Fundamentals

Let us look more closely at the processes that "fit" each combination of demands presented in Fig. 5.3. In the first combination—low coordination demands and low environmental demands—process demands are relatively low. In fact, Galbraith (1982) has argued that these firms would do better if members of the top team see themselves not as business managers, but rather as portfolio managers, pushing managerial decisions and heavy coordination demands away from them into the diversified businesses at a lower level in the organization. Nonetheless, I argue that in order to maintain high levels of performance, these top teams must master some fundamental processes.

Given the complex technical, social, and political tasks the top team must perform, the team must have some minimal task and maintenance skills. Certainly, teams must be able to call meetings and have everyone attend, follow agendas, surface information relevant to decisions, and follow through on commitments. Work must be allocated to those most able to carry it out and without undue overlap with other team members.

In order to support the task behaviors aimed at coordination and decision making, a minimal level of maintenance activity is also required. If work is to be delegated, there must be some level of trust that other people can execute their part of the task completely and will honor their commitments to do so (Gabarro, 1978). Furthermore, openness of communication is needed so that conflict can be surfaced and resolved, and decisions can be made with accurate information.

Finally, even under conditions of low coordination and environmental demands, top teams must be able to manage their internal politics. Conflict, coalition formation, and negotiated settlements may be the only mechanism to resolve the differing viewpoints inherent in organizations (Pfeffer, 1981), but when politics begins to distort judgment it can prove detrimental to the team (Eisenhardt & Bourgeois, 1988). The extreme case of this problem is seen when a successor to the CEO or Chairman is being sought. The succession process may be associated with distortions about firm performance, competitive pressures, managerial expertise, and future scenarios (Kets de Vries, 1988). It is suggested that top teams will be better performers to the extent that they work through the succession decision in a structured fashion, and that this process is separated from ongoing decision making (Nadler & Tushman, 1988). Political behavior also can be controlled through appropriate modeling on the part of the CEO, and through rewards and objectives that are based on firm-level output, thus stressing corporate rather than personal or group-level objectives (Kets de Vries, 1988; Nadler & Tushman 1988).

High Coordination Demands and Low Environmental Demands—Internal Processes

More sophisticated task and maintenance processes are needed as coordination demands increase (Condition 2). Here, top managers face more social, technical, and political complexity. Executives must manage interrelated businesses, and decisions are not easily delegated to lower levels. The top team needs to become expert at developing compromise among divisional, functional, and personal agendas. In contrast to Condition 1, the organizational units must be more tightly coupled, resulting in the need for negotiated agreements among units and an organizational vision to pull all units in the same direction. A good example of an organization in this condition is the telephone company before deregulation.

The internal perspective is most applicable to groups that are in this condition during convergent periods. Faced with difficult and complex internal demands, and low external demands, I hypothesize that these groups will be high performing to the extent that they become homogeneous with respect to tenure in the company, education, and age. This similarity facilitates the cohesion, communication, and coordination needed within the team.

Homogeneous group composition works to create strategies that reinforce the need for more similar others, and such similarity facilitates smooth task and maintenance processes. People who are different are most likely to leave, just as the deviants in the early social psychology experiments were most likely to face negative sanctions from group members (Asch, 1956; Bales, 1958).

Other literature from social psychology suggests that over time this cohesion and communication will strengthen conformity to group norms and lessen the flow of information that conflicts with the group vision (Janis, 1972; Kiesler, 1978; McGrath, 1984). As similarity increases consensus, decision making becomes easier, members come to have high levels of trust in one another, participation increases (except when it threatens relationships in the group), members stay in the group longer, and adjustment to the group is easier (Brown & Garland, 1971; Dutton & Duncan, 1987; Janis, 1982). Similar people participate in social trade-offs that are low in cost, support the validity of each other's beliefs, and usually affirm the worth of each other's decisions (Byrne, 1971; Kiesler, 1978). Once similar people develop a smooth process, they attempt to maintain it by bringing in more similar individuals. Over time such groups exhibit less external activity and become very invested in the status quo (Katz, 1982; Pfeffer, 1981).

This set of interactions appears to work in the organization's favor under conditions of high coordination and low environmental demands. When the organization is in a convergent period, and the environment is not changing, the top group is needed primarily to manage symbolically. Similarity of viewpoint in this case helps to insure that the organization moves in a unified direction, coalescing around the given strategy. Success likewise breeds strong commitment, which helps to insure continued success and motivates members to deal with the negotiation, compromise, and high information processing needed for integration.

Low Coordination Demands and High Environmental Demands—External Processes

Top teams facing low coordination demands and high environmental demands (Condition 3) develop very differently. Academic institutions are a very good model of an organization that expects its members to monitor trends in the larger academic environment, and to make reputations for themselves in that external world—reputations that translate into internal rewards and power—and yet demands relatively low levels of internal coordination. The contrast in Conditions 2 and 3 highlights some of the interrelationships between internal and external processes.

The internal cohesion that optimizes demands in Condition 2 has been shown to lead to external stereotyping and an illusion of invincibility vis-à-vis the "enemy" (Janis, 1982; Sherif, Harvey, White, Hood, & Sherif, 1961). This internal cohesion and the positive feelings that empower team members who share a common language and view of the world are related to a decrease in the external monitoring process and a tendency to shut off or distort external information that does not fit the group's vision (Caldwell &

O'Reilly, 1982; Janis & Mann, 1977). This process works for the organizations facing Condition 2, but would be harmful for those in Condition 3.

External monitoring and communication with outsiders who have different values, priorities, and viewpoints, which is needed to meet environmental demands in Condition 3, breeds conflict within the group as the multiple perspectives are juxtaposed and evaluated (Dougherty, 1987). Because teams in Conditions 3 have relatively low coordination demands, however, this conflict can be easily managed.

Performance in Condition 3 is predicted therefore more by the external perspective. More specifically, the model here is a heterogeneous top team that engages in high levels of external scanning, modeling, and influence. The top-team members develop broad, dense, external networks, with a simplified internal process and structure. Benetton, which has moved many organizational activities outside its boundaries (e.g., production and sales), yet optimizes external scanning of those activities and market trends, is a good example of the new network organization (Galbraith, 1988). Power in such an organization is based less on internal politics and more on access to powerful outsiders who control resources that are critical to the team.

High Coordination Demands and High Environmental Demands—High Complexity

Teams facing both high coordination and environmental demands, Condition 4, face the most difficult challenge. Computer companies, for example, face turbulent markets and are vertically integrated businesses. The sophisticated processes that are necessary here cannot be facilitated by a homogeneous team, because heterogeneity is needed to track a diverse and changing environment. At the same time, diverse views and values need to be harnessed for a unified set of decisions, as team members must coordinate closely. Although teams in Condition 2 may be overbounded (internally focused, with an intricate internal structure, strong shared views, and high conformity to group norms, but low and possibly distorted external models and interaction), and teams in Condition 3 may be underbounded (high levels of external activity and identification with external groups, but little internal structure, low team identity, and minimal interaction), these characteristics fit their internal and external demands (Alderfer, 1976).

Teams in Condition 4 must combine complicated internal processes with high external activity. Team members in these groups deal with high levels of conflict and ambiguity, as well as cope with the stress of internal and external demands. To meet these demands, team members must have high levels of social skills, be able to negotiate and compromise, be able to pool information from multiple sources, and to blend analysis and action (Bourgeois &

Eisenhardt, 1988; Quinn, 1982). These teams may need all the mechanisms described in the external perspective, including external initiatives, committees, interlocking directorates, and movement between buffering and an open boundary. Teams such as this pay a price for this increased level of activity in the form of stress, high turnover, and burnout. Team members in this kind of organization need to have very high levels of a wide range of skills, making them difficult to find, develop, and keep.

All these matches between process and task demands may work during convergent periods, but the same processes may not be useful during reorientations. In fact, processes that are appropriate for evolutionary periods, may hold only potential for failure during revolutionary periods.

PREPARING FOR THE REVOLUTION

It is difficult enough for a CEO to develop a team to meet current coordination and environmental demands. Harder still is organizing to meet the fact that these demands change over time. Organization revolutions require that an organization move into Condition 4. In order to accomplish large-scale change, that is, top-team members must be able to handle the large coordination demands required to make sure that all organizational components are transformed to mesh with one another and to fit the new strategy (Nadler & Tushman, 1988). Similarly, the team must have a good model of the competitive and market changes that will threaten, or already have threatened, its competitive position and performance. Teams that are in Conditions 1, 2, and 3 face different challenges as they move to shift processes and change structures and carry out a revolution.

The Impossible

Perhaps the most difficult task is moving from Condition 1 to Condition 4. Top teams that have not developed either the internal process for dealing with high levels of conflict, uncertainty, and change; or the external processes to monitor, model, influence, and mold the external and organizational environment, may not be able to acquire the requisite skills in the time available. This may be an instance where there is a need to bring in a new team both to signal a change and to move the organization in the "right" direction. In order to adapt, teams in this position would have to be able to change in the ways described for Conditions 2 and 3.

Increasing External Awareness

Teams in Condition 2 also face a difficult challenge. The very commitment and uniformity that creates success during convergence is now maladaptive.

Research indicates that individuals and groups may become so bound by their previous actions for example, that they remain committed to a strategy even after it has met failure (Staw, 1976). This process of escalating commitment has been termed *entrapment* (Rubin & Brockner, 1975) or having too much invested to quit. In the face of mounting evidence of failure, a team may become even more committed to the original strategy.

A team that is homogeneous also has less chance of detecting trends across a diverse and complex environment (Dutton & Duncan, 1987). Limited examination of the environment, a tendency to ignore warning signals, or an inability to monitor a broad and diverse set of cues may mean that a team picks up on environmental changes and declining performance later than competitors. Once signals are strong enough to get through to the group, the trends they are signalling may be quite well developed and perhaps even urgent. Urgency may provide momentum for a reorientation, or, if the trend is well established and is perceived as infeasible to solve, may propel the team into rigidity of response that accompanies threat (Dutton & Duncan, 1987; Staw et al., 1981).

The similarity of outlook, which once aided the group, now forestalls the recognition of external change and internal failure, thus increasing the probability that these events will be difficult to deal with and will be perceived as threats rather than opportunities. Reactions to threat often limit a group's ability to be creative, to change its processes and procedures, in short, to adapt. On the positive side, this team is in the best position to be able to make internal changes and motivate the rest of the organization, if it discovers external trends quickly enough.

The external perspective offers some insight into how teams in this condition can prepare for the revolution. By increased external initiatives, management of the team's boundaries, and including external representatives, the team should be able to predict external change better and to adapt to it. These teams can also prepare themselves for environmental change through exercises such as scenario construction, which enhance it ability to detect and act on technical discontinuities and economic downturns. The price, however, may be increased conflict and lower cohesion in the team, more stress for team members, and extra time and expense.

Increasing Internal Integration

Teams in Condition 3, because of their external vigilance, are more apt to pick up on environmental change that needs to be attended to; they are least able, however, to mobilize themselves, and the rest of the organization, to do anything. Members in such groups and organizations have external loyalties and are not accustomed to a high degree of internal coordination or negotiated settlements. In this condition, steps need to be taken to shift organization and team members to focus their energies inward, rather than outward. This switch may be difficult, because by its nature an unbounded team does not tend to promote loyalty among its members, and the task of coalescing the changed external information and viewpoints into a new, strategic direction may seem beyond the team's ability.

In Condition 3, the internal perspective offers some suggestions to prepare for the revolution. Rewards that are tied to the organization, and that are related to joint, internal activities, will push team members to learn the skills required for coordination. The team structure might benefit from a senior member who is responsible for internal coordination and control. In many university settings, for example, an external dean may represent the school to important constituencies and raise money, while an internal dean makes sure that the school is running effectively. This internal dean often sets up committees dealing with various institutional functions (e.g., personnel decisions and strategy formulation), so an internal structure promotes the interaction and problem-solving skills needed to run the institution. Finally, a process consultant can be used both to prepare for the revolution and to cope with it. The process consultant monitors internal processes and can help to move the team up the learning curve to smooth, efficient interactions. Once again, these precautions have costs. Team members may see such activities as tangential to their more important external activities and resent the time given to internal exercises.

Coping With the Revolution

Top teams in Condition 4 are best equipped to deal with the revolution. These teams have been paying the price for simultaneously dealing with internal and external demands all along. The payoff certainly would be felt during revolutionary periods, in that external trends can be detected earlier, and the internal processes are in place to respond to those trends. Will the revolution therefore be painless? Unlikely—no major change is painless. Environmental change still requires some change in the composition of the top team in that new external contingencies may need to be monitored and influenced. Nevertheless, Condition 4 teams are most prepared for the revolution.

So can CEOs prepare their teams for the revolution? The answer is a modified yes. It can be done, but there are heavy costs involved, and luck plays a role. For example, Franklin Roosevelt's style as President was to act as if there were many coordination and environmental demands. He gave groups and individuals overlapping responsibilities and problems so that responses could be debated and experimentation promoted. This practice was very frustrating for some of those who worked with him, yet Roosevelt's cabinet was well-equipped to cope with the New Deal. This management team groped its way toward economic solutions never before considered within the domain of government. The strong emphasis on experimentation proved to be highly productive in this case (Wrightsman, 1985).

Should all teams move into Condition 4? No. Top teams need to decide whether cutting down on their efficiency in the shortrun has major effectiveness benefits in the long term. This can be decided only in light of the rate of technological and industry change, which, in turn, determines the likelihood of a revolution (the minicomputer industry vs. the cement industry, for example), the ease and cost of replacing the top team, and the CEO's ability to push against group processes that can take on a life of their own. If an industry requires reorientation only every 100 years or so, it is not clear that preparing for it on a routine basis makes any sense. It is for future researchers to outline the trade-offs more carefully, and evaluate the wisdom of making them.

And after the revolution? The team again enters a convergent period and must move to coalesce around its new strategy. This is not the time to make more major changes, but rather a period to refining the ones that have just been made (Virnay & Tushman, 1986). It is a time to move into the internal process mode, then to enter the condition suggested by the previous discussion.

CONCLUSION

Top-management teams face technical, social, and political complexities that create coordination and environmental demands. To cope with these demands, the team must concurrently develop some minimal level of internal process skills and manage political behavior. Teams facing higher coordination demands also must create meaning and cohesion through shared visions, biases, and information. This is often accomplished through homogeneity of team membership, which allows for similarity of values and attitudes. Consensus decision making, negotiation, and coordination are all facilitated when this homogeneity exists. Furthermore, under conditions of positive performance the team begins to become more uniform and believe that its view is indeed the "right" one. Dissonant views are quieted, and information is collected to support the directives from the top.

This interaction of group composition and process creates high performance under conditions of high internal coordination and low environmental demands. When environmental demands are high, and internal coordination demands are low, however, this emphasis on homogeneity and coordinated interaction among members is replaced by a need for heterogeneity and high levels of environmental scanning, modeling, and influence. Top teams facing high levels of both coordination and environmental demands must adopt complex structures (multiple committees, say), and follow complex processes (such as the ability to negotiate), to deal with demands that pull the team in multiple directions.

The traditional social psychology paradigm, coupled with the external perspective, provides a means to model successful processes during evolutionary, and convergent periods. These perspectives also allow us to foreshadow the difficulties involved in shifting these processes in preparation for revolutionary periods.

Teams must manage both complex coordination and environmental demands during revolutionary change. Convergent periods and a long history of success, however, may encourage top teams to focus on optimizing either internal or external processes. This optimization may allow for efficient operation in the short term, but will inhibit long-term effectiveness in industries that require frequent reorientation and change.

Top teams can indeed prepare for the revolution by maintaining a balance of internal and external process skills, yet there are costs that make this strategy inappropriate for many organizations. It must also be remembered, however, that there are high costs to replacing the top team. The pairing of the internal and external perspectives allows us to better understand how existing teams can improve their chances of survival. These perspectives also help to explain the behavior of top teams that are striving to deal with rapid technological change, global economies, and the complex interactions among the organizational elite.

ACKNOWLEDGMENTS

I would like to thank John Carroll, Don Hambrick, and Michael Tushman for their helpful commentary on earlier drafts of this chapter.

REFERENCES

Adams, J. S. (1980). Interorganizational processes and organization boundary activities. In B. Staw & L. Cummings (Eds.), *Research in organizational behavior* (Vol. 2, pp. 321–355). Greenwich, CT: JAI Press.

Alderfer C. P. (1976). Boundary relations and organizational diagnosis. In M. Meltzer & F. R. Wickert (Eds.), *Humanizing organizational behavior* (pp. 109–133). Springfield, IL: Charles Thomas.

Aldrich, H. E. (1979). *Organizations and environments.* Englewood Cliffs, NJ: Prentice-Hall.

Allen, T. J. (1984). *Managing the flow of technology: Technology transfer and the dissemination of technological information within the R & D organization.* Cambridge, MA: MIT Press.

Ancona, D. G. (1987). Groups in organizations: Extending laboratory models. In C. Hendrick (Ed.), *Group processes and intergroup relations* (pp. 207–230). Beverly Hills, CA: Sage.

Ancona, D. G., & Caldwell, D. F. (1987). Management issues facing new-product teams in high technology companies. *Advances in Industrial Relations* (Vol. 4, pp. 199–221). Greenwich, CT: JAI Press.

Ancona, D. G., & Caldwell, D. F. (1988). Beyond task and maintenance: Defining external functions in groups. *Group and Organization Studies, 13,* 468–494.

Asch, S. E. (1956). Studies of independence and conformity: A minority of one against a unanimous majority. *Psychological Monographs, 70*(9), (Whole no. 416).

Astley, W. G., & Van de Ven, A. H. (1983). Central perspectives and debates in organization theory. *Administrative Science Quarterly, 28,* 245–273.

Bales, R. F. (1958). Task roles and social roles in problem-solving groups. In E. Maccoby, T. M. Newcomb, & E. L. Hartley (Eds.), *Readings in social psychology* (3rd ed., pp. 437–447). New York: Holt, Rinehart & Winston.

Bettenhausen, K., & Murnighan, J. K. (1985). The emergence of norms in competitive decision-making groups. *Administrative Science Quarterly, 30,* 350–372.

Boeker, W. (1988). *Executive succession: The role of organizational performance and chief executive power.* Columbia Business School Working Paper.

Bourgeois, L. J., (III). (1980). Performance and consensus. *Strategic Management Journal, 1,* 227–248.

Bourgeois, L. J., & Eisenhardt, K. M. (1987). Strategic decision processes in high velocity environments: Four cases in the microcomputer industry. *Management Science, 34,* 816–835.

Brett, J. M., & Rognes, J. K. (1986). Intergroup relations in organizations: A negotiations perspective. In P. Goodman (Ed.), *Designing effective workgroups* (pp. 202–236). San Francisco, CA: Jossey-Bass.

Brown, B. R., & Garland, H. (1971). The effects of incompetency, audience acquaintanceship, and anticipated evaluative feedback on face-saving behavior. *Journal of Experimental Social Psychology, 7,* 490–502.

Byrne, D. (1971). *The attraction paradigm.* New York: Academic Press.

Caldwell, D. F., & O'Reilly, C. A. (1982). Boundary spanning and individual performance: The impact of self monitoring. *Journal of Applied Psychology, 67,* 124–127.

Cartwright, D., & Zander, A. (Eds.). (1968). *Group dynamics: Research and theory* (3rd ed.). New York: Harper & Row.

Chandler, A. D. (1962). *Strategy and structure: Chapters in the history of American industrial enterprise.* Cambridge, MA: MIT Press.

Cohen, M. D., & March, J. G. (1974). *Leadership and ambiguity: The American college president.* New York: McGraw-Hill.

Cummings, T. G. (1978). Self-regulating work groups: A socio-technical synthesis. *Academy of Management Review, 11,* 625–634.

Dougherty, D. (1987). *New products in old organizations: The myth of the better mousetrap in search of the beaten path.* Unpublished doctoral dissertation, Sloan School of Management, MIT, Cambridge, MA.

Dutton, J. E., & Duncan, R. B. (1987). The creation of momentum for change through strategic issue diagnosis. *Strategic Management Journal,* 8(3), 279–296.

Eisenhardt, K. M., & Bourgeois, L. J., III (1988). The politics of strategic decision making in top teams: A study in microcomputer industry. *Academy of Management Journal, 31,* 737–770.

Filley, A. C. (1975). *Interpersonal conflict resolution.* Glenview, IL: Scott, Foresman.

Gabarro, J. J. (1978). The development of trust, influence, and expectations. In A. G. Athos & J. J. Gabarro (Eds.), *Interpersonal behavior* (pp. 290–303). Englewood Cliffs, NJ: Prentice-Hall.

Galbraith, J. (1982, Winter). Designing the innovating organization. *Organizational Dynamics,* 5–26.

Galbraith, J. (1988). [Presentation at a business meeting].

Gersick, C. J. C. (1988). Time and transition in work teams: toward a new model group development. *Academy of Management Journal, 31*(1), 9–41.

Gladstein, D. (1984). Groups in context: A model of task group effectiveness. *Administrative Science Quarterly, 29,* 499–517.

Goodman, P. (Ed.). (1986). The impact of task and technology on group performance. In P. Goodman (Ed.), *Designing effective work groups* (pp. 120–167). San Francisco, CA: Jossey-Bass.

Greiner, L. E. (1972, July–August). Evolution and revolution as organizations grow. *Harvard Business Review,* 37–46.

Hackman, J. R. (1983). The design of work teams. In J. W. Lorsch (Ed.), *Handbook of organizational behavior* (pp. 315–342). Englewood Cliffs, NJ: Prentice-Hall.

Hackman, J. R., & Morris, C. G. (1975). Group tasks, group interaction process and group performance effectiveness: A review and proposed integration. In L. Berkowitz (Ed.), *Advances in experimental social psychology* (Vol. 8, pp. 45–99). New York: Academic Press.

Hackman, J. R., & Walton, R. E. (1986). Leading groups in organizations. In P. Goodman (Ed.), *Designing effective work groups* (pp. 72–119). San Francisco, CA: Jossey-Bass.

Hall, R. H. (1976). A system pathology of an organization: The rise and fall of the old Saturday Evening Post. *Administrative Science Quarterly, 21,* 185–211.

Hambrick, D. C., & Mason, P. A. (1984). Upper echelons: The organization as a reflection of its top managers. *Academy of Management Review, 9,* 195–206.

Hatvany, N. G., & Gladstein, D. (1982). A perspective on group decision making. In D. A. Nadler, Tushman, M. L., & Hatvany, N. G., *Managing organizations: Readings and cases* (pp. 213–227). Canada: Little, Brown.

Helmich, D. L., & Brown, W. B. (1972). Successor type and organizational change in the corporate enterprise. *Administrative Science Quarterly, 17,* 371–381.

Herold, D. (1979). The effectiveness of work groups. In S. Kerr (Ed.), *Organizational behavior* (pp. 179–193). Columbus, OH: Grid.

Janis, I. (1982). *Groupthink.* Boston: Houghton-Mifflin.

Janis, I. L. (1972). *Victims of groupthink.* Boston, MA: Houghton Mifflin.

Janis, I. L., & Mann, L. (1977). *Decision making: A psychological analysis of conflict, choice and commitment.* New York: The Free Press.

Jay, A. (1976, March). How to run a meeting. *Harvard Business Review,* 3–16.

Katz, R. (1982). The effects of group longevity on project communication and performance. *Administrative Science Quarterly, 27,* 81–104.

Katz, R., & Tushman, M. (1981). An investigation into the managerial roles and career paths of gatekeepers and project supervisors in a major R&D facility. *R&D Management, 11,* 103–110.

Kets de Vries, M. F. R. (1988, January–February). The dark side of CEO succession. *Harvard Business Review,* 56–60.

Kiesler, S. B. (1978). *Interpersonal processes in groups and organizations.* Arlington Heights, IL: AHM Publishing.

Lieberman, S., & O'Connor, J. F., (1972). Leadership and organizational performance: A study of large corporations. *American Sociological Review, 37,* 117–130.

Likert, R. (1981). *New patterns of management.* New York: McGraw-Hill.

Lindblom, C. E. (1959). The science of "muddling through." *Public Administration Review, 19,* 78–88.

Lott, A., & Lott, B. (1965). Group cohesiveness as interpersonal attraction: A review of the relationships with antecedent and consequent variables. *Psychological Bulletin, 64,* 259–309.

McGrath, J. E. (1984). *Groups: Interaction and performance.* Englewood Cliffs, NJ: Prentice-Hall.

Michel, J. G., & Hambrick, D. C. (1988). *Diversification posture and the characteristics of the top management team.* Columbia Business School, Working Paper.

Miller, D., & Friesen, P. (1980). Archetypes of organizational transitions. *Administrative Science Quarterly, 25,* 268–299.

Nadler, D. A., Tushman, M. L. (1986). Organizing for innovation. *California Management Review, 128*(3), 74–92.

Nadler, D. A.. & Tushman, M. L. (1988, June 6). What makes for magic leadership. *Fortune,* pp. 261–262.

Nelson, R., & Winter, S. (1981). *An evolutionary theory of economic change.* Cambridge, MA: Harvard University Press.

Pennings, J. M. (1980). *Interlocking directorates.* San Francisco, CA: Jossey-Bass.

Peters, T. J. (1978). Symbols, patterns, and settings: An optimistic case for getting things done. *Organizational Dynamics, 7,* 3–23.

Pfeffer, J. (1981). Management as symbolic action: The creation and maintenance of organizational paradigms. In L. L. Cummings & B. Staw (Eds.), *Research in organizational behavior* (Vol. 3, pp. 1–52). Greenwich, CT: JAI Press.

Pfeffer, J. (1986). A resource dependence perspective on intercorporate relations. In M. S. Mizruchi & M. Schwartz (Eds.), *Structural analysis of business* (pp. 117–132). New York: Academic Press.

Pfeffer, J., & Salancik, G. R. (1978). *The external control of organizations: A resource dependence perspective.* New York: Harper & Row.

Phillip, H., & Dunphy, D. (1959). Developmental trends in small groups. *Sociometry, 22,* 162–174.

Quinn, J. B. (1982). Managing strategies incrementally. *Omega, 10,* 613–627.

Roberts, E. R., & Fusfeld, A. R. (1983, May). Staffing the innovative technology-based organization. *CHEMTECH: The Innovator's Magazine,* 266–274.

Romanelli, E., & Tushman, M. (1986). Inertia, environments and strategic choice: A quasi-experimental design for comparative-longitudinal research. *Management Science, 32,* 608–621.

Rubin, J. Z., & Brockner, J. (1975). Factors affecting entrapment in waiting situations: The Rosencrantz and Guildenstern effect. *Journal of Personality and Social Psychology, 31,* 1054–1063.

Rumelt, R. P. (1974). *Strategy, structure and economic performance.* Boston: Harvard University Press.

Samuelson, B. A., Gailbraith, C. S., & McGuire, J. W. (1985). Organizational Performance and Top-Management Turnover. *Organizational Studies, 3,* 275–291.

Schein, E. H. (1985). *Organizational culture and leadership.* San Francisco, CA: Jossey-Bass.

Schein, E. H. (1988). *Process consultation: Its role in organization development* (Vol. I). Reading, MA: Addison-Wesley.

Shaw, M. (1971). *Group dynamics: The psychology of small group behavior.* New York: McGraw-Hill.

Sherif, M., Harvey, O. J., White, B. J., Hood, W. R., & Sherif, C. W. (1961). *Intergroup conflict and cooperation: The robbers' cave experiment.* Norman, OK: University Book Exchange.

Song, J. H. (1982). Diversification strategies and the experience of top executives of large firms. *Strategic Management Journal, 3*(4), 377–380.

Staw, B. M. (1976). Knee-deep in the big muddy: A study of escalating commitment to a chosen course of action. *Organizational Behavior and Human Performance, 17,* 27–44.

Staw, B. M., Sandelands, L. E., & Dutton, J. E. (1981). Thread-rigidity effects in organizational behavior: Multi-level analysis. *Administrative Science Quarterly, 22,* 587–605.

Steiner, I. D. (1972). *Group process and productivity.* New York: Academic Press.

Stephan, W. G. (1984). Intergroup relations. In G. Lindzey & E. Aronson (Eds.), *Handbook of social psychology* (Vol. 2, 3rd ed., pp. 599–658). New York: Random House.

Sutton, R. I., & Rousseau, D. M. (1979). Structure, technology, and dependence on a parent organization: Organizational and environmental correlates of individual responses. *Journal of Applied Psychology, 64,* 675–687.

Terreberry, S. (1968). The evolution of organizational environments. *Administrative Science Quarterly, 12,* 590–613.

Thomas, E. J., & Fink, C. F. (1963). Effects of group size. *Psychological Bulletin, 60,* 371–384.

Tushman, M. (1977). Special boundary roles in the innovation process. *Administrative Science Quarterly, 22,* 587–605.

Tushman, M. L., & Anderson, P. (1986). Technological discontinuities and organizational environments. *Administrative Science Quarterly, 31,* 439–465.

Tushman, M. L., Newman, W. H., & Romanelli, E. (1986). Convergence and upheaval: Managing the unsteady pace of organizational revolution. *California Management Review, 29,* 1–16.

Tushman, M., & Romanelli, E. (1985). Organizational evolution: A metamorphosis model of convergence and reorientation. In L. L. Cummings & Barry M. Staw (Eds.), *Research in organizational behavior* (Vol. 7, pp. 171–222). Greenwich, CT: JAI Press.

Tushman, M., & Virany, B., (1986). Changing characteristics of executive teams in an emerging industry. *Journal of Business Venturing, 3,* 261–274.

Vancil, R. F., & Green, C. H. (1984, January–February). How CEOs use top management committees. *Harvard Business Review,* 65–73.

Van de Ven, A. H., & Walker, G. (1984). The dynamics of interorganizational coordination. *Administrative Science Quarterly, 29,* 598–621.

Virany, B. B., & Tushman, M. (1986). Changing characteristics of executive teams in an emerging industry. *Journal of Business Venturing, 3,* 261–274.

Von Hippel, E. A. (1977, Winter). Has a customer already developed your new product? *Sloan Management Review,* 63–74.

Vroom, V. H., & Jago, A. G. (1974). Decision making as a social process: Normative and descriptive models of leader behavior. *Decision Sciences, 5.*

Wagner, G. W., Pfeffer, J., & O'Reilly, C. A. (1984). Organizational demography and turnover in top management groups. *Administrative Science Quarterly, 29,* 74–92.

Weiner, N., & Mahoney, J. A., (1981). A model of corporate performance as a function of environmental, organizational and leadership influences. *Academy of Management Journal, 24,* 453–470.

Wrightsman, L. S. (1985). The social psychology of U.S. presidential effectiveness. In S. Oskamp (Ed.), *Applied social psychology annual (6): International conflict and national public policy issues.* Beverly Hills, CA: Sage.

Perceptions of Leadership and Their Implications in Organizations

Robert G. Lord
Karen J. Maher
Department of Psychology, The University of Akron

Surveys of both academics and practitioners indicate that leadership is the most important topic within the realm of organizational behavior (Rahim, 1981). Leadership has also been studied extensively, with over 3,000 references to this topic listed in Stogdill's (1974) *Handbook of Leadership.* Yet there remains in the literature considerable disagreement as to whether leaders actually have discernible impact on organizational performance (Day & Lord, 1988; Meindl & Ehrlich, 1987), and there is concern that much of the work on leadership lacks an adequate scientific foundation (Calder, 1977).

We believe that most of the deficiencies and disagreements in the leadership literature are related to three crucial issues. First, researchers have often mistakenly treated leadership perceptions and a leader's impact on group or organizational performance as isomorphic issues (Lord, De Vader, & Alliger, 1986). However, the relationship between performance and perception is a complex issue. At any point in time, perceptions are partially dependent on past performance, yet they provide a cognitive context that influences future performance. In other words, people look backward at past behaviors or past performance to form leadership perceptions. Once leadership perceptions are formed (or revised), an important cognitive context that indirectly affects future performance at both individual and organizational levels is created. Thus, we believe that perceptions are the key link between past and future performances.

A second crucial issue is that there has been a lack of comprehensive theory in both the perception and performance domains. As Calder (1977) noted, the leadership field has been guided more by implicit and poorly articulated notions based on everyday experience (implicit theories of leadership in Calder's terms) than by coherent scientific principles.

A third crucial issue is that researchers have not carefully specified the hierarchical level in organizations to which leadership theories apply. As many organizational theorists have noted, lower level and upper level leadership are qualitatively different (Katz & Kahn, 1978; Mintzberg, 1973; Pavett & Lau, 1983).

This chapter addresses each of these three crucial issues. The chapter elaborates on the implications of a perceptual viewpoint for explaining the indirect effects of leadership on performance. The following section presents a comprehensive and explicit theory of leadership perceptions that is derived from recent work in the social–cognitive area. This provides a more precise view of leadership perceptions than work derived from everyday experience with leadership. The chapter argues that leadership perceptions depend on both recognition-based and inferential processes and that both of these processes can occur using automatic or controlled modes of processing. The chapter then examines the differential application and implications of this viewpoint to lower and upper hierarchical levels, elaborating on the fundamental role of perceptual processing at each of these levels and how perceptions relate to performance. Although perceptions have much in common at each level, we argue that different processes are emphasized at different hierarchical levels.

LEADERSHIP PERCEPTIONS

Basic Perceptual Processes

Leadership perceptions are pervasive phenomena. By first grade, children can clearly differentiate leaders from nonleaders and can articulate the factors that separate these two groups of people (Matthews, Lord, & Walker, 1987). The leader/nonleader distinction becomes even more important for older students, and adults view leadership as having fundamental importance in many contexts (military, political, business, sports, religion, etc.).

To explain leadership perception, we must specify both the factors that distinguish leaders from nonleaders and the perceptual processes used by followers. Early work on leadership perceptions focused only on the former, as many researchers searched for universal traits that distinguished leaders from followers (Mann, 1959). Although early trait research was severely criticized, recent meta-analytic techniques (Lord et al., 1986) show there are traits that generally are associated with leadership. Other researchers (Calder, 1977) have identified both behaviors and events as evidence upon which leadership perceptions are based. Thus, events, behaviors, and traits are crucial distinguishing features of leaders. However, it is these features as perceived and utilized by others, not as they occur in any objective sense, that are crucial in explaining leadership perceptions (Hollander & Julian, 1969; Lord et al., 1986). These features may be made salient by leaders, but they must also be noticed by perceivers. Further, perceivers must encode these features in a way that is personally meaningful, and use them to differentiate others in terms of leadership.

Although we often think about or discuss leadership, at other times we seem to attribute leadership without deliberate thought through normal task-related activities in many different contexts. That leadership perceptions are formed when people's attention and motivations are focused on task activities suggests that such perceptions involve what cognitive psychologists call *automatic processes*—processes that occur without awareness, without intent, without much effort, and without interference with other cognitive tasks. Our ability to think about or discuss leadership also implicates the involvement of *controlled processes*—processes that require awareness, intent, effort, and that interfere with other activities. We think this distinction between controlled and automatic processes (Hasher & Zacks, 1979; Shiffrin & Schneider, 1977) is fundamental to understanding leadership perceptions.

Lord (1985) developed a social information-processing model of leadership processes in which he asserted that leadership perceptions can be explained by two qualitatively different processes. Leadership can be recognized from the qualities and behaviors revealed through normal day-to-day interactions with others, or it can be inferred from the outcomes of salient events. For example, someone who is intelligent, honest, outgoing, understanding, and verbally skilled is likely to be recognized as having strong leadership qualities. Alternatively, leadership is likely to be inferred when a person is seen as being directly responsible for a favorable performance outcome. Both inferential and recognition-based processes can be either automatic or controlled. A theory explaining recognition-based processes is developed in the following section. This section is followed by a discussion of inferential processes.

Recognition-Based Processes

Recognition-based perceptual processes help us form leadership perceptions from the normal flow of interpersonal activities. Because social interactions often place high processing demands on actors (Ostrom, 1984), it makes sense to think of recognition-based processes that occur in normal task oriented interaction as proceeding more automatically. *Automatic processes* would compete less with ongoing interaction than would controlled processes. Recognition-based processes also depend on exposure to the behaviors of others and knowledge of their underlying traits. Thus, they involve the use of preexisting knowledge about leadership in particular contexts. Such knowledge has been referred to as *implicit leadership theories* (ILT) by many academic researchers (Lord, Foti, & De Vader, 1984).

One theory about how recognition-based leadership perceptions are formed under these situations was suggested by Lord et al. (1984). They viewed leadership as being a cognitive category that was fundamentally important in many different situations. Following Rosch's (1978) theory of cognitive categorization, they argued that leadership is a fairly general, superordinate category; and they saw the situation (or context) as being essential in refining this category to a more useful, basic level (e.g., business leader). This emphasis on context to help specify basic-level leadership categories is consistent with Bond and Brockett's (1987) work showing that people index personality traits according to context. Thus, basic-level leadership categories might simply consist of the traits and behaviors appropriate to a leadership role in a particular context.

According to the leadership categorization theory of Lord et al. (1984), categorizations are made based on the match of characteristics of a person to abstractions or prototypes derived from features common to category members. Thus, leadership is a cognitive knowledge structure held in the memory of perceivers that is based on an assimilation of their experience with prior leaders in particular contexts. Essentially, perceivers use degree of match to this ready-made structure to form leadership perceptions. For example, in a business context someone who is well-dressed, honest, outgoing, intelligent, and industrious would be seen as a leader. Whereas in politics someone seen as wanting peace, having strong convictions, being charismatic, and a good administrator would be labeled as a leader. Such prototype-matching processes can be made easily, perhaps automatically (Alba, Chromiak, Hasher, & Attig, 1980), and this same basic leadership perception process can be used under high and low information load conditions (Maurer, 1987). Several laboratory studies now show that the fit of a person's behavior to observer's prototypes of leadership affects the leadership ratings (Cronshaw & Lord, 1987; Fraser & Lord, 1987; Lord et al., 1984).

A more *controlled process* that is also important in forming leadership perceptions is explicit, conscious evaluation by others. In contexts where leadership is important, leadership qualities are often directly discussed. For example, sports commentators and political analysts frequently comment on leadership qualities, and leadership may be formally evaluated through procedures such as assessment centers. Although such procedures involve an explicit focus on leadership, they can still be considered a recognition-based process because they use traits and behaviors of the leader rather than outcomes and environmental events (occurrences that are relevant to groups or organizations but do not require the presence of the leader) as a basis for leadership perceptions. In fact, we suspect that the same basic prototype-matching process is used to form leadership perceptions (classify people as leaders or nonleaders) from either directly experienced (face-to-face contact) or indirectly experienced, socially communicated behavioral information.

Interestingly, once others are categorized as leaders, observers can rely on existing category structures to describe a leader's behaviors or form expectations about future behavior. Thus, a simple act of categorization may provide a powerful cognitive structure that shapes the nature of interactions among people. If a subordinate categorizes a supervisor as an effective leader, this simple labeling process causes the subordinate to expect behavior consistent with effective leadership in future interactions. Information contained in such categories may also provide a self-standard that indicates to leaders themselves how they should behave (Carver, 1979). Moreover, such effects seem to be independent of the means by which a person is categorized. Because categorization can affect perceptions of leaders and their actual behavior, the content and structure of leadership categories is of both practical and theoretical importance, therefore it is discussed at length in the following section.

Content and Structure of Leadership Categories. Lord et al. (1984) argued that leadership is a cognitive category that is hierarchically organized in a manner similar to other object and person categories (Cantor & Mischel, 1979; Rosch, 1978). Leaders are distinguished from nonleaders at the highest, superordinate level based on a highly abstract, but general, prototype. Lord et al. argued that context information is combined with the leadership construct to develop more refined, basic-level conceptualizations of leadership. From a content analysis of the way leadership was used in the popular press, they identify 11 different contexts that are used to specify types of leaders (military, educational, business, religious, sports, world political, national political, financial, minority, media, and labor leaders).

Based on categorization theory, one would expect that the attributes that were most widely shared among these basic-level categories would define the superordinate-level leadership prototype. This is exactly what they found based on an extensive analysis of college students' leadership categories. The most frequent attributes across the basic-level categories, with the proportion of categories to which they applied listed in parentheses, were: intelligent (.91), honest (.64), outgoing (.55), understanding (.45), verbally skilled (.45), aggressive (.36), determined (.36), caring (.27), decisive (.27), dedicated (.27), educated (.27), and well-dressed (.27). Thus, for example, intelligence was thought to characterize leaders in 10 of the 11 contexts (the sole exception being national political leader).

The fact that few of these attributes applied to all 11 basic-level categories is consistent with the principle of overlapping similarity among categories labeled "family resemblance" by Rosch (1978). What this means is that leaders in different contexts do not share exactly the same set of traits, even though they are all recognized as being leaders. This principle fits well with the frequently mentioned "situationally contingent" nature of leadership. It also suggests that leaders may have difficulty moving from some contexts to others. More specifically, if there is a high degree of overlap among the traits characterizing leaders in two contexts (e.g., business and finance), leaders may be able to move from one context to the other without much difficulty. However, if there is minimal overlap (e.g., sports and financial leaders), one would expect substantial problems for real-world leaders attempting to cross these contextual boundaries.

Mobility of Leaders.   Because the issue of moving across contextual boundaries (basic-level leadership categories) has never been directly addressed in the leadership literature, we discuss it in a bit more depth and provide some illustrative data. Based on a perceiver-oriented view of leadership, we would expect that leaders could function better in any context if they fit with the commonly held prototypes of followers. This is because they would more easily be categorized as leaders, enhancing their social power and ability to influence others. Also, they would generally conform more to subordinates' expectations, allowing them to build up credit that permits greater future deviations from group norms (Hollander, 1964, 1985). For this reason, we would predict that where prototypes are similar, common perceptual standards would make transitions across contextual boundaries easier for leaders than where prototypes are dissimilar.

Fortunately, the data to compare contexts in terms of prototype similarity are available from the previously discussed Lord et al. (1984) study of the 11 basic-level leadership categories. To do this, we simply used their data to create a context by trait matrix in which entries were one if a trait was found by Lord et al. to apply to a category and zero if it did not apply. This was done for the 35 most prototypical traits for the superordinate category of leader based on the Lord et al. study. We then calculated measures of association for the 11 basic-level leadership categories across these 35 traits. Chamber's r_e coefficients were calculated, as this measure of association gives the best approximation to the underlying correlations with dichotomous data (Alexander, Alliger, Carson, & Barrett, 1985). The resulting matrix is shown in Table 6.1. These indices reflect the degree of prototype similarity between contexts, and they imply an ease of transfer across some boundaries (business and finance or education and religion) but not across others (military and business or sports and business). It should be noted, however, that there are also other factors (e.g., technical competence, style, type of power, nature of

TABLE 6.1
Similarity of Leadership Prototypes From Different Contexts

	B	F	MIN	E	R	S	NP	WP	L	MED	MIL
Business	—										
Finance	.83 **	—									
Minority	.50	.67 *	—								
Education	.57	.72 *	.28	—							
Religion	.34	.54	.49	.80 **	—						
Sports	.18	.32	.28	.36	.37	—					
Natnl. Pol.	.20	−.06	−.47	.21	.06	−.07	—				
World Pol.	.50	.67 *	.20	.75 **	.49	.28	.76 **	—			
Labor	.57	.32	−.09	.36	.09	.36	−.07	−.09	—		
Media	.50	.25	−.16	.28	.00	−.09	.10	.47	.55 *	—	
Military	.11	.25	−.16	−.09	−.34	.28	−.16	.20	.28	−.16	—

$N = 35$
*p < .05. **p < .01.
Note: Significance values were obtained from a chi-square analysis of the 2 X 2 contingency tables from which Chamber's r_e statistics were calculated.

subordinates) that would affect ease of movement across these contextual boundaries that are not reflected in Table 6.1.

In spite of this caveat, there are some surprising findings in Table 6.1. There were few high values, with only 8 of 55 associations reaching significance. There were many low values, however, and 13 pairs of contexts (24%) were actually negatively related. Together, these results indicate that there is definitely not one homogeneous pattern of leadership traits across contexts. Several contexts were generally not associated with other contextual prototypes: military leaders, sports leaders, national political leaders (which was only significantly correlated with world political leader), labor and media (which were significantly associated only with each other). This suggests that contrary to popular myths, politics, sports, and the military may not be helpful contexts in which to learn general leadership skills. It is interesting to note the strong negative relationship between minority and national political leadership prototypes. This indicates that minority leaders may have considerable difficulty moving into the political realm. Characteristics prototypical of the category of minority leader are humanitarian, persistent, cooperative, and having strong character. Whereas the most prototypical characteristics for national political leaders are being good administrators; wanting peace; having strong convictions; and being charismatic, goal-oriented, and responsible. This may explain some of the difficulties Jesse Jackson faced in moving into national politics.

To further explore similarities, we performed a cluster analysis on the data in Table 6.1 using the SPSSX cluster program with a pattern similarity measure. This analysis indicated that there were only two general clusters: business, finance, minority, religion, and education; and national and world politics. The first cluster can be seen by looking at the triangle formed by the first five contexts in Table 6.1. Many of these associations are significant, indicating substantial overlap or prototypical leadership traits across these settings. Apart from these two clusters, prototypes were not very similar. Even within the main cluster, the relationships are only moderate.

Thus, even moving across closely related contexts (e.g., religion to minority) is something that requires careful planning and an adjustment process. To some extent, crossing any contextual boundaries may require retraining or relearning of leadership skills, and for most transitions such relearning would have to be substantial for leaders to successfully fit into the prototypes held by followers. For example, training might stress teaching leaders to emphasize the traits they possess that are consistent with prototypes in a new situation. Emphasizing a partial rather than perfect fit is consistent with family resemblance, as opposed to the classical, critical feature model of categorization. Without such training, commonly held prototypes within contexts may impede the movement of leadership talent across contexts.

The previous discussion shows how the issue of leadership mobility can be addressed from a perceptual viewpoint. There are some obvious limitations to the prior analysis that need further research. First, data came from undergraduates who lack experience in many of the contexts for which they described leaders, and therefore may provide different descriptions than experts in these contexts (Lurigio & Carroll, 1985). Second, categorical systems may be built around other distinctions besides context. For example, hierarchical level, tasks, and subordinate characteristics may also be incorporated into categorical systems. Current research in this area is exploring expert/novice differences and the effects of hierarchical levels (Baumgardner, Lord, & Forti, 1989) on the structure of leadership categories. There is an obvious need for research investigating the effects of other factors on these categorical systems.

We turn now to a discussion of the inferential processes of leadership perception. In this model, information on past performance is used to infer leadership. Such information processes provide an alternative to recognition-based processes for forming leadership perceptions. As we noted in the introduction, once leadership perceptions are formed through either process, they provide a cognitive context that can impact on future performance. For example, at lower levels, leadership perceptions affect a supervisor's ability to motivate and socialize subordinates. At the highest organizational levels, leadership perceptions affect top management's ability to create a corporate culture and strategic vision. We focus on such indirect effects on performance because they are closely tied to leadership perceptions, and have often been ignored by traditional work in the leadership area. At both levels, we choose to ignore the direct effects of leader behavior on subordinate or organizational performance (instructing subordinates on how to perform tasks or making strategic decisions), which have been the traditional focus of leadership research.

Inferential Processes

Inferential processes are used to link leadership perceptions to key organizational events. Performance outcomes for major organizational tasks (e.g., corporate profit statements for businesses or winning championships in sports) are often key events, and many studies show that performance feedback does indeed affect leadership perceptions (Lord, 1985). In short, success enhances the perception of leadership, whereas failure can limit perceptions of leadership. Further, causal ascriptions to leaders are a basic part of this process. As traditional attribution theorists would imply (Kelley, 1973), if people are seen as being more causal in determining favorable outcomes, then the perception that they are leaders is enhanced; if they are seen as being less causal for good performance, their leadership ratings are not as high. Similarly, when outcomes are negative, causal ascriptions to actors produce lower leadership ratings than do ascriptions to other factors. Interestingly, the attributional component in inferential processes may involve either automatic or controlled processing. People may think carefully about causality trying to assess the relative impact of facilitative or inhibiting factors, or they unknowingly may be influenced by factors in the situations that make some causal sources more salient than others (see Taylor & Fiske, 1978, for a discussion of the role of salience in causal attributions).

An experimental study by Phillips and Lord (1981) illustrates both automatic and controlled attributional processes. They had subjects make leadership ratings after watching a specially developed videotape of a group problem-solving task and receiving bogus feedback on the performance of the videotaped group. As expected, even though all subjects viewed the same videotaped interaction, good performance feedback led to higher leadership ratings of the target person than did poor performance feedback. This effect, however, also depended on causal ascriptions. When other information given to subjects provided a plausible explanation for performance outcomes, this performance cue effect was diminished, as were causal ascriptions to the leader. For example, when subjects were told that groups in the stimulus tape performed well and that these groups were high in ability and motivation, or when subjects were told that groups performed poorly and that these groups were low in ability and motivation, the role of the leader could be discounted. When information provided subjects was inconsistent with the observed outcome, (pairing low ability and motivation information with good performance feedback or high ability and motivation information with poor performance feedback) the performance cue effect was strengthened, as were causal ascriptions to the leader. This logical integration of information, consistent with Kelley's augmenting and discounting configural factors, is suggestive of controlled processing.

However, causal attributions and leadership ratings were also affected by a less rational, more perceptually based causal factor in the Phillips and Lord study. The videotapes shown to subjects were made from two alternative camera angles that made the target subject either more or less salient. Although these films were concurrent, resulting in exactly the same behaviors being clearly visible on the videotapes, this salience manipulation affected causal attributions and leadership perceptions. Subjects shown the salient leader videotapes rated the leader as being more responsible for group outcomes and altered their ratings more based on bogus performance feedback. When subjects were shown the videotapes with the less salient leader, they rated the leader as being less causally responsible and their ratings were less based on the bogus performance feedback. This experimental factor seemed to involve more automatic processes, reflecting perceptually dominated (Lowe & Kassin, 1980) rather than deliberate, reflective processes.

To see how these experimental results might parallel real-world processes, consider the example of Lee Iacocca and Chrysler. When Iacocca became CEO, Chrysler had poor products and limited financial resources. Given these inhibiting factors, Chrysler's turnaround was naturally explained in terms of Iacocca's leadership. Such reasoning shows a logical integration of information and is consistent with controlled processing. That is, people might reason that some extraordinary quality of Iacocca (i.e., leadership ability) allowed him to overcome these inhibiting factors. However, Iacocca also made himself very salient by testifying to Congress and being personally featured in numerous television ads. This salience may have also triggered more automatic causal processes that supported his causal importance and enhanced leadership perceptions. Thus, both controlled and automatic attributional processes may have guided perceivers' inferences that Lee Iacocca had exerted substantial amounts of leadership at Chrysler. An inferential model would apply to observers' perceptions of Iacocca because they were judging leadership based on the outcome of events (i.e., Chrysler's turnaround), rather than on face-to-face contact. For people who interacted directly with Iacocca, recognition-based processes would also affect leadership perceptions.

So far, we have described two perceptual processes, inferential and recognition-based, by which people can be perceived as leaders. We expect that in most instances perceptions are formed and modified over time, and because of this time-distributed nature of perceptions, a mixture of processes may be used. For example, initial impressions may be formed based on recognition of prototypical behaviors, but these perceptions may be revised later using inferential processes to integrate information on performance. This procedure relies on simple, automatic processes to confirm prior conclusions, when new information is consistent with prior categorizations. However, it is likely that more controlled processes are used to integrate information that is inconsistent with prior expectations (Wong & Weiner, 1981). In such cases, observers first carefully assess the causal role of leaders in producing inconsistent performance outcomes. Observers then use performance to revise leadership ratings if the leader is seen as a cause. To illustrate this process, consider an executive who is hired based on his or her fit to a leadership prototype, subsequently, effective performance (consistent with the prototype) is accepted at face value, and automatically assimilated into the leadership category. If the executive has failed to perform well, however, there is a controlled search for factors that may have led to the poor performance. We believe that many leaders are aware of this phenomenon, and do much to appropriately manage the "image" they have created. For example, a U.S. President may associate himself with successes, while letting subordinates (press secretaries, Cabinet members) explain failures.

To summarize, we have argued that there are essentially four different types of processes involved in forming leadership perceptions. These processes, which are shown in Table 6.2, can be either inferential or recognition based, and they may involve either predominantly automatic or controlled modes of processing information. The inferential/recognition dimension corresponds to the type of information used by perceivers (i.e., event or outcome information vs. trait or behavioral information, respectively). The automatic/controlled dimension corresponds to the type of processes (and the amount of attentional resources they require) that are used to form perceptions from stimulus information.

We believe that most sources of information can be fit into the categories in Table 6.2. However, one important source of leadership information, that conveyed by television and similar media, does not fit very well. For exam-

TABLE 6.2
Alternative Types of Processes Used to Form Leadership Perceptions

Models of Perceptual Process	Data	Mode of Cognitive Process	
		Automatic	Controlled
Inferential	Events and outcomes	Perceptually guided, simplified causal analysis	Logically based, comprehensive causal analysis
Recognition	Traits and behavior	Prototype matching based on face-to-face contact	Prototype matching based on socially communicated information

ple, viewing a political leader on television involves a complex and rich source of information similar to face-to-face contact, suggesting automatic processing. However, viewing television does not create the concurrent task and social information processing demands that normally occur during face-to-face contact in organizations. This implies that television viewers would have sufficient spare processing capacity to utilize more controlled processes. Thus, media such as television may be consistent with either automatic or controlled processing.

IMPLICATIONS

In this section we address implications of leadership perceptions for leadership theory and offer some practical examples for both the recognition-based and inferential models of leadership perceptions in business settings. We believe these models may be applied differentially to lower and upper levels of the corporate hierarchy. Lower level leadership emphasizes automatic, recognition-based processes shown in Table 6.2. We believe this to be the case because the effectiveness of lower level leaders is often not clearly identifiable. Frequently, lower level leaders do not produce a complete product or engage in decision making that results in visible effects. If outcomes of lower level leaders were clearly identifiable, inferential models would apply. Upper level leadership emphasizes the remaining three processes in Table 6.2. First, we discuss how recognition-based leadership perceptions may impact at lower hierarchical levels. We present implications of the automatic recognition-based mode of processing in three areas: dyadic relations between leaders and subordinates, generation of leader behavior, and self-leadership. Second, we examine how the inferential model of leadership perception is related to executive power and the transmission of corporate culture at the highest levels of the organization.

Lower Level Leadership Perceptions

Dyadic Relations Between Leaders and Subordinates. The dyadic relation between leaders and subordinates at lower hierarchical levels has been the primary focus of most leadership theory and research. Traditional research addressed the direct impact of leader behavior on subordinate behavior. Traits possessed by the leader and behaviors reflecting those traits were thought to be the primary determinants of subordinate performance. For example, task-oriented leaders were thought to be able to motivate subordinates by clarifying paths to work goals. However, researchers soon realized that leader behavior originated, in part, in subordinates. That is, leaders responded differently to different subordinates (Dansereau, Graen, & Haga, 1975) and leaders altered their behavior depending on the performance of subordinates (Farris & Lim, 1969; Greene, 1975; Lowin & Craig, 1968). In fact, it is actually more appropriate to conceptualize dyadic relations as a mutual influence process (Herold, 1977). Moreover, the perceptual processes of leaders (Green & Mitchell, 1979) and subordinates (Calder, 1977; Hollander & Julian, 1969) were seen as key mediating processes that linked the behavior of one dyadic member to the response of the other.

Figure 6.1 illustrates both the traditional and more current theories of dyadic leadership. The top portion of this figure illustrates the traditional theories of leadership in which the effects of leader and subordinate behavior were emphasized. The lower portion reflects the theoretical shift that has occurred in the past decade to study leader and subordinate perceptions in dyadic interactions. According to this social–cognitive view, mutual influence can be conceptualized as a cyclical process involving behaviors and interpretations of those behaviors that unfolds over time. This process is represented in Fig. 6.1 by a combination of two loops. The first loop shows that subordinate behavior affects perceptions by the leader, which affect subsequent leader behavior (Arrows 1 and 3). The second loop shows that subordinate perceptions of leader behavior mediate its effect on subsequent subordinate behavior (Arrows 2 and 4 in Fig. 6.1). Together these two loops describe the cyclical interaction of behaviors and cognitions (Arrows 1 to 3 and 2 to 4, repeat).

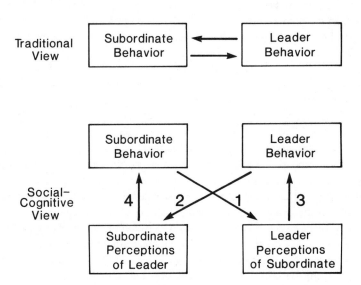

FIG. 6.1. A schematic view of the linkages between leaders and subordinates.

What is needed to translate Fig. 6.1 into a viable theory of leadership is a precise specification of the cognitive processes that underlie the two lower boxes. This specification of subordinate cognitive processes has already been provided in the prior sections of this chapter. Detailing the cognitive processes of leaders that produce their perceptions of subordinates falls outside the scope of this chapter, but we can note that there are parallels to both the recognition and inferential models we have already discussed. Work on performance appraisal (Feldman, 1981) suggests that supervisors can recognize good subordinates using relatively simple categorization processes. For example, General Motors traditionally identified good subordinates by their fit to the organizational culture (Yates, 1983). Other work based on attribution theory (Green & Mitchell, 1979; Mitchell, Green, & Wood, 1981; Mitchell & Wood, 1980) suggests that the causal analyses of leaders are crucial links by which they draw inferences about subordinates based on their performance.

Thus, there are separate and somewhat parallel lines of research that find that perceptions play an important role in understanding dyadic interactions, but both are one-sided perspectives because neither addresses the effects of both subordinate and leadership perceptions of the other's behavior. We think that substantial progress in understanding dyadic relationships could be made by using both recognition-based and inferential processes to explain the type of reciprocal interdependence shown in Figure 6.1. Some progress on joint models of leader and subordinate perceptions has been provided by Martinko and Gardner (1987) who developed an interactive attributional model to explain how reciprocal interdependence develops over time. However, their work neglects both recognition-based processes and the more automatic type of inferential processes described earlier. We think that automatic processing provides the most reasonable explanation for perceptions based on face-to-face contact between superiors and subordinates. Thus, work on reciprocal influence should emphasize such processes, rather than the controlled processes typically used in laboratory studies of causal attributions.

Generation of Leader Behavior. At lower levels where leaders' performance outcomes are often unclear, subordinate perceptions of leaders typically involve recognition-based processes shown in Table 6.2. Because these perceptions occur in face-to-face situations where attention is focused on task activities, leadership perceptions occur automatically. This process has been explained in an earlier section of this chapter. However, these prototype-matching processes can also affect a manager's own behavior, thus producing an additional effect on the leader–subordinate interaction process.

We have thus far illustrated that subordinates use prototypes to understand and predict the behavior of their superiors. Because these leadership prototypes are widely held and understood, leaders themselves also may be aware of these prototypical leader behaviors and traits, and make use of this knowledge to guide their own behavior. Thus, managers compare their own behavior to self-generated behavioral standards (cf. Carver, 1979) derived from leader prototypes. If managers have a clear idea of the appropriate leader prototype, such a comparison could provide a means of self-evaluation and feedback. Prototype matching can therefore provide information as to the appropriateness of a manager's behavior and can directly guide behavior generation through behavioral scripts (Lord & Kernan, 1987). Strict adherence to a prototypical set of behaviors, however, may be an overly restrictive way to behave, and may be inappropriate in certain instances. The point we wish to make, however, is that prototypes help subordinates understand and form behavioral expectations of leader behavior, whereas managers use these same prototypes to help guide their own self-presentations.

Given that recognition-based leadership perceptions are pervasive in organizations, some prescriptive statements can be made regarding managerial behavior. The category of an effective leader is widely held by subordinates in a given context. Therefore, it would benefit the manager to learn what traits and behaviors are prototypical of effective leadership and make an effort to behave in congruence with this prototype when feasible. As such, leadership training programs should aim toward identifying subordinate's perceptions of effective leadership in particular contexts. Although behaviors and traits associated with effective leadership are thought to be consistent across situations by popular writers (e.g., Peters & Waterman, 1982), there may be important differences across organizations, levels of the same organization, or across different task domains (Lord & Alliger, 1985). Thus, managers new to an organization, or those transferring to different departments within an organization, should be sensitive to different prototypes that affect subordinate perceptions of effective leadership in these domains. This may explain why attempts to bring in executives from outside a company often fail. (See Yates', 1983, discussion of this problem at General Motors.)

Self-Leadership. It has been suggested (Kerr & Jermier, 1978; Manz, 1986; Manz & Sims, 1980) that certain characteristics of the subordinate, the task, and the organization may serve as substitutes for formal leadership behaviors. Manz and Sims (1980, 1987) suggested that leader–subordinate interactions are integral in promoting self-leadership among subordinates through modeling and reinforcement. We believe leadership perceptions may be important in the formation and maintenance of self-leadership behaviors. Interestingly, this perspective is consistent with much of the recent emphasis on quality circles and Japanese-style management techniques.

A self-leadership perspective implies that leader traits and behaviors have less impact on subordinate behavior to the extent that self-leadership is present. If one accepts the idea that employees can be motivated through self-leadership, then the traditional view depicted in the upper portion of Fig. 6.1 is not directly relevant because the leader's behaviors that usually serve to direct subordinates (e.g., initiating structure) are internalized by subordinates. Many mentor–protege relationships are characterized by this process. Over time, the protege typically develops an internal model of the mentor's thought processes and can identify what the mentor would do in any given situation. When proteges begin to rely on this internal model rather than consulting their mentor, self-leadership substitutes for the traditional effects of leaders shown in Fig. 6.1.

However, when self-leadership is interpreted in social–cognitive terms (the lower portion of Fig. 6.1), it can be seen that leadership still has an influence over the subordinate. This influence does not occur directly through overt leader behavior, but through perceptions of leadership that have been internalized by the subordinate, thereby affecting the degree to which the subordinate engages in self-leadership behavior. Again, the importance of context may play a role in leadership perceptions. The recognition-based model of leadership perception may be differentially important across contexts to the extent that self-leadership is present.

The self-leadership model may not imply an absence of leader influence on the subordinate, but may instead imply an absence of direct leader influence through behavior (as in the top panel of Fig. 6.1). Indirect leader influence through an internalization of an effective leadership prototype, however, may be an important component in what is termed *self-leadership.*

In summary, we have argued that the recognition-based, automatic processes shown in the upper left quadrant of Table 6.2 are most useful for understanding the interaction between leaders and subordinates at lower hierarchical levels. Leadership perceptions formed through such processes provide a context within which much of the motivation and socialization of subordinates may occur. This process usually occurs automatically, through face-to-face contact with the leader, but it can also involve controlled processes when information about a manager's behaviors is obtained indirectly through socially communicated information that has already been labeled and interpreted by others. Individuals, of course, can also think carefully about leaders, but perceptions are colored by initial categorizations.

Executive-Level Leadership Perceptions

Executive-level leadership emphasizes the processes in the remaining quadrants of Table 6.1. For the most part, executives do not interact on a face-to-face basis with organizational members except with their immediate team of managers. Here recognition-based, automatic processes would also be important. The CEO, for example, interacts directly with the board of directors and vice-presidents. First-line managers, however, typically never interact directly with the CEO. Usually top executives often have only indirect influence with most organizational members through symbolism, images, and policies that impact on the organization as a whole.

An assumption common to most leadership theory is that leadership, in some form, is instrumental in contributing to organizational effectiveness. Recently, however, academicians have questioned this assumption when applied to chief executives. It is asserted that leadership is inconsequential to organizational performance (Meindl & Ehrlich, 1987; Pfeffer, 1977). The primary database for these arguments is from leadership succession studies (Brown, 1982; Salancik & Pfeffer, 1977). This view holds that leadership has meaning only through the attributions of observers (Calder, 1977). Others (Pfeffer & Davis-Blake, 1986; Smith, Carson, & Alexander, 1984), however, disagree with the assertion that executive leadership has no impact on organizational outcomes. Specifically, Day and Lord (1988) addressed several methodological limitations of the succession studies, and reevaluated the original results based on these criticisms. They concluded that leadership can explain 20% to 45% of the variance in organizational outcomes. Barrick, Day, Lord, and Alexander (1988) used a different method to show that high-performing executives have significant impact (in dollars) on the performance of a sample of Fortune "500" companies, thus demonstrating the utility of executive leadership. Their results indicated that the overall utility of having an above average executive was over $25 million for Fortune "500" firms.

Hambrick and Finkelstein (1987) have attempted to integrate the diverging views of the degree of executive impact on organizational outcomes. They argued that the degree of managerial discretion can explain the differences in these two perspectives: Only if managers have discretion would there be a relationship between executive leadership and performance. One of our main points is that leadership perceptions play a large role in determining managerial discretion. To be effective, executive leaders must make use of perceptually derived power to substantially influence factors that impact on organizational performance, either directly or indirectly. Perceptions create power by expanding what Hambrick and Finkelstein (1987) called the zone of acceptance of powerful constituencies in organizations. Further, if the outcome of actions within the zone of acceptance is favorable, executive influence will be enhanced. If the outcome is unfavorable, the influence of the leader will eventually decline.

The processes shown in Table 6.2 help to provide an explanation of how an executive's zone of acceptance may be expanded or contracted. Recognition-based processes and inferential processes are both important. If an executive fits an effective leader prototype held by members of powerful constituencies (e.g., the board of directors), then the leader's zone of acceptance will expand through automatic, recognition-based perceptual processes. Also, if socially communicated information about the leader's behaviors is compared to a leader prototype a recognition-based, controlled mode of processing may be used. This type of processing may occur, for example, if a CEO is discussed in *The Wall Street Journal.* Once categorized in terms of leadership, subsequent actions and their associated outcomes may be interpreted in light of these perceptions through inferential processes. If leaders are seen as being responsible for events, leadership perceptions will be affected substantially by good or bad outcomes. Responsibility may be assessed automatically, if the leader is saliently associated with an event. Recall our example of Iacocca appearing on television to promote Chrysler automobiles. Alternatively, a more controlled process may operate if perceivers infer that the leader caused the event or outcome because of his or her level of discretion. This type of processing may occur when leaders affect factors outside the organization. When Iacocca went to the government and labor unions for help in saving Chrysler, he was perceived as being responsible for engineering the rescue of the company.

Our comments on how a leader's zone of acceptance is expanded or contracted have practical importance for both substantive and symbolic actions. Leadership perceptions affect the amount of discretion executives are allowed in several substantive (e.g., resource allocation, administrative choice, market selection) and symbolic (e.g., language and other actions used to affect organizational values) domains. (See also Tushman & Romanelli, 1985.) We suggest that substantive, direct actions are related to perceptions of power, while symbolic, indirect actions are primarily associated with perceptions related to organizational culture. We expand on each of these topics in the following sections.

Leadership Perceptions and Power.   Power is fundamental in understanding organizational behavior (Pfeffer, 1981). Our analysis of inferential and recognition-based models of leadership perception helps to clarify the distinction between enacted power and potential power (Provan, 1980). *Enacted power* refers to demonstrated influence over outcomes that have already occurred and may serve to expand (or contract) the zone of acceptance. *Potential power* refers to one's capacity to influence future outcomes. Potential power is synonymous with an expanded zone of acceptance. Potential power is reflected in the recognition-based model of leadership perception, in which power is derived from sets of behaviors or traits that may be compared to an "effective leader" prototype that is accessed and used to interpret a leader's behavior. In addition, however, potential power also reflects outcomes of past inferences and, as such, can serve as an input to leadership perceptions. An executive who has been associated with successful events will be perceived as having greater influence on future events, as illustrated by the inferential model in the top half of Table 6.2.

The following example illustrates how the zone of acceptance can be expanded through perceptual processes. Reagan's association with the successful return of the American hostages held in Iran in 1980 capitalized on automatic inferential processes to increase his potential power over government activities. Reagan's fit with common prototypes of political leaders also helped to increase his power through more recognition-based processes (as reflected in the lower right quadrant of Table 6.2). Subsequently, on a domestic level, Reagan was able to make drastic changes in the budget and initiate a large-scale tax reform plan. On an international level, Reagan was supported in the Grenada invasion and in the attack on Libya. A President who did not make optimal use of inferential and recognition-based processes likely would not have been supported in these events. Thus, both inferential and recognition models of leadership perceptions can be combined to enhance power and enlarge the zone of acceptable behavior for a leader.

In summary, much of the power and leadership literature has focused on substantive behaviors and strategies of executives that directly affect organizational outcomes. The point we wish to make is that perceptions of these behaviors in terms of leadership play an equally large part in affecting organizational outcomes. We believe that adequate power is required for effective implementation of substantive actions favored by leaders, particularly when these actions fall outside the normal zone of acceptance for key constituencies. Moreover, leadership perceptions are the key cognition linking past, present, and future events to an executive's power. Thus, they help determine the extent to which top executives can directly affect organizational performance.

Leadership Perceptions and Organizational Culture. Understanding the cognitive processes that underlie leadership perceptions can also help us understand how an executive can have discretion in shaping an organization's culture. To an outside observer, organizational culture may be one of the most salient aspects of the organization, yet one of the most enigmatic. An organization's culture may have one of several forms and serve many functions. Forms of culture include rituals and ceremonies (Trice & Beyer, 1984), stories (Martin, 1982), logos and corporate jokes (Dandridge, Mitroff, & Joyce, 1980). IBM, for example, was well known for the "blue suit, white shirt" aspect of its culture. Culture serves several useful functions in organizations. A shared culture leads to shared interpretations of organizational events, awareness of expected behaviors, uncertainty reduction, inspiration for employees, and appropriate in-group and out-group boundaries between hierarchical levels (Siehl & Martin, 1984).

Culture is developed, maintained, and changed by actions in the symbolic domain (Hambrick & Finkelstein, 1987; Pfeffer, 1981). It has been suggested that executive leaders play a primary role in cultural transmission and maintenance through symbolic action (Pondy, 1978). Schein (1985) argued it is possible that the primary activity of leaders is the creation and management of culture. Further, Schein suggested that culture transmission is achieved through certain qualities possessed by the leader, such as vision and emotional strength. This perspective is reminiscent of the traditional trait view of leaders discussed previously. In short, many theorists agree that culture and leadership traits are strongly intertwined.

We agree with Schein that leadership traits are important in cultural transmission. However, we argue for a more process-oriented view of the executive's impact on organizational culture, where leadership perceptions are based both on traits and outcomes. Leadership perceptions reflect one of the primary processes by which symbolic management of culture is maintained. In fact, Schein's emphasis on the role of leadership qualities in transmitting culture seems to reflect what we have called socially communicated, recognition-based leadership perceptions in the lower right quadrant of Table 6.2. Leaders also affect organizational outcomes through the inferential model of leadership perceptions, where perceptions are linked to organizational events. Referring again to the top half of Table 6.2, causal ascriptions for events are consciously attributed to the executive leader based on symbolic activities he or she performs in relation to that event, reflecting the inferential model of leadership perceptions.

Work on leadership perceptions suggests that executives should be aware of the strong relationship of such perceptions to culture, and the importance of image management. The chief executive "manages" attributional processes (either knowingly or unknowingly) which affect leadership perceptions. Stories communicated throughout the organization can be powerful forms of culture transmission (Martin, 1982). For example, at a large insurance organization, the CEO regularly stood in the cafeteria line with organizational members from all hierarchical levels. This story was often relayed to new employees, serving as a form of information about the organization's culture consistent with other aspects of the culture, such as an open-door policy.

Likewise, when an organization undergoes a major change (e.g., takeover, diversification, restructuring), related changes in the executive's symbolic actions also may be required. For example, if the organization is forced to initiate pay cuts or large scale payoffs during restructuring, the CEO may choose to convey that he or she has also taken a pay cut to symbolize fairness in implementing these changes. Insensitivity to such issues can create major difficulties for top executives. General Motors Chairman Roger Smith was perceived very negatively when, in 1982, he and his colleagues voted themselves increased bonuses just after the corporation had extracted $2.5 billion in wage concessions from the United Auto Workers (Yates, 1983, p. 107).

Although other theories of organizational culture have acknowledged the important role of executive behavior in culture transmission, many have not addressed how leadership perceptions influence culture development and maintenance. The concept of transformational leadership (Bass, Avolio, & Goodheim, 1987), however, does address this issue. A transformational leader goes beyond the employment contract by shaping subordinates' value systems. In other words, subordinates internalize the leader's beliefs. Following this line of reasoning, transformational leadership may be an analog of self-leadership applied at an organization-wide level. A leader's values may be adopted by members and form the basic culture of the organization. In summary, it is not only executive behaviors, per se, that affect culture. Rather it is how these behaviors are perceived by organizational members that perpetuate or change a given culture.

CONCLUSION

In this chapter, we have presented a recognition-based model and an inferential model of leadership perceptions. Perceptual processing may be both automatic and controlled with each of these models. Furthermore, we have argued that these models have differential importance at different hierarchical levels. At lower levels where dyadic interactions are most crucial and performance information is often ambiguous, recognition-based leadership perceptions derived from face-to-face contact help the manager motivate and socialize employees. At the executive level, leadership perceptions emphasize the other three processes shown in Table 6.2. These perceptions affect a leader's potential for innovative substantive action through their link with a leader's power. Such perceptions also affect a leader's ability to manage an organization's culture. In short, at both upper and lower levels perceptions create an important context that may have powerful indirect effects on performance.

Although the distinction between leadership at upper and lower levels actually may be more of a continuum than a dichotomy, others have noted real differences in the requirements at these two levels. We have emphasized differences in typical perceptual processes associated with leadership at each level. An important consequence of such differences is that at some point in a manager's career, one would expect difficulties in transition from lower to upper levels that parallel difficulties in crossing contexts, as we noted previously. To successfully manage such transitions, executive-level leaders must attend to the different perceptual processes associated with executives, as compared to lower level leaders.

In presenting our models, we have attempted to integrate the leadership literature with social information processing theory. We have chosen not to present lists of practical implications for managers, but have instead elected to develop a framework readers can use to draw their own prescriptions from our discussion of leadership perceptions.

ACKNOWLEDGMENTS

We would like to thank Terri Baumgardner, David Day, Michelle Rohrback, and Dan Svyantek for helpful comments on an earlier draft of this chapter.

REFERENCES

Alba, J. W., Chromiak, W., Hasher, L., & Attig, M. S. (1980). Automatic encoding of category size information. *Journal of Experimental Psychology: Human Learning and Memory, 6,* 370–378.

Alexander, R. A., Alliger, G. M., Carson, K. P., & Barrett, G. V. (1985). The empirical performance of measures of association in the 2 × 2 table. *Educational and Psychological Measurement, 45,* 79–87.

Barrick, M. R., Day, D. V., Lord, R. G., & Alexander, R. A. (1988). *Assessing the utility of executive leadership.* Unpublished manuscript, University of Akron, Akron, OH.

Bass, B. M., Avolio, B. J., & Goodheim, L. (1987). Biography and the assessment of transformational leadership at the world-class level. *Journal of Management, 13,* 7–19.

Baumgardner, T. L., Lord, R. G., & Forti, J. C. (1989). *A prescription for aspiring leaders: Implications of expert-novice schema differences and alternative leadership hierarchical models.* Unpublished manuscript, University of Akron, Akron, OH.

Bond, C. F., Jr., & Brockett, D. R. (1987). A social context-personality index theory of memory for acquaintances. *Journal of Personality and Social Psychology, 52,* 1110–1121.

Brown, M. C. (1982). Administrative succession and organizational performance: The succession effect. *Administrative Science Quarterly, 27,* 1–16.

Calder, B. J. (1977). An attribution theory of leadership. In B. M. Staw & G. R. Salancik (Eds.), *New directions in organizational behavior* (pp. 179–204). Chicago: St Clair Press.

Cantor, N., & Mischel, W. (1979). Prototypes in person perception. In L. Berkowitz (Ed.), *Advances in experimental social psychology* (pp. 4–52). New York: Academic Press.

Carver, C. S. (1979). A cybernetic model of self-attention processes. *Journal of Personality and Social Psychology, 37,* 1251–2171.

Cronshaw, S. F., & Lord, R. G. (1987). Effects of categorization, attribution, and encoding processes on leadership perceptions. *Journal of Applied Psychology, 72,* 97–106.

Dandridge, T. C., Mitroff, I. I., & Joyce, W. F. (1980). Organizational symbolism: A topic to expand organizational analysis. *Academy of Management Review, 5,* 77–82.

Dansereau, F., Graen, G. & Haga, W. J. (1975). A vertical dyad linkage approach to leadership within formal organizations: A longitudinal investigation of the role making process. *Organizational Behavior and Human Performance, 13,* 46–78.

Day, D. V., & Lord, R. G. (1988). Executive leadership and organizational performance: Suggestions for a new theory and methodology. *Journal of Management, 14,* 111–122.

Farris, G. F., & Lim, F. G., Jr. (1969). Effects of performance on leadership, cohesiveness, influence, satisfaction, and subsequent performance. *Journal of Applied Psychology, 53,* 490–497.

Feldman, J. M. (1981). Beyond attribution theory: Cognitive processes in performance appraisal. *Journal of Applied Psychology, 66,* 127–148.

Fraser, S. L., & Lord, R. G. (1987, March). *Stimulus prototypicality and general leadership impressions: Their role in leadership and behavioral ratings.* Paper presented at the meeting of the Southeastern Psychological Association, Atlanta, GA.

Green, S. G., & Mitchell, T. R. (1979). Attributional processes of leaders in leader-member interactions. *Organizational Behavior and Human Performance, 23,* 429–458.

Greene, C. N. (1975). The reciprocal nature of influence between leader and subordinate. *Journal of Applied Psychology, 60,* 187–193.

Hambrick, D. C., & Finkelstein, S. (1987). Managerial discretion: A bridge between polar views of organizational outcomes. In B. M. Staw & L. L. Cummings (Eds.), *Research in organizational behavior* (Vol. 9, pp. 369–402). Greenwich, CT: JAI Press.

Hasher, L., & Zacks, R. T. (1979). Automatic and effortful processes in memory. *Journal of Experimental Psychology: General, 108,* 356–388.

Herold, D. M. (1977). Two-way influence processes in leader-follower dyads. *Academy of Management Journal, 20,* 224–237.

Hollander, E. P. (1964). *Leaders, groups, and influence.* New York: Oxford University Press.

Hollander, E. P. (1985). Leadership and power. In G. Lindzey & E. Aronson (Eds.), *The handbook of social psychology* (pp. 485–537). New York: Random House.

Hollander, E. P., & Julian, J. W. (1969). Contemporary trends in the analysis of leadership perceptions. *Psychological Bulletin, 71,* 387–397.

Katz, D., & Kahn, R. L. (1978). *The social psychology of organizations* (2nd ed.). New York: Wiley.

Kelley, H. H. (1973). The processes of causal attribution. *American Psychologist, 28,* 107–127.

Kerr, S., & Jermier, J. M. (1978). Substitutes for leadership: Their meaning and measurement. *Organizational Behavior and Human Performance, 22,* 375–403.

Lord, R. G. (1985). An information processing approach to social perceptions, leadership and behavioral measurement in organizations. In B. M. Staw & L. L.

Cummings (Eds.), *Research in organizational behavior* (Vol. 7, pp. 87–128). Greenwich, CT: JAI Press.

Lord, R. G., & Alliger, G. M. (1985). A comparison of four information processing models of leadership and social perceptions. *Human Relations, 38,* 47–65.

Lord, R. G., De Vader, D., & Alliger, G. (1986). A meta-analysis of the relation between personality traits and leadership perceptions: An application of validity generalization procedures. *Journal of Applied Psychology, 71,* 402–410.

Lord, R. G., Foti, R., & De Vader, C. (1984). A test of leadership categorization theory: Internal structure, information processing, and leadership perceptions. *Organizational Behavior and Human Performance, 34,* 343–378.

Lord, R. G., & Kernan, M. C. (1987). Scripts as determinants of purposeful behavior in organizations. *Academy of Management Review, 12,* 265–277.

Lowe, C. A., & Kassin, S. M. (1980). A perceptual view of attribution: theoretical and methodological implications. *Personality and Social Psychology Bulletin, 6,* 532–542.

Lowin, A., & Craig, J. R. (1968). The influence of level of performance on managerial style: An experimental object-lesson in the ambiguity of correlational data. *Organizational Behavior and Human Performance, 3,* 440–458.

Lurigio, A. J. & Carroll, J. S. (1985). Probation officers' schemata of offenders: Content, development and impact on treatment decisions. *Journal of Personality and Social Psychology, 48,* 1112–1126.

Mann, R. D. (1959). A review of the relationships between personality and performance in small groups. *Psychological Bulletin, 56,* 241–270.

Manz, C. C. (1986). Self-leadership: Toward an expanded theory of self-influence processes in organizations. *Academy of Management Review, 11,* 585–600.

Manz, C. C., & Sims, H. P., Jr. (1980). Self-management as a substitute for leadership: A social learning theory perspective. *Academy of Management Review, 5,* 361–367.

Manz, C. C., & Sims, H. P., Jr. (1987). Leading workers to lead themselves: The external leadership of self-managing work teams. *Administrative Science Quarterly, 32,* 106–129.

Martin, J. (1982). Stories and scripts in organizational settings. In A. H. Hastorf, & A. M. Isen (Eds.), *Cognitive social psychology* (pp. 255–306). New York: Elsevier/North-Holland.

Martinko, M. J., & Gardner, W. L. (1987). The leader/member attribution process. *Academy of Management Review, 12,* 235–249.

Matthews, A. M., Lord, R. G., & Walker, J. B. (1987). *The development of leadership perceptions in children.* Manuscript submitted for publication.

Maurer, T. J. (1987). *Differential information processing capacity: The effect on level of processing in leadership perception.* Unpublished master's thesis, University of Akron, Akron, OH.

Meindl, J. R., & Ehrlich, S. B. (1987). The romance of leadership and the evaluation of organizational performance. *Academy of Management Journal, 30,* 91–109.

Mintzberg, H. (1973). *The nature of managerial work.* New York: Harper & Row.

Mitchell, T. R., Green, S. G., & Wood, R. E. (1981). An attributional model of leadership and the poor performing subordinate: Development and validation. In B. M. Staw & L. L. Cummings (Eds.), *Research in organizational behavior* (Vol. 3, pp. 197–235). Greenwich, CT: JAI Press.

Mitchell, T. R., & Wood, R. E. (1980). Supervisor's responses to subordinate poor performance: A test of an attribution model. *Organizational Behavior and Human Performance, 25,* 123–138.

Ostrom, T. M. (1984). The sovereignty of social cognition. In R. S. Wyer, Jr. & T. K. Srull (Eds.), *Handbook of social cognition* (pp. 3–38). Hillsdale, NJ: Lawrence Erlbaum Associates.

Pavett, C. M., & Lau, A. W. (1983). Managerial work: The influence of hierarchical level and functional specialty. *Academy of Management Journal, 26,* 170–177.

Peters, T. J., & Waterman, R. H., Jr. (1982). *In search of excellence: Lessons from America's best-run companies.* New York: Harper & Row.

Pfeffer, J. (1977). The ambiguity of leadership. *Academy of Management Review, 2,* 104–112.

Pfeffer, J. (1981). *Power in organizations.* Marshfield, MA: Pitman.

Pfeffer, J., & Davis-Blake, A. (1986). Administrative succession and organizational performance: How administrator experience mediates the succession effect. *Academy of Management Journal, 29,* 72–83.

Phillips, J. S., & Lord, R. G. (1981). Causal attributions and perceptions of leadership. *Organizational Behavior and Human Performance, 28,* 143–163.

Pondy, L. R. (1978). Leadership is a language game. In M. W. McCall, Jr. & M. M. Lombardo (Eds.), *Leadership: Where else can we go?* (pp. 87–99). Durham, NC: Duke University Press.

Provan, K. G. (1980). Recognizing, measuring, and interpreting the potential/enacted power distinction in organizational research. *Academy of Management Review, 5,* 549–559.

Rahim, A. (1981). Organizational behavior course for graduate students in business administration: Views from the tower and battlefield. *Psychological Reports, 49,* 583–592.

Rosch, E. (1978). Principles of categorization. In E. Rosch & B. B. Lloyd (Eds.), *Cognition and categorization* (pp. 28–49). Hillsdale, NJ: Lawrence Erlbaum Associates.

Salancik, G. R., & Pfeffer, J. (1977). Constraints on administrator discretion: The limited influence of mayors on city budgets. *Urban Affairs Quarterly, 12,* 475–498.

Schein, E. H. (1985). *Organizational culture and leadership.* San Francisco: Jossey-Bass.

Shiffrin, R. M., & Schneider, W. (1977). Controlled and automatic human information processing: Perceptual learning, automatic attending, and a general theory. *Psychological Review, 84,* 127–190.

Siehl, C., & Martin, J. (1984). The role of symbolic management: How can managers effectively transmit organizational culture? In J. G. Hunt & others (Eds.), *Leaders and managers: International perspectives on managerial behavior and leadership* (pp. 227–239). New York: Pergamon Press.

Smith, J. E., Carson, K. P., & Alexander, R. A. (1984). Leadership: It can make a difference. *Academy of Management Journal, 27,* 765–776.

Stogdill, R. M. (1974). *Handbook of leadership.* New York: The Free Press.

Taylor, S. E., & Fiske, S. T. (1978). Salience, attention, and attribution: Top of the head phenomena. In L. Berkowitz (Ed.), *Advances in experimental social psychology* (pp. 250–289). New York: Academic Press.

Trice, H. M., & Beyer, J. M. (1984). Studying organizational cultures through rites and ceremonies. *Academy of Management Review, 9,* 653–669.

Tushman, M. L., & Romanelli, E. (1985). Organizational evolution: A metamorphosis model of convergence and reorientation. In B. M. Staw & L. L. Cummings (Eds.), *Research in organizational behavior* (Vol. 7, pp. 171–222). Greenwich, CT: JAI Press.

Wong, P. T. P., & Weiner, B. (1981). When people ask "why" questions, and the heuristics of attributional search. *Journal of Personality and Social Psychology, 40,* 650–663.

Yates, B. (1983). *The decline and fall of the American automobile industry.* New York: Empire.

Putting Information Technology in its Place: Organizational Communication and the Human Infrastructure

Arthur D. Shulman
Communication Research Institute of Australia and Washington University, St Louis

Robyn Penman
David Sless
Communication Research Institute of Australia

The importance of communication to organizations is now widely accepted. For some, the relationship is a major contributory one: communicating is organizing (e.g., Farace, Monge, & Russell, 1977; Tompkins & Cheney, 1985; Weick, 1969). For others it is one of equivalence: organizations are their communication (e.g., Barnard, 1968; McPhee, 1985; Mintzberg, 1983). This recognition has led organizational and social psychologists to focus on ways of understanding and improving the communicative capacities and practices of organizations. As part of this major trend in the last few decades, there has been wide-scale exploration of the role of information technologies in the organizational communication process. This chapter evaluates the results of this exploration and indicates the future pathways. In this evaluation we are only concerned with those technologies that are commonly called *interactive* (e.g., computer networking, telecommunications, videoconferencing). We also include hardware, software, and the standard operating procedures as components of these technologies.

Three different stances have been taken on the role and impact of information technology on organizational communication. There are those, described variously as optimists (e.g., Hirschheim, 1985), technologists (e.g., Shulman, 1981), or utopians (e.g., Bryant, 1988), who view information technology as the solution to all, or almost all, of our problems. At the other extreme are those described as pessimists (e.g., Hirschheim, 1985) or devolutionists (e.g., Shulman, 1981). From this gloom-and-doom position, the new information technologies are seen as the source or exacerbation of all our current problems (e.g., Doswell, 1983; Hoos, 1983). Although this belief predicts the opposite of the first, it is in fact based on a similar technocratic faith. In both instances, the technology is assumed to take on an existence independent of human users, but that still determines human behavior. The third position, one of pragmatism, lies somewhere between the first two. Pragmatists believe that technology has a role to play but it is not necessarily good or bad. Instead, the positive or negative impact of information technology depends on the use to which it is put. This third position is the one adopted by most social, organizational, technological assessment, and human factor psychologists who assume that there is a relationship between technology and human performance.

Unfortunately, the research literature does not help us to resolve these different claims: There is empirical evidence to support each one of them. In other words, research has failed to produce consistent findings about the role of information technology in organizational communication. For every research study that shows a particular impact of information technology, there is either another study that shows the reverse (e.g., see Markus & Robey, 1988; Robey, 1986, 1987) or a study that concludes that the impacts are more complex than had been previously assumed (Siegel, Dubrovsky, Keisler, & McGuire 1986). The wealth of contradictory and confusing studies in this field makes the applied social psychologist's role close to a nightmare.

Regardless of the confusion in the research literature, information technology is now a way of life for most organizations and individuals. Social psychological research has neither significantly helped nor hindered the introduction of information technology into organizations. Although there are numerous reasons why this came about (see, e.g., Rice, 1984), an obvious practical reason is that by the time researchers produced results, the users were already onto the next generation of technology. For the researchers, the technologies themselves became moving targets (Tornatzky, 1986). This can be clearly illustrated with the research on the effects of specific information technology terminals (e.g., computer, enhanced telephones, facsimile, work stations). The end user is no longer concerned with this research because the specific terminals are no longer seen as separate entities. This chapter is, therefore, not concerned with separate information technology items, but with the integrated totality. This chapter is also concerned with where and how this totality fits in the organizational communication process.

We argue here, that the promise of new and better information technology is causing confusion and contradiction because it is based on a misleading view of both information and the broader process of communication. As a result, there has been a long succession of missed research opportunities; not because researchers were slow in taking up the challenge of information technology but because it was not the right challenge. One underlying reason for a failure to see and take the real opportunities can be traced to the inappropriateness of the models and methods of study used: models and methods based in an empiricist tradition. The inappropriateness of this tradition has been well argued by Lawler, Mohrman, Mohrman, Ledford, and Gummuning (1985) for the area of organizational research, by Lange and Reese (1983) for technological assessment research, and by Penman (1982) for communication research. The empiricist tradition has a narrow conception of empirical data based on the kinds of data most typically found in the physical sciences. But within a human context, data has a rich array of potential meanings that requires the researcher's active interpretation. Data rich in meaning, so typical of communication research, needs to be treated quite differently from physical science or technology data. But the models and methods commonly employed within the empiricist tradition do not distinguish methodologically between the human and technological infrastructure. As such, researchers operating in that tradition are inadvertently led to adopt some kind of technological determinism.

The inadequacies and limitations of this empiricist approach are illustrated in the next section where past research is reviewed. This critical review provides the basis for the third section of this chapter where a key distinction is made between the technological and human infrastructures (Sless 1985). This distinction provides the basis for a radically different position that is commensurate with recent theoretical developments in the social sciences leading to a new paradigm shift (see, e.g., Gergen, 1982; Toulmin, 1982). These developments give rise to a different conception of communication that in turn leads us to ask new questions about information technologies and organizational communication. These new questions also allow us to put information technology in its place—as a potential aid to the real business of human communication, not as a substitute for it.

A PROGRESSION OF HYPOTHESES

Over the past two decades there have been three distinct hypotheses advanced about the impact of information technology on organizational communication. In the first hypothesis, information technology was seen as a substitute for various forms of human communication. In the second hypothesis, information technology was seen as adding something to the organizational process; it acted in an innovative role. In the third hypothesis, the effects of information technology were seen to be contingent on either temporal or structural/task factors.

The three different beliefs described in the introduction interweave these three hypotheses. For each hypothesis, we can find researchers adopting any one of the three basic beliefs. But as we demonstrate, none of these hypotheses have received strong, consistent empirical support, and researchers are beginning to have serious doubts about the conventional view of information, and therefore its supporting technology, in organizations.

Information Technology as Substitution

During the 1970s, a major concern was with how and where information technology could act as a cost-effective substitute for face-to-face communication. At this beginning stage there was no attempt to establish that information technology could achieve better communication results; the concern was only with the possibility of economically efficient replacement of human communicative activities. Two types of substitution were considered: process and function. Each consideration used different research methods, but both types of approaches had their problems.

Process Substitution.   Process substitution studies hypothesized that information technology could substitute for another "mode," or channel, or interaction, rather than a specific function per se. Questions of process substitution were often addressed in laboratory simulations. In fact, it is likely that the propensity to use laboratory methodologies gave rise to the early concentration on process substitution. The work of the Communication Studies Group at University College, London, is a good illustration of research in this stage (e.g., Christie, 1987; Hough, 1976; Short, Williams, & Christie, 1976; Williams, 1974). Research in this area took extant face-to-face communication practices, typically meetings, as their standard against which to judge outcomes of the introduction of information technology. Any information technology that yielded similar outcomes compared with the standard was judged to be potentially efficient.

Unfortunately, studies using other methods have either been unable to duplicate their findings or give conflicting results (Rice, 1984; Shulman & Steinman, 1978). In general, the positive outcomes found in the laboratories are not readily demonstrable when the systems that were studied are used as real substitutes in real organizations (e.g., Conrath, 1973; Conrath & Blair, 1974). Quite frequently, this incompatibility of research findings and practice has been attributed to "too many unknowns." But from our point of view it is far more easily attributable to the untenability of the basic hypotheses and methods.

In the first instance, the technology employed to test the hypotheses was constructed to minimize substitution problems. Prototype terminals and instructional formats were as user friendly as possible—atypical of the normal terminals and instructions to be found in organizations. And some of the testing was conducted in an atmosphere of euphoric expectations. In other words, the experimental materials and setting were such that a null or negative hypothesis could not be fairly tested.

Second, the methods employed (e.g., scenario testing, taste trials, and laboratory simulations) distance the researcher from important contextual factors that apply in real life. For example, the work of the Communication Studies Group assumed: (a) meetings could be classified in terms of tasks; (b) meetings existed in isolation of a history of meetings and other nonrelated interaction; (c) tasks could be treated as independent; (d) prior experience with information technologies played little part in behaviors being tested; and (e) process was ignored in favor of outcomes. In the light of more recent social psychological research on meetings (e.g., Hackman, 1986; Kelly & McGrath, 1985; McGrath & Kelly, 1986), these assumptions are quite extraordinary. They all deny the critical role played by temporal and structural contexts in the organizational communication process.

Function Substitution. The function substitution approach hypothesized that automation would result in the same outcome with reduced labor costs. Examples of this included the substitution of on-the-spot monitoring of processes normally done by middle management (Pfeffer, 1978), and the automation of inventory monitoring. Questions of function substitution directed researchers to set up studies where issues of job redesign including utopian enhancement, doomsayer deskilling, and retrenchment could be assessed. These questions could not be easily addressed in laboratory situations. Rather, investigators had to wait until the technology was in place and then rely upon in-situ methodologies of case studies and field investigations.

The Rand office automation panel surveys conducted by Gutek, Bikson, and Mankin (1984) illustrate this methodology and the consequent problems. By the time this study was completed, the organizations had brought in more advanced technology making the research findings redundant. But more importantly, the nature of the methods and the vested interests of the sponsors and the equipment vendors (who Swanson, 1984, found to be the major source of advice to customers), minimized the possibility of disproving the substitutability assumption. It was not a matter of asking whether the technology could substitute for function or not, but of how efficient that substitution would be.

One exception to this association between the design of the study and the form of substitution studied, are the field trials of prototype technology in which both process and function substitution are studied together over time. These expensive longitudinal trials tend to have short lives, ending when the major goal, that of demonstrating that the information technology can increase efficiency, is achieved. The Telecom Australia Field Investigations of Customer Services (Shulman, Wearing, & Craick, 1982) serve as an example of this. The researchers concentrated on improving the user friendliness of a prototype intelligent telephone (IT). These improvements had to be made without affecting the distribution shape of the cells made. Simultaneously, the researchers also studied function substitution; they looked for increases in productivity through the automation of call recording procedures. Both improvements and increases in productivity were found (Shulman, Craick, & Wearing, 1983). The longitudinal trials also showed that the patterns of use changed with experience and as a function of the equipment design and instructions. But perhaps more important for researchers, the trials revealed that the user's prior expectations and predictions did not correspond well to their actual use of the new IT. These last findings point to the obvious limitations of methods that rely on forecasts made by potential or novice users.

Like the studies originally conceived to maximize findings of substitution of process, these combined process and function substitution field trials were not designed to confirm doomsayer predictions. This is partly due to the fact that both sponsors (i.e., government or manufacturer) and cooperating businesses are mainly interested in taking part in endeavors that have promise for increasing efficiency through the substitution of process or function without exposing themselves to foreseen risks.

Despite the lack of empirical support for this substitution hypothesis, many continue to believe that technology can be used as a substitute for face-to-face communication. A striking example of this can be found in a recent paper on group decision support systems by DeSanctis and Gallupe (1987): "A GDSS aims to improve the process of group decision making by removing communication barriers, providing techniques for structuring decision analysis, and systematically directing the pattern, timing and content of discussion" (p. 589). Here, we have an example that not only perpetuates the belief in substitutability, but introduces the added element that technology will improve the organizational communication process. At no point in their argument do DeSanctis and Gallupe question the tenability of their optimistic assumption. Given our conclusions about the failure of earlier substitution studies to properly test for pessimistic predictions, these later developments are falling into the same trap. Thus, despite the wealth of studies that raise serious doubts about substituting technology for aspects of human communication, the belief continues to the present time.

Further limitations of these studies are exposed in the next section which discusses the actual nature of communication processes in organizations. For the moment it is sufficient to point to the lack of concern in these studies with what actually happens in human communication processes. These studies have simply assumed that they already understand the human communication processes for which they are seeking a technological substitute. But they are not alone. A similar problem can be discerned in studies seeking support for the next major hypothesis.

Information Technology as Innovation

Those believing in the substitution hypothesis assumed that the organizational structure would remain constant when technology was substituted for human activities. Initially, this was the case. The new information technologies were adopted without any changes to organizational structure and the machines were left in the hands of the technicians. But once the new technologies were incorporated, users and researchers alike gradually realized that the machines were being used in organizations as opportunities or excuses for structural innovation by management (Gutek et al., 1984). The new technologies were being used to help the strategic planning and operation of the organization, and control shifted from the technicians to central management. As Bailey (1987) noted, this change in control and conception of technology also led to a change in terminology: from the Management of Information Systems to Information Technology Management.

At the same time, management itself was also being relocated. Such relocations occurred both upwards (centralization) and downwards (decentralization). Regardless of direction, the middle managers previously involved with monitoring of process were no longer needed and the coordination structures could be reorganized along regional or product lines. Researchers took up this centralization–decentralization issue with fervor. They believed that information technology was causing the centralization of control by allowing senior management to process more information, thereby eliminating the need to delegate such control downward. They mistook the actions of managers for effects of the technology. In his review of the literature on this topic, Pfeffer (1978) succinctly summed up the debate on this issue: "No topic has sparked more debate, with perhaps less enlightenment, than the possible effect of computers on centralization" (p. 70). Similar conclusions have been reached by Keen (1981). In all, we can conclude that the empirical evidence about the effect of information technology on centralization is mixed.

Putting aside methodological issues, the inconclusive nature of the research can be attributed to an unresolved conceptual problem—what constitutes control and what constitutes centralization or decentralization? As Pfeffer (1978) argued, the way in which these concepts are defined will bring about different conclusions. For example, he suggested that, given certain definitions, it is conceivable that information technology can make possible the appearance of decentralization while maintaining effective centralized control over organizational operations. Just such a situation was demon-strated in Fleischer and Morell's (1985) study where, from the position of management, a new computer system was seen as decentralizing but, from the position of office workers, was seen as centralizing control by management.

Heedless of the research debate, management continued to explore orga-nizational design and control and discovered further opportunities for re-organizing firms to give strategic advantage in the marketplace. Many organi-zations saw the potential for using information technology, not only as organizational innovator, but to provide new, value-added services/products, such as inventory control, automatic ordering and various database develop-ments (see Porter & Millar, 1985). These developments led researchers to extend the original organizational innovation hypothesis to make informa-tion technology "a competitive weapon" (Parsons, 1983). This is analogous to the developments we observed in the substitution hypothesis: Initially, information technology was seen as a potentially more efficient substitute for face-to-face communication, then it became a better one.

Information technologies are now being seen as a strategic resource requir-ing sophisticated management policies (see Bailey, 1987). Information tech-nology is no longer thought to just provide us with organizational innovations, it also offers managerial ones. The technology-as-innovation hypothesis has not, however, provided the manager or researcher with the pathway to bring about this innovative potential. Moreover, although there is extensive liter-ature for this hypothesis on the outcome possibilities, there is no unequivocal set of results (Buchanan & Brody, 1982; Robey, 1987). This state of affairs has led Tornatzky to conclude that in spite of "the possibilities for social science, and psychology in particular, . . . there have been no contributions to date" (1986, pp. 76–77).

Information Technology Outcome as Contingency

The research using the substitution and innovation hypotheses sought to demonstrate universal patterns of change. Belief in the possibility of universal patterns rests on the assumption of some form of technological imperative or determinism. Recent reviews and empirical findings cast serious doubts on this notion (e.g., Attewell & Rule, 1984; Bjørn-Andersen, Eason, & Robey, 1986). Perhaps the most conclusive finding to emerge from these reviews is that the impact of information technologies varies from study to study. Put another way, the impact of information technology depends on the tech-nology and the organization.

Such findings have led to the contingency hypothesis. Although many variations of the contingency hypothesis exist, their major theme is that organizational outcomes are positively related to the fit between the organization's structure and the technology it uses. For example, Gutek, Sasse, and Bikson (1986) studied the implementation of computer-based office information technologies in 55 offices and its relation to organizational structure— defined in terms of the primary occupational function of the unit (e.g., clerical, managerial)—and the nature of the technology—defined in terms of its physical attributes (e.g., age, micro/mini). They found some support for covariation of structure and technology, but little support for a relationship between organizational outcome (e.g., productivity and satisfaction) and this covariation.

Others have suggested that the contingency effects of information technology and organizational structure on output change as a function of temporal stage of implementation, changing loci of technology use, experience with the technology and the nature of managerial control. For example, Shulman (1981) proposed that the impact of technology is contingent on organizational structure as represented by managerial styles across five phases of technological innovation. Robey (e.g., 1987) hypothesized that the temporal progression of integrating and using information technology required the simultaneous consideration of both a substitution and innovative phase, and a consideration of how they were related. Tornatzky (1986) has taken this hypothesis one step further by proposing a number of stages in the process of adopting and implementing information technologies.

The models previously mentioned, however, recognize that there is no single best way for maximizing fit between technology and structure. In fact, the current state of our knowledge about possible ways of maximizing fit is quite limited. According to Tornatzky (1986), we can only predict that the more difficult technologies will be those "that are extremely complex, they are costly, their relative advantages are sometimes obscure, and they are often incompatible with past ways of doing business" (p. 63).

To date, then, the contingency hypothesis and related context fit hypothesis (see review of organizational imperative studies by Markus & Robey, 1988) have had little empirical support. Furthermore, they ignore the processes by which congruence can be achieved (Gutek et al., 1986). Suffice to say that the contingency hypothesis will probably remain attractive to researchers hopeful of eventually finding the elusive key element that will make heterogeneous findings homogeneous. However, the real limitations of the contingency hypothesis, as well as the two previous approaches, become apparent when it is realized that information and the relevant technologies are not just about rational control of the organizational environment.

Information Technology in Transition

All the previous hypotheses rest on certain implicit beliefs about the nature of information technologies and their use in organizations. Specifically, it has been assumed that information technologies can increase efficiency and that the use of information technology would be rationally based. Neither of these implicit assumptions about the nature and use of information technology have received convincing empirical support. In the past few years a number of disparate authors have been questioning a range of earlier assumptions about the technology.

First, some of the more experienced social psychologists in the field started to recognize that their previous programs were not producing results that held outside of the research setting. For some (e.g., Christie & DeAlberdi, 1985; Makin, Bikson, & Gutek, 1985), it was a recognition that past studies had tended to focus on the use of specific technologies (e.g., audio-conferencing) in isolation from other modes (e.g., face-to-face) that were often available to persons operating in the work setting. For Christie (1987), there was also the recognition that studying specific hardware and software for particular activities may be analytically neat, but in reality the activities are multipurpose and nonindependent. Because availability and purposes are managerial issues, not technological, they concluded that future studies will have to consider more thoroughly the decisions, policies, and change strategies within which the innovation are embedded. In other words, future studies need to focus on the human, rather than the technological, infrastructure.

Second, investigators started to seriously question whether the well-controlled experimental procedures could capture the dynamic changing nature of the knowledge base that users gain with increased familiarity with the information technology. Studies by Carroll (1985) provide an example of this. The classic experimental design was violated by having novice and experienced users provide an on-going stream of rationales and world views for their actions as they worked through various software programs. It is doubtful that classic stimulus–response design would have captured the changing dynamic of the interface. For Carroll (1985) and Carroll and Mack (1982) the user is not passive, but engaged in active exploration processes, and the role of the software becomes one of stimulating invitations to see the task in a new light.

Third, recent work in organizational psychology and sociology strongly points to the untenability of the assumption of rational decision making in organizations (e.g., Burrell & Morgan, 1979; Perrow, 1984; Schön, 1983). Feldman and March's (1981) argument, while concerned with seemingly rational uses of information per se, is of particular relevance to information technology. From a review of empirical studies of information in organizations and supporting case histories, they draw a picture of information behavior that is hard to rationalize using formal theories of rational choice. Instead, they show that organizations systematically gather more information than they need or use and that this gathering is not necessarily strictly functional.

Instead, information can have, what they describe as, a *symbolic* role. As such, the information technology also takes on some of these symbolic features and is used for other than rational-choice purposes.

Feldman and March's argument has been extended to technology by Barley (1986) and Wiesband and Kiesler (1985); each using nonexperimental procedures. Barley (1986) used observational techniques to study the meanings given to computerized tomography (CT scanners) technology. He found that when similar CT technologies were accompanied by similar introductory processes in different organizations, they still occasioned different outcomes. For Barley, the technology became a social object whose meanings were defined by the context of their use. Similarly in the Weisband and Kiesler (1985) study, the meanings of the technology were defined by their context. Using interview data, they were able to identify that the most predominant meaning theme was a nonrational party-line script reflecting the manager's position in the organization (central office vs. field).

All of these studies raise two central points for our argument: Information use is not necessarily guided by rational choice as conventionally conceived, and information can serve symbolic as well as instrumental purposes. Information is not just an instrument for efficient, rational management. However, although these studies rightly point to different roles for information, it is still necessary to fully consider the broader and more complex communication process.

RECONSIDERING COMMUNICATION AND THE HUMAN INFRASTRUCTURE

Perhaps the most striking feature of all the literature reviewed here, with the possible exception of the last transition stage, is its faith that we all understand and share the same view of communication and information. The three hypotheses take the communication process for granted, and the concept of information as given and uniformly accepted. Unfortunately, neither assumption is warranted. Both information and communication are highly problematic. Moreover, the particular conception of communication and information that is embedded in the literature is itself misleading. In this section, we review the common conceptions of information and communication and then reconsider these concepts in a new framework that is more appropriate to the real problems being faced in organizations.

Common Conceptions of Information and Communication

When one reviews the various literatures concerned with information (e.g., information economics, information management, organizational management), the most striking finding is the extraordinary variety of ways in which the concept is used. First, there are authors who simply assume that they and the reader fully understand the nature of information, without any formal definition (e.g., Department of Science, 1985, pp. 1, 13). Second, for those authors who do define the term (and interestingly most social psychologists do not), there appears to be almost as many different definitions as authors. Moreover, at least two distinct approaches are adopted: Either information is treated "as if" it was something else or the "essence" of the concept is given.

The "as if" approach has most typically likened information to a resource or commodity (e.g., Kochen, 1970). In fact, this style of definition has been seen by some as a way out of the problem of more rigorous definition. For example, in the U.S. National Commission on Library and Information Science report (1982), it was said that the term *information* simply eluded description. For the committee, the resolution was to treat information "as a commodity, as a tool for better management of tangible resources, as an economic resource in and of itself." Unfortunately, this description flies in the face of a number of arguments from the communication literature. Even as far back as 1948, Wiener argued that information could not be seen as a commodity in any sense as it cannot be used up; it is continually available. Information is also continually changing and highly sensitive to context and user factors that are outside the control or influence of any economic or management system (Sless, 1985, 1986b).

On the other hand, the "essence" definitions have described information variously as meaningful content (e.g., Machlup, 1983), cerebral activity or knowledge (e.g., Cronin, 1986), data (e.g., Conrath, Higgins, Thachenkarg, & Wright, 1981; Drucker, 1988; Stigler, 1961) or uncertainty reduction (e.g., Krippendorf, 1984). Shannon and Weaver's (1949) definition, however, remains popular (i.e., information is the signal sent or received). This definition was originally developed to deal with electronic systems and, unfortunately, has been applied in a wide variety of human contexts, including that of information economics (e.g., Machlup & Mansfield, 1983). But this notion of information is insufficient for accounting for the human phenomena of communication (e.g., Penman, 1985; Sless, 1986a).

There is far less confusion surrounding the term *communication*. In most of the research literature, communication has been conceived of as a transmission process: a process of sending and receiving information or messages. This is simply the full version of Shannon and Weaver's original model and the key elements still remain in contemporary researchers' definitions of communication (e.g., Berlo, 1960; Siegel et al., 1986; Williams, 1984). This transmission view of communication is also the one most prevalent amongst laypeople. This has been well demonstrated by Reddy's (1979) analysis of our everyday language about language. From this analysis he identified the "conduit metaphor": People put thoughts into words and send these word packages along one conduit to another, who then unpacks the ideas from the words. This metaphor is implied in such common phrases as "she didn't get her message across" and "I didn't get a single idea out of his words."

Given the nature and prevalence of this transmission view, it is no wonder that organizations have wholeheartedly embraced the new information technologies. With the new information technologies we are presumably able to speed up the transmission and to increase the storage of ideas much more than we could if we were relying on simple human "connections" and the fallible human mind (e.g., Crawford, 1982). But as the research demonstrates, there is no evidence that information technology can act as a substitute for human communication, let alone do it better. As one of us has described elsewhere, the major consequence of the introduction of new information technologies within organizations has not been better communication, only faster misunderstandings (Sless, 1986b).

Researchers operating within the prevalent view of communication have fared little better than the organizations implementing the technology. The failure to predict the consequences of information technology on organizational communication has arisen because of the failure to distinguish conceptually between human communication and the hardware of information technologies. The additional failure to control the "flow" and use of information in organizations has also arisen through the same flawed assumption.

The belief that communication is a tool—an instrument for getting your message across—has led to false and exaggerated expectations about what communication can do. And as such has also led many practitioners and researchers alike along an unproductive pathway with substantial hidden costs. For example, in 1983 the UK Inland Revenue office redesigned their tax form to "look better," assuming that the appearance of the form would reduce the error rates by taxpayers completing the form. The falsity of the belief was demonstrated when it was found that there had been no change in the high error rates—a rather expensive discovery (Sless, 1986b). Other examples of ineffective and costly management decisions based on false expectations about communication as a tool are shown in recent studies demonstrating that new computer systems can result in lower profitability and reduced production (Dougherty, 1988).

In other words, how we think about communication is not simply a matter of scholarly indulgence; it determines the decisions and actions we all take in our practical communicative activities. This point is not just relevant to the conceptions people have about communication. As McGrath and Kelley (1986) also point out, it has profound implications for the continuing use of our traditional methodologies. From our point of view, then, it makes good common sense to seriously consider what may be an appropriate view of communication.

Two Infrastructures

In the transmission view of communication, the technological and human aspects of the infrastructure of communication are treated as if they were part of the same phenomenon. We argue that they are substantially different. The concept of rationality allows us one way of distinguishing between the technological and human infrastructures. Clearly, information technology systems are governed in their operations by formal scientific theories of rationality. But as Feldman and March (1981) argued, empirical studies of the human use of information in organizations portray a pattern that is incompatible with these formal theories of rational choice.

If we wish to maintain some notion of rationality in human organizations then we need to accept that there may be more than one form. This is congruent with a long philosophical tradition, from Aristotle's work in the Nichomachean Ethics (see, e.g., Sensat, 1979) to the work of contemporary critical and social theorists such as Habermas (e.g., 1975), that distinguishes between the form of rationality necessary for knowing about things in the world and the form of rationality necessary for knowing of the world. The capacity to deal rationally with technical problems is different in kind from the capacity to deal rationally with human problems (Sensat, 1979).

Knowing about things in the world uses the "scientific" rationality of empiricism, with the ultimate aim to arrive at necessary and universal truths about the physical world in which we exist and to apply this knowledge to technical problems. Knowing about things of the world requires a different form of rationality that is appropriate to understanding human problems. This form of rationality is rarely discussed in the social sciences. We agree with Habermas (e.g., 1971) that modern social science and practice has lost its orientation to human questions: What remains is an exclusively technical perspective.

These two different forms of rationality allow us to distinguish between two different infrastructures in the organization's communication environment—a technological and human infrastructure. The technological infrastructure arises from the application of scientific rationality to serve technical interests and includes the machines of information technology. Alongside is a human infrastructure arising from communicative action and practical knowledge. The human infrastructure consists broadly of what we describe as culture: our languages, knowledge of human custom and practices, and our modes of social organization.

Paradoxically, information technology has been created to facilitate communicative action and practical knowledge. But the technical rationality of the machines is different in kind from the human rationality of languages and culture that they are designed to serve; the two spheres operate on different conceptual and rational planes. Although information technologies can provide us with new and varied opportunities for communications, not even the most sophisticated information technologies can do anything directly to improve our communication practices.

The key point so far, then, is that most contemporary research has failed to make the distinction between these two infrastructures and has applied technical means of knowing to human problems. This is well illustrated by the assumptions of causality that underlie most research in this area (see, e.g., the review by Markus & Robey, 1988). Strictly speaking, causality is a concept that belongs only to the technical realm, where external events can directly cause or determine other events. When we enter the human realm and attribute humans with any agency or intention in their communicative actions, then we cannot assume simultaneously that those actions are caused by external events. From our theoretical position, causality has no place in the human infrastructure. Although inappropriate technical concepts, such as causality, continue to be used to understand the human realm, the real problems will never be addressed, let alone resolved. And the real problems can never be addressed until we discard the technical, instrumental view of communication prevalent in our research and society alike.

New Conceptions of Information and Communication

In reconceptualizing communication we need to start from the one clear conclusion that can be derived from 40 years of communication research: Communication is a messy and uncertain business. Communication is always partially ineffective, potentially wasteful, and to some degree beyond the control of any one individual or organization. Here, we are concerned with developing a description of communication that can account for these practical observations. Much of the confusion in the research literature, as well as in practice, rests on the failure to make a critical conceptual distinction between information and communication. Sless (1981) has developed an extensive argument regarding the differences and we draw heavily on this here.

Information. We start by taking the common sense view of information as an entity that exists in some form or other in the physical world. In this sense, all things that exist in the physical world are potential sources of information. As such, information has the properties of the physical world and exists regardless of our perception of it. In other words, information is something independent of humans. It is inanimate, incapable of acting or exhibiting agency. When the human agent enters the scene and reads the information a fundamental change takes place. In the relationship between human agent and information something new is created that we usually call meaning. Information does not contain meaning per se. Meaning is brought about in the relationship between the reader and the information being read.

The concept of information has some similarities with common sense views that also see information as an entity. But our view does not falsely attribute the "entity" with meaning independent of the human reader. Those views that equate information and meaning are making a category mistake in the same way that Ryle (1963) argued for the mind/body dualism. Ryle illustrated what he meant by a category mistake by telling a story about someone who was taken on a tour of a university; including the lecture theaters, laboratories, and libraries. After the tour the visitor turned to the guide somewhat confused and said, "You have shown me lots of things, but where is the university amongst these?" The visitor was making a category mistake, assuming the university to be another part, rather than the whole. Similarly, those who expect meaning to be a property of information, mistakenly believe meaning to be a part that can be separately identified, rather than the outcome of an interaction between information and human agent. The problem of a category mistake in the field of information technology is that meaning is taken as belonging to the category of the physical world, when it actually belongs in the human world.

When meaning is assumed to exist independent of humans, it is easy (although false) to conceive of technical/mechanical means for storing, transferring, and transforming this meaning. When meanings are seen as stored in words or other signals, then the more signals we can create and preserve, presumably the more ideas we transfer and store. This very mistaken view has, according to Reddy (1979), significant social consequences: If we do not cultivate our abilities to create and reconstruct meanings we will end up with a culture less sophisticated rather than more. On the other hand, if we take meaning to be a process in the human infrastructure, we are correctly placing the responsibility for meaning creation and manipulation in human hands, not mechanical ones.

Communication.   For communication to occur, a further condition is necessary: A communicative intent must be inferred in the information being read. By this we mean that if we believe the information in our environment was generated by someone else in order to communicate then the necessary and sufficient conditions exist to describe the phenomenon as communication. It is important to note here, that it is the inferrence of the "other" and their intent that is critical, not the physical presence nor that the "other" really had a communicative intent.

The distinction between inferring meaning from information and within communication can be illustrated with Sless' (1981) example of the wink/twitch. Suppose you were in a conversation with someone who, every time he or she finished an utterance, closed and then opened one eye, just once, very quickly. If you took this movement to be an unfortunate twitch, you would probably do your best to ignore it. On the other hand, if you took the movement to be a wink, you would infer quite a different meaning, such as the speaker was not treating his or her own words seriously. Our attribution of communicative intent, then, changes a twitch to a wink: That is, it changes our meaning generation and the way we interact with the other.

Communication then is also a relational phenomenon, but one involving more than one person, whether assumed or real. Thus, the communication process incorporates the meaning generation process, but in a particular way. The communication process incorporates more than one "reader" and this adds complexity to the meaning generation process. It is the way in which these people are in relation with each other that provides the basis for our conception of communication. In keeping with new developments in communication theory and research, we need to conceive of "a form of communication which consists only in the flow of activity between people, not in the sequential occurrence of things; in a process, not in a series of products" (Shotter, 1986a, p. 205). Rather than a sequential series of discrete events, passing from one person to another, communication is a flow of common, joint activity. In this new view, we are our communication. In creating our communication and creating our world with it, we are at the same time creating ourselves. Such a circular proposition gives full recognition to the claim of equivalence made at the very beginning of this chapter—organizations are their communication.

Interestingly, this very same circular notion is incorporated in recent developments in systems theory. Maturana and Varela (1980) proposed the notion of *autopoiesis* to describe what they believe is a critical feature of many systems, especially human, social ones—that of self-reproduction. The capacity for some systems to be self-generating is seen to arise solely out of the interactions of the components of the system. Moreover, this process not only creates its own internal structure but also sets its own boundaries. Communication, as an autopoietic process, is self-generating, structure-creating, and boundary-setting. In acting in this process we find ourselves in a rather more difficult place than conventionally proposed. Communication activity is not only self-generating, it is also self-specifying. It is self-specifying in the sense that our past activities point to the directions of our present activities. "Rather than acting 'out of' an inner plan or schema, we can think of ourselves as acting 'into' our own present situation" (Shotter, 1986a, p. 203).

The meanings generated in this process arise from unique patterns of interaction between the participants; patterns beyond the control or intention of any individual party. The meanings are also subject to continual modification with the evolving temporal context. As we act into our communicative situation we are at the same time changing it by that action. In continually bringing about a new state affairs, joint communicative actions and the implicated meanings are always emergent and never finished. As Sless (1986a) poignantly put it: "Understanding is the dead spot in our struggle for meaning: it is the momentary pause, the stillness, before incomprehension continues" (p. i). This is not to suggest the possibility that meanings could be complete, if only. . . . On the contrary, meanings are essentially unfinishable.

A critical point in our argument, then, is that meaning is inherently indeterminate. We cannot guarantee, predict or fully control the direction of the process or the nature of the meaning inferred. Instead, the "organized settings" we are led into by our past actions and implicated meanings act as constraints (in contrast to determinants) on the range of possible future meanings. These constraints provide temporary closure in an otherwise unstable and indeterminate social world. In this way, although there may be potential for an infinite range of meanings, in practice this is limited by the closure we impose. Thus, our key concern is not one of determining (or even believing in) the stability of meaning, but of understanding the points and procedures for closures. Meaning cannot be controlled or predicted, but it can be managed and constrained.

The essential indeterminacy of meaning logically leads us to challenge the metaphysics of foundationalism (see Rorty, 1980)—a metaphysics that assumes there can be a stable foundation, a certain objective, and unchangeable knowledge base. Such a challenge should give no cause for alarm. There have been numerous arguments about the failure of the foundationalist's tradition to make sense of the vicissitudes of human social life (see, e.g., Maxwell, 1984). This failure is readily attributable to the features of communication already described, particularly its central role in bringing about our understandings of our world and the essential indeterminancy of these understandings. From our point of view, it is logically impossible to establish foundations for, and derive predictable long term generalizations, from anything as inherently unstable as human social life (see, e.g., Macintyre, 1985). This, then, is the real key to the failure of past research on information technology reviewed in his paper. The past research attempted to predict the impact of technology on organizational activity, when that activity itself is inherently unstable.

MISMANAGING AND MANAGING MEANING

In this section we argue that the management of meaning is central to managing information technology within organizations. This view contrasts with more conventional views and practices in which central attention is given to the management of the technology itself.

Technology is in one sense very easily managed: It is reliable, predictable, and does not answer back (except when Murphy's law operates). By contrast, human beings in organizations are unreliable, unpredictable, and frequently answer back. It is at the points where information technology and people meet—where meanings are generated—that the problems of management and control of information technology arise. Therefore, it is at that point—at the interface between people and technology—that the effort of management should be directed. The reasons for this can best be illustrated through examples of meaning mismanagement.

Mismanaged Meaning

Over the last 3½ years, the Communication Research Institute of Australia has conducted research on administrative systems in both government and business organizations that use large-scale information technology systems. We have usually been invited to work in these organizations at points where there have been recognized problems of communication. Out of this experience, spanning many particular case histories, we have put together a composite picture of organizational management of information technology, and, by using the conceptual framework articulated in this paper, we have identified three key features that lead to failure: definitions of system boundaries and users, definitions of information, and software languages.

Definitions of System Boundaries. The conventional pattern of system development methodologies used by systems analysts tends to focus on the hardware and programming aspects of the system. Technical boundaries rather than human ones are set. In practice, of course, no system has such narrow boundaries. For example, any large-scale data-processing system for government organizations dealing with a public client group has boundaries that extend into the living spaces of those clients. In other words, the providers of information for a data-processing system are also part of the system. The technical framework of the typical system designer, however, excludes the broader human boundaries in various ways.

In the first instance, the technical frame of the system designers leads to the assumption that the communication process in which the system fits, is actually the process itself. In other words, most information technology systems are designed with a transmission view of communication. This is hardly surprising because the Shannon and Weaver model of communication is implicit in the training of communications engineers and technologists. With such a view of communication, it is almost inevitable that human users will be seen as nothing more than another transfer device in the great technological system.

System designers operating within this technical frame are also unable to conceive of a user as being different from themselves. The images of the users that system designers seem to have in mind when they create their system tend to display the characteristics of either themselves or the machines they work with. In most instances, these assumptions regarding the user are false. For example, the Australian Taxation Office, like many systems that collect financial data through forms, asks the form filler to provide totals so that the system can run an edit check on its own data processors to ensure that no mistakes have been made in data entry. This simple programming device is based on an image of the form filler as someone who can reliably add up figures. This is an understandable image among programmers, but not, as it turns out, a particularly well-informed image when it is compared with what is known about the low level of numeracy in the population (Castles, 1986). In one test by the Institute of an Australian tax form that requires such additions, it was found that 27% of all errors arose from incorrect additions.

The technical frame in which both the system and the users are usually defined by system designers has direct and serious implications for the way in which technology can be used in the communication process. In particular, the narrowness of the frame, the false conceptions of the process, and the false images of projected users severely limit the capacity of the technology to contribute to the overall communication process. The net result is frequently a high incidence of failures and mistakes during normal operations of the system.

Perrow (1984) has documented a number of the serious consequences of a narrow technical approach to complex system design; including such disastrous system failures as the Three Mile Island nuclear plant meltdown. However, these failures cannot be fully averted with the simple application of human factors engineering (Perrow, 1984). Human factors engineering, with its reductionist scientific methodology, only focuses on the mental and physical capacities of human system operators, it does not consider the other equally important social and organizational factors that also affect system operation or failure. Sless (1988) has made a similar point about the recently emergent field of software ergonomics. While, in many instances, software ergonomics can bring about gains, this is chiefly because user interfaces are so poorly designed that any consideration of the human being will lead to an improvement. Using the example of screen design, however, Sless (1988) argued that: "Tackling the screen design layout is like using polyfilla to repair cracks due to poor foundations: It has short term cosmetic effects" (p. 5). A broader social/communicative perspective is called for. One in which "[t]he operator is not then a transfer device in the loop, ready for replacement, but a formulator of worlds, of system representations" (Perrow, 1983, p. 539).

Definitions of Information. We noted earlier that there are almost as many definitions of information as there are researchers anxious to lay claim to information as a territory to investigate. In the day-to-day life of organizations it is also possible to discern three radically different conceptions of information, interestingly parallel with the three major types of epistemology to be found in philosophy. These different conceptions of information provide one of the most interesting sources of disagreement and conflict within organizations.

The simplest, the naive empiricist view—usually found among systems designers—asserts that there is information in the world that the administration collects and processes. In this view, information is analogous to fruit growing on trees: The administration picks the fruit and makes sure that it is not bruised or damaged in the collection process. This notion of information accords well with system engineering conceptions of information flow and storage.

The second view of information, the Platonic view—usually, but not always, found among those who interpret legislation or company policy—asserts that information in the world is a shadowy reflection of the conceptually pure category to be found in the legislation or policy. In this view, information collected on forms or other data-collection methods is inherently corrupt; the administration has to apply rigorous conceptual standards to the corrupt data in order to determine the truth. As one administrator put it: "Either we accept the world as people describe it or we deal with the world as it really is."

The third view of information, the constructionist view—sometimes found among those who deal directly with the public or customers—asserts that information is something created by the organization. In this view, the information provided on data-collection forms comes into existence because the form requires it. One can see this on forms that ask for estimates where actual figures are not available. The constructionist view is potentially quite threatening to the other two views because it casts doubt on the absolute legitimacy of the bureaucratic process to specify meanings. It suggests that the bureaucracy should negotiate meanings with its clients: In other words, it should give its clients some power in the decision-making process. Loss of control or power is not something that comes easily to bureaucracy. Nor can it, using traditional administrative methods, effectively negotiate meanings with its clients.

Many battles are fought, for example, over the issue of question order on data-collection forms. The naive empiricist will usually fight for an order to suit the needs of data processing. After all, if information is just out there to be picked it does not matter what order it is picked in, so one might as well organize it to suit the machine. The Platonist will argue for an order that is consistent with the structure of the legislation, to protect the purity of the legislation in a corrupt world. The constructionist will draw attention to the effect of question order on information providers. The real battle here is usually between the Platonists and empiricists, with the constructionists losing early on to superior forces. Unfortunately, the superiority of the force lies only in numbers, not in argument. The constructionist position is the only one that takes account of the user/reader of the form and the only one that recognizes the instability of meaning.

The effect on data-collection systems of such debates, all of which lie outside of the capacity of the technology to control, can be horrendous. It is not unusual to discover forms in regular use that have extremely high error rates. For example, in a test of the errors on a sample of 200 forms used in a large insurance company, over 1,500 errors were found and not one form was error free (Fisher & Sless, 1988). These high error rates can be directly attributable to the application of an empiricist or Platonist view. When the same forms were redesigned following constructionist principles, the error rate was reduced by 97% (Fisher & Sless, 1988).

Software Languages. Despite the veneer of scientific precision, software systems involve extensive manipulation and use of metaphors (Sless, 1988). For example, such terms as *delete, abort, escape,* or the Macintosh *trash can* do not actually describe what the machines do when they are asked to execute these commands. Nor are the screen *menus* really menus. All of these terms are metaphors that allow us to think of something in ways other than what it actually is. In normal language, metaphors can help to extend our understanding of something but not with precision. They allow us to take something familiar and make it into something new. In computer technology, metaphors are used to take something unfamiliar and turn it into the familiar. As such we expect something like the Macintosh trash can to behave like the trash can we are all familiar with. But it does not. If, for example, we put a disc icon into the trash can, the disk is ejected from its drive. Real trash cans are not like that. Thus, the particular use of metaphor in computer language can be quite misleading and a source of many misunderstandings.

But misunderstandings cannot be avoided. In fact, the more accessible a computer language becomes to ordinary language users, the more susceptible it will be to the normal range of interpretations and misunderstandings found in natural language use. The uncertainties in the meaning generation process are as inherent in computer languages as any other language. This is seldom recognized, with the consequence that little allowance is made for adequate user training in order to control the interpretations made by users. This is illustrated in almost every software manual where users are simply expected to know and uniformly interpret a range of obscure technical expressions. Little attempt is made to manage meanings because they are thought to be self-evident.

Cole, Lansdale, and Christie (1985) and Lansdale (1985) provide a summary of what little recognition there is of the metaphor problem. But they only see metaphors as one type of device within a range—including models, analogies, advance organizers, and command languages—rather than as as the central device around which all the others are constructed. There is simply no way of developing a user interface without employing metaphors. The work of Lakoff and Johnson (1980) and Lakoff (1987) demonstrates very clearly how everyday and specialized languages are intimately dependent on metaphor. We cannot choose whether or not to use metaphors in computers. The only choices we have is which metaphors and how we use them. The inherent possibility for different interpretations is always there. Building systems without deliberately managing the meanings generated at the user interface—as if such meanings were unproblematic or easily controllable—leads to serious failures in information technology systems.

Managing Meanings

These considerations of information system failures gives us the basis for suggesting some of the things that need to be done to ensure a degree of success in the design of information technology systems, and therefore the use of the systems. However, there is more to proper management of meaning that just system design. Here, we also consider issues to do with system implementation and with management over time.

System Design and the End User. Systems need to be designed and used with the problematic nature of communication in mind. Understanding the sources of uncertainty and the possibilities for misunderstandings is a first step to designing a system that is human compatible. More specifically, however, it is essential that knowledge of the end user is incorporated into the design of the technology, rather than imposing the technology onto the end user.

The critical importance of understanding the end user has been demonstrated in a range of studies undertaken by the Institute on data-processing systems. We have shown substantial reductions in error rates on data gathering instruments when these instruments have been designed for the end user (e.g., Fisher & Sless, 1988; Sless, 1985). Such design work relies on sensitive empirical data gathering (albeit, not experimental). The aim of this data

gathering is diagnostic rather than predictive: It identifies unintended interpretations, confusions, inappropriate responses, and the like. By repeated
testing, redesign, and retesting, a system can be produced that constrains the
range and number of errors (Sless, 1979). This diagnostic testing and design
is ideally the province of the social scientist, not the design engineer.

The applied social psychologist has an important interventionist role to
play in information system design. This is quite different from the research
role adopted over the past few decades. In that role, the applied social
psychologist took the system as given and tested for various impacts. Here we
are suggesting that that they should be proactive, ensuring the system is
compatible with the needs and requirements of the end user. This process
needs to be concerned with the proper projections of readers or end users of
the information system, with the design of languages used in the systems, and
the meanings ascribed to the technology itself. With the design of such
languages, the social psychologist is essentially engaged in a creative communication process in which multiple interpretations are envisaged and negotiated with users. This allows for some control—through understanding and
negotiation not through prediction.

Management of Implementation. Users' expectations and beliefs about the
technologies create meanings about the technology that will affect acceptance and use. These meanings and expectations cannot be predicted from
experiments, but can be inferred from past practices and the organizational
context. As Shneiderman (1987) astutely observed: "The social and political
environment surrounding the implementation of a complex information system is not amenable to study by controlled experimentation. . . . The experienced project leader knows that organizational politics and the preferences
of individuals may be more important than the technical issues in governing
success of an interactive system" (p. 393). Perrow (1984) has argued
similarly.

Thus, in system implementation we need to focus on managing meanings
in the human infrastructure of the organization; rather than on the mechanical implementation in the technological infrastructure. Again, this is a valid
role for the applied social psychologists operating within a communication
framework. This means investigating the diversity of meanings that are in
use, where possible containing them, and where not, making allowances for
variability in interpretation. The key methodological considerations for this
are described at the end of this chapter.

Once it is realized that the meanings attributed to the technology will play
a role in its use, then it is also possible to focus management efforts in that
direction. It is particularly important in this management process to guard
against and control false expectations arising from false beliefs. At the beginning of this chapter we described three different sets of beliefs held by re-

searchers regarding information technology: optimistic, pessimistic, and pragmatic. These same sets of beliefs are also held by implementors and users of information systems. And it is these beliefs that need to be managed in order to avoid the problems that arise from false expectations. It is also important to manage the false expectations raised by recent authors who refer to information technology systems as decision-making systems (e.g., Huber & McDaniel, 1986). This is yet another form of animism in which the technology is attributed with the capacity to make decisions rather than the human creators and users of those systems.

False expectations lead to ineffective management. For example, if we take an optimistic view of the technology and assume that its rationality will lead us to better communication, then we need to take no effort whatsoever in the communication process. We can pass the effort over to the machine. Unfortunately, this will not only not remove the problematic, capriciousness nature of human communication but will in fact exacerbate the very features of communication that the technology is supposed to remove. This problem is well illustrated in the banking industry. Over the past 20 years, massive automatic data-processing systems have been installed with the expectation of greater efficiency and accuracies in transactions—in other words, the machines will do all the work and do it better. Unfortunately, the costs of normal banking transactions have doubled with automation (Rubin & Hubert, 1986) and the transactions are still as error prone. The human–communication problems of data provision and entry have not been removed by automation. These problems remain to be properly addressed by applied social psychologists and others operating within a communication framework.

From a management point of view, our major concern is with generating and managing better expectations. Better expectations are those that are based on a realistic conception of the communication process and its inherently problematic nature. When we take misunderstandings to be the norm rather than the exception we are more alert for the problems and more able to manage them. In this sense, then, better expectations take the technology to be both an enabling and constraining device, depending on how well it is designed, implemented and used.

When we are concerned with strictly information-based activities (cf. communication), information technology systems provide us with a range of opportunities for modeling and rehearsal of information activities. When we are concerned with communication activities per se, the technology once again provides us with certain opportunities. In particular, the various technologies offer people opportunity for greater access, different types of access—such as voice, data, and graphics—and facility for faster access. But it only provides us with more and faster opportunities for communication. It does not provide us with communication per se, let alone better communication. The problems inherent in the communication process are not removed by that technology. In fact, with the current limited state of development of these technologies problems in the communication process are more likely to be exacerbated than minimized. This is particularly evident in the general poor quality of interface designs.

Applied social psychologists could directly contribute to the development of strategies for meaning management in the implementation and use of the technologies. Such strategies would include the development of a way of talking about the technology that was congruent with its real limits and possibilities. As an example, in the computer-aided design programs at the Institute, we refer to the Macintosh as "a sophisticated pencil" in order to emphasize that fancy computer-aided design will not improve a bad form any more than the use of an expensive pencil. Such language strategies need to be tested on the projected end users of the system, where possible, before implementation across an organization.

Management Over Time.   The introduction of information technology appears to be most successful when it is at least accompanied by the planned management of its meaning in the workplace. For example, Ettlie's (1985) study showed that technological change was more likely to be judged successful when such change was preceded or accompanied by management explaining the likely effects on employees' jobs and future. But such research tends to treat explanations of purpose and consequences as stable; whereas it is clear that these explanations, like other acts of communication, change their meaning over time (see, e.g., Ross & Staw, 1986; Shulman et al., 1982).

The instability of meaning and its particular sensitivity to changing temporal contexts raises a number of longer term management problems. Some of these problems have been recognized in the past few years; albeit not in a meaning management framework. For example, there has been an increasing call by practitioners and theorists alike to develop ongoing procedures that include employees in all phases of planning, implementation and usage of new technologies (Robey, 1986). This involvement presumably will not be short in duration, for as pointed out by Yin (1979), the management of any technological change is likely to take years to play itself out—if it ever does.

The need for a longer term meaning management policy is also congruent with the popular view of managers as responsible for developing and guiding corporate culture (e.g., Peters & Waterman, 1982). But unlike Peters and Waterman, who treat culture as a dominant form, we agree with Meyerson and Martin's (1986) analysis that the meanings of new technologies within corporate culture can take a variety of forms. The extent of consensus can vary depending on location and history, and some areas will be more tolerant of ambiguity than others. In addition, we need to consider that not only are meanings unstable and variable across people and contexts, they are also essentially indeterminate.

Given this indeterminacy and instability, the management of meaning can be construed as one of autopoietic deviation, amplification, and counteraction. As Nord (1985) has pointed out, managing involves understanding both the conditions where small deliberate changes—as in bringing in a new information technology in a complex system—can produce a self-sustaining (deviation–amplifying) change in the complex system, and the conditions where the change will be overwhelmed by the system (deviation-counteracted) (Nord, 1985, pp. 188–189). When new technology is managed as if it were an innovation, then deviation amplification occurs. When new technology is managed as if it were a substitution, then deviation—counteraction occurs. Either style of management depends on managing meanings.

A role for the applied social psychological researchers is one of documenting and affecting this amplification and deviation–counteraction of meaning. While managers and researchers can offer new meanings, they also need to wait for and then vigorously amplify already existent, valued meanings. Obviously, for researchers, such lying in wait cannot be done through a one-off entry into an organization, and research designs that do not allow for an historical unfolding are inappropriate. Hackman (1986) suggested that valued meanings can be amplified by capitalizing on the presence of "multiple nonindependent enabling conditions"; such as available expert coaching and supporting reward structures. But there is no one best way of structuring the amplification. The same outcome can be achieved by a variety of means (equifinality) and multifinal possible outcomes can emerge in any situation. For Hackman (1986), such equifinal and multifinal possibilities require qualitatively different kinds of models and qualitatively different methods for assessing the validity and usefulness of those models. For Hackman, as it is for Nord (1985), such approaches would still be "scientific" but follow a different drummer. The question remains as to what type of drummer and what type of tune.

METHODS AND MEANINGS

Throughout this chapter we have emphasized the inappropriateness of the classical methodologies for advancing our understandings of the place of information technologies within the human communication infrastructure. Although such critiques are not new to the discipline (e.g., Harré & Secord, 1973), some are becoming quite sophisticated and convincing (e.g., Shotter, 1986b). Others, while resonating with the emergent, indeterminate view expressed in this chapter, are not yet quite ready to let go of the traditional methods (Hackman, 1986; McGrath & Kelly, 1986; Nord, 1985). There is no doubt that it is difficult to let go of such methods, if for no other reason than they provide a legitimation of our activities. The reporting of so-called scientific results makes the accounts we give more acceptable to the community of researchers and laypeople alike (and we do not deny this important political role). Unfortunately, the very same scientific results have not been overly useful to the users of the technology.

The traditional, empiricist methodology is largely inappropriate for understanding communication and the meaning generation process. The continually changing and inherently uncertain nature of the process eludes objective measurement and prediction. Yet despite the unstable nature of communication, alternative methods, and rigorous ones, are still possible. Here we propose two key concepts that are essential ingredients in a methodology concerned with understanding communication and meanings: that of position and accounts (see Penman, 1988). In discussing these concepts we point to the type of research questions that need to be addressed with these new methods—if we are to understand the real place of information technology in organizational communication.

Position

In undertaking research into the communication process, we not only have to recognize the instability of what is being researched but also that we are using the very same process as that being researched. Given this, the peculiar nature of communicative environments and our relation to such environments needs to be taken into account. We can describe this relationship with the use of a metaphor based on the idea of a landscape within which are located both the researcher and the object of study (Sless, 1986a). How the landscape appears to the researcher very much depends on the position from which they view it. As the position they occupy changes so does the scene, and as certain views become visible others disappear.

However, the landscape of communication is more like the surface of a giant trampoline than terra firma. Our very presence as researchers subtly transforms and changes the landscape. No matter where we move, a new horizon springs up around us, occluding the view, so that we always must speculate about what lies beyond. Despite, the deformation of the landscape by the researcher, the changes are subject to underlying regularities and principles. When a trampoline yields as we walk across it, the feeling may be one of uncontrollable and chaotic movement but we know that the trampoline is obeying strict physical laws of elasticity that do not change. The regularity is at a level that we as walkers have not yet grasped. In much the same way there is a regularity to our understandings of communication that are difficult to grasp. In our trampoline metaphor, it may seem as if the researcher is uncontrollably distorting the landscape of communication. However, there is a subtle relationship between the position taken in that landscape and the view of it. Recognition of this relationship between research position and and our view of communication is the first step in gaining control of the flexible communicative landscape. And it is this type of control that the applied social psychologist needs in order to effectively manage meanings in the organizational context.

Unfortunately, in the contemporary literature accounts of the position of the researcher are conspicuous by their absence (Markus & Robey, 1988). Social psychologists working in this area have typically (with some exceptions) assumed the position of neutral, outside observer—an assumption commensurate with the empiricist epistemology employed. Even the proactive approach of action researchers has not moved the researchers out of the objective, observer position. Yet no such position is possible in our communication landscape. We are always standing somewhere and deriving a certain view as a function of where we are standing. Recognition of this opens up exciting research possibilities that rely on us asking the question "how does it look from different positions?". We have already discussed one application of this general question in the section on system design. There we pointed out that a system looks very different from the position of the end user as compared to the position of the system designer. When it is further recognized that there are multiple end users with different needs and capacities, the complexities of the problem and the research potentials are opened up. A range of studies are needed to look at these different end user positions and the consequences for effective use of information technologies. Possible methodological approaches for these studies include Shotter's (1984) grammatical logic based on the notion of person and Sless' (1986a) logic of the various positions of readers and authors of communicative texts/messages. Such approaches allow us to appreciate the relationship between the range of meanings and our own position for mapping them.

Accounts

At the same time as recognizing the problem and potential of position, we must also consider the difference between providing an account or a theory of communication. A theoretical order would demand "a single supposedly universal, context-free standpoint for the description of an orderly sequential progress to an outcome" (Shotter, 1987, p. 235). But a theoretical order is not congruent with the assumptions and arguments developed here. The essential indeterminancy of communication and the capacity of persons in the process to act as agents rather than reactors means that outcome is rarely, if ever, predictable. Moreover, the fact that researchers of the communication process must engage in the very same process means that there is no context-free, objective standpoint to take. In contrast, an account is simply a description of activity that renders the activity as something visibly rational and reportable for all practical purposes (Garfinkel, 1967). With accounts, no problematic claims of objectivity or predictability are required.

Given that accounts or stories are also the means by which organizational members construct their organizational world and their activities within it, it makes some sense to investigate this in a compatible frame. In the past few years increasing recognition has been given to the importance of account gathering in various contexts. For example, Read (1987) has described the use of account gathering in his work on the narratives that people use to make sense of their worlds. In his documentation, using causal scenarios, he also points to a range of questions that need to be asked in this area. Ross and Staw's (1986) work, mentioned earlier, also provides an illustration of a case narrative method. In that study they were able to demonstrate the way in which various stakeholders of Expo '86 changed their rationales and interpretations.

When we are concerned with the role of information technology in organizational settings we need to be concerned with questions on how the meanings attributed to information technologies are maintained and amplified by organizational members. We need also to be concerned with how these meanings change with the physical characteristics and distribution of the technology from different positions and with how these meanings are related to changing patterns of technology use. Questions about how these meanings are related to specific states of individuals, in particular their levels of technological and communicative competence, are also at issue.

But it is important to emphasize that in asking questions about meanings we, as researchers, are involved in the very same process of meaning generation. Thus, in our account gathering we are not gathering the truth in any objective or absolute sense. Instead, our accounts indicate a range of possible interpretations, including our own. It is in the use of a logic of positions that some order and comparative base can be given to the range of a possible interpretations. Our approach to questions of meanings are likely to be the most rigorous when we are aware of our position in the changing communication landscape.

SUMMARY

Past social psychological research on the impact of information technology in organizational communication can be seen as a progression of hypotheses in which information technology was portrayed:

- as a substitute for various forms of functions and processes of communication;
- as an innovator of functions and processes communication; and
- as affecting organizational communication in complex ways that were contingent on either temporal or structural/task factors.

Because of the lack of reliable evidence supporting these three hypotheses, the contribution of applied social psychology has been marginal. In this chapter we have reviewed some of the reasons for this and how we could make substantial contributions by re-examining the underlying values and premises of these hypotheses and associated research.

We found that the false promise of new and better information technology is based on a misleading view of information and the broader process of communication. We put forward alternative, emergent conceptions of information and communication to account for this state of affairs.

In this emergent view a clear distinction was made between the technological infrastructure and the human communication infrastructure. The traditional interests of applied social psychology are within the human communication infrastructure. In this view, the meanings attributed to technology are unstable, indeterminate, and position specific. This view led us to ask new questions, see new problems, and point to various appropriate methodologies that can put information technology in its place. Information technology is a potential aid to the real business of human communication, not a substitute for it. And the real business of human communication in organizations is managing meanings.

The problems in this area cannot be identified or researched within the traditional, monadic approach of the psychologist. Nor can they can be identified or researched within the empiricist tradition derived from the physical sciences. Instead, the problems and their resolutions need to be thought about as complex relational processes in which misunderstandings are the norm rather than the exception. And where our perception of both the problems and their resolution are dependent on the position we adopt in the communication landscape.

REFERENCES

Attewell, P., & Rule, J. (1984). Computing in organizations: What we know and what we don't know. *Communications of the* ACM, 27(12), 1184–1192.

Bailey, T. (1987). Some perspectives on the management of information technology. *Australian Journal of Management, 12,* 2, 159–182.

Barley, S. R. (1986). Technology as an occasion for structuring evidence from observations of CT scanners and the social order of radiology departments. *Administration Science Quarterly, 31,* 78–108.

Barnard, C. (1968). *The functions of the executive.* Cambridge, MA: Harvard University Press (Original published 1938)

Berlo, D. (1960). *The process of communication.* New York: Holt, Rinehart & Winston.

Bjørn-Andersen, N., Eason, K., & Robey, D. (1986). *Managing computer impact: An international study of management and organizations.* Norwood, NJ: Ablex.

Bryant, A. (1988). The information society: Computopia, dystopia, myopia. *Prometheus, 6,* 61–77.

Buchanan, D. A.,& Brody, D. (1982). Advanced technology and the quality of working life: The effects of word processing on video typists. *Journal of Occupational Psychology, 55,* 1–11.

Burrell, G., & Morgan, G. (1979). *Sociological paradigms and organizational analysis.* London: Heinemann.

Carroll, J. M. (1985). Miminalist design for active users. In B. Shackel (Ed.), *Interact '84* (pp. 39–44). Oxford: North Holland.

Carroll, J. M., & Mack, R. L. (1982). *Metaphor, computing systems and active learning.* IBM Research Report, Yorktown Heights, NY.

Castles, A. (1986). Australian mathematical competence. *CARE Newsletter, 3,* 3.

Christie, B., & De Alherdi, M. (1985). Electronic meetings. In B. Christie (Ed.), *Human factors of information technology in the office* (pp. 95–126). Chichester, England: Wiley.

Christie, B. (1987). The technological and work context: The office as the prototypical electronic work place of the 1990s. In A. Gake & B. Christie (Eds.), *Psychophysiology and the electronic workplace* (pp. 32–62). Chichester, England: Wiley.

Cole, I., Lansdale, M., & Christie, B. (1985). Dialogue design guidelines. In B. Christie (Ed.), *Human factors of information technology in office* (pp. 212–241). Chichester, England: Wiley.

Conrath, D. (1973). Communications environment and its relationship to organizational structure. *Management Science, 20,* 586–603.

Conrath, D., & Blair, J. H. (1974, August). The computer as an interpersonal communication device: A study of augmented technology and its apparent impact on organizational communication. In *Proceedings of the Second International Conference on Computer Communication.* Stockholm, Sweden.

Conrath, D. W., Higgins, C. A., Thachenkarg, C. S., & Wright, W. M. (1981). The electronic office and organizational behavior—Measuring office activities. *Computer Networks, 5,* 401–410.

Crawford, A. B. (1982). Corporate electronic mail—A communication-intensive application of information technology. *Management Information Science Quarterly, 6,* 1–14.

Cronin, B. (1986), The information society. *Aslib Proceedings, 38,* 121–129.

Department of Science. (1985). *National information policy for Australia: Discussion paper.* Commonwealth Government of Australia.

DeSanctis, G., & Gallupe, R. B. (1987). A foundation for the study of group decision support systems. *Management Science, 33,* 589–609.

Doswell, A. (1983). *Office automation.* Chichester, England: Wiley.

Dougherty, B. (1988, July 18). DEC warns of hidden costs. *Financial Review,* p. 63.

Drucker, P. F. (1988, January–February). The coming of the new organization. *Harvard Business Review,* pp. 45–53.

Ettlie, J. E. (1985, August). *Organizational adaptations for radical process innovations.* Paper presented at Academy of Management, San Diego CA.

Farace, R. V., Monge, P. R., & Russell, H. M. (1977). *Communicating and organizing.* Reading, MA: Addison-Wesley.

Feldman, M. S., & March, J. G. (1981). Information in organizations as signal and symbol. *Administrative Science Quarterly, 26,* 171–186.

Fisher, P., & Sless, D. (1988). *Improving information management in the insurance industry.* Occasional Paper, Communication Research Institute of Australia.

Fleischer, M., & Morell, J. (1985). The organizational and managerial consequences of computer technology. *Computers in Human Behavior, 1,* 83–93.

Garfinkel, H. (1967). *Studies in ethnomethodology.* Englewood Cliffs, NJ: Prentice-Hall.

Gergen, K. (1982). *Toward transformation in social knowledge.* New York: Springer-Verlag.

Gutek, B. A., Bikson, T. K., & Mankin, D. (1984). Individual and organizational consequences of computer-based office information technology. In S. Oskamp (Ed.), *Applied social psychology annual* (Vol. 5, pp. 231–254). Beverley Hills: Sage.

Gutek, B. A., Sasse, S. H., & Bikson, T. K. (1986, August). *The fit between technology and work group structure: The structural contingency approach and office automation.* Paper presented at Technology: Its Meaning, Measurement and Impact in the Age of Computerized Work, Academy of Management Conference, Chicago.

Habermas, J. (1971). *Knowledge and human interests.* Boston: Beacon Press.

Habermas, J. (1975). *Legitimation crisis.* (T. McCarthy, trans). Boston: Beacon Press.

Hackman, J. R. (1986). The psychology of self-management in organizations. In M. S. Pallack & R. O. Perloff (Eds.), *Psychology and work: Productivity, change and employment* (pp. 86–136). Washington DC: American Psychological Association.

Harré, R., & Secord, P. (1973). *The explanation of social behaviour.* Totowa, NJ: Littlefield Adams.

Hirschheim, R. A. (1985). *Office automation: A social and organizational perspective.* London: Wiley.

Hoos, I. R. (1983). Can we avoid the negative effects of information technology? In N. Szyperski, E. Grochla, U. M. Richter, & W. Weitz (Eds.), *Assessing the impact of information technology* (pp. 31–54). Braunschweig/Wiesbaden Friedr: Vieweg & Sohn.

Hough, R. W. (1976). *Teleconferencing systems: A state of the art survey & preliminary analysis.* Final Report for the National Science Foundation, Grant No. SSH 74-22611.

Huber, G., & McDaniel, R. (1986). The decision-making paradigm of organizational design. *Management Science, 32,* 572–589.

Keen, P. (1981). Communication in the 21st century: Telecommunications and business policy. *Organizational Dynamics, 10,* 54–67.

Kelly, J. R. & McGrath, J. E. (1985). Effects of time limits and task types on task performance and interaction of four-person groups. *Journal of Personality and Social Psychology, 49,* 395–407.

Kochen, M. (1970). Stability in the goal of knowledge. In T. Saracevic (Ed.), *Introduction to information science* (pp. 44–55). New York: Bowker.

Krippendorf, K. (1984). Paradox and information. *Progress in Communication Sciences, 6,* 45–71.

Lakoff, G. (1987). *Women, fire & dangerous things.* Chicago: University of Chicago Press.

Lakoff, G., & Johnson, M. (1980). *Metaphors we live by.* Chicago: University of Chicago Press.

Lansdale, M. (1985). Beyond dialogue design guidelines: The role of mental models. In B. Christie (Ed.), *Human factors of information technology in the office* (pp. 242–270). Chichester, England: Wiley.

Lange, B., & Reese, J. (1983). Impact research and research policy: An analytical framework. In N. Szyperski, E. Grochla, U. M. Richter, & W. Weitz (Eds.), *Assessing the impact of information technology* (pp. 31–54). Braunschweig/Wiesbaden Friedr: Vieweg & Sohn.

Lawler, E. E., Mohrman, A. M., Mohrman, S., Ledford, G., & Gummuning, T. G. (1985). *Doing research that is useful for theory and practice.* San Francisco: Jossey Bass.

Machlup, F. (1983). Semantic quirks in the study of information. In F. Machlup & U. Mansfield (Eds.), *The study of information* (pp. 641–671). New York: Wiley.

Machlup, F., & Mansfiled, U. (Eds.). (1983). *The study of information.* New York: Wiley.

Macintyre, A. (1985). *After virtue.* London: Duckworth.

Makin, D., Bikson, T. K., & Gutek, B. (1985). Factors in successful implementation of computer-based office information systems. A review of the literature with suggestions for O.B.M. Research. *Journal of Organizational Behavior Management, 6,* 1–20.

Markus, M. L., & Robey, D. (1988). Information technology and organizational change: Causal structure in theory and research. *Management Science, 34,* 583–598.

Maturana, H., & Varela, F. (1980). *Autopoiesis and cognition.* Dordrecht, Holland: D. Reidel.

Maxwell, N. (1984). *From knowledge to wisdom.* Oxford: Blackwell.

McGrath, J. E., & Kelly, J. R. (1986). *Time and human interaction.* New York: Guilford Press.

McPhee, R. D. (1985). Formal structure and organizational communication. In R. D. McPhee & P. K. Tomkins (Eds.), *Organizational communication: Traditional themes and new directions* (pp. 149–177). Beverly Hills, CA: Sage.

Meyerson, D., & Martin, J. (1986, June). Questioning the assumptions of value engineering: Alternative views of the cultural change process. *Proceedings of the International Conference on Organization Symbolism and Corporate Culture* (pp. 171–188), Montreal.

Mintzberg, H. (1983). *Power in and around organizations.* Englewood Cliffs, NJ: Prentice-Hall.

National Commission on Libraries and Information Science. (1982). [Report to the U.S. Government.]

Nord, W. (1985). Can organizational culture be managed? A synthesis in P. Frost, L. Moore, M. Louis, L. Lundberg, & I. Martin (Eds.), *Organizational culture* (pp. 187–196). Beverley Hills, CA: Sage.

Parsons, G. L. (1983, Fall). Information technology: A new competitive weapon. *Sloan Management Review,* pp. 3–13.

Penman, R. (1982). Problems in human communication studies: Another argument. *Australian Journal of Communication, 1–2,* 52–56.

Penman, R. (1985). The impact of information technology on society: Two possible futures. In T. Smith, G. Osborne, & R. Penman (Eds.), *Communication and government* (pp. 349–362). Canberra: CCAE Press.

Penman, R. (1988). Communication reconstructed. *Journal of Theory in Social Behavior, 18,* 301–310.

Perrow, C. (1983). The organizational context of human factors engineering. *Administrative Science Quarterly, 28,* 521–541.

Perrow, C. (1984). *Normal accidents.* New York: Basic Books.

Peters, T. J., & Waterman, R. H. (1982). *In search of excellence: Lessons from America's best run companies.* New York: Harper & Row.

Pfeffer, J. (1978). *Organizational design.* Arlington Heights, IL: AHM.

Porter, M. E., & Millar, V. E. (1985, July–August). How information gives you competitive advantage. *Harvard Business Review,* pp. 149–160.

Read, S. J. (1987). Constructing causal scenarios: A knowledge structure approach to causal reasoning. *Journal of Personality and Social Psychology, 52,* 288–302.

Reddy, M. (1979). The conduit metaphor. In A. Ortony (Ed.) *Metaphor and thought* (pp. 301–322). London: Cambridge University Press.

Rice, R. E. (1984). Development of new media research. In R. E. Rice (Ed.), *The new media* (pp. 15–31). Beverley Hills, CA: Sage.

Robey, D. (1986). *Designing organizations* (2nd ed.). Homewood, IL: Richard D. Irwin.

Robey, D. (1987). Implementation and the organizational impacts of information systems. *Interfaces, 17,* 72–84.

Rorty, R. (1980). *Philosophy and the mirror of nature.* Oxford: Blackwell.

Ross, J., & Staw, B. M. (1986). Expo 86: An escalation prototype. *Administrative Science Quarterly, 131,* 274–279.

Rubin, M. R., & Hubert, M. T. (1986). *The knowledge industry in the U.S. 1960–1980.* Princeton, NJ: Princeton University Press.

Ryle, G. (1963). *The concept of mind.* Harmondsworth: Penguin.

Schön, D. A. (1983). *The reflective practitioner: How professionals think in action.* London: Temple Smith.

Sensat, J. (1979). *Habermas & Marxism.* London: Sage.

Shannon, C. E., & Weaver, W. (1949). *Mathematical theory of communication.* Urbana, IL: University of Illinois Press.

Shneiderman, B. (1987). *Designing the user interface: Strategies for effective human-computer interaction.* Reading, MA: Addison-Wesley.

Short, J., Williams, E., & Christie, B. (1976). *The social psychology of telecommunications.* London: Wiley.

Shotter, J. (1984). *Social accountability and selfhood.* Oxford: Blackwell.

Shotter, J. (1986a). A sense of place: Vico and the social production of social identities. *British Journal of Social Psychology, 25,* 199–211.

Shotter, J. (1986b). Realism and relativism, rules and intentionality, theories and accounts. *British Journal of Social Psychology, 25,* 199–211.

Shotter, J. (1987). The social construction of an "us": Problems in accountability and narratology. In R. Burnett, P. McGhee, & D. Clarke (Eds.), *Accounting for personal relationships: Explanation, representation and knowledge* (pp. 225–247). London: Methuen.

Shulman, A. D. (1981). Humanizing technology. In H. Meltzer & W. Nord (Eds.), *Making organizations humane and productive: A handbook for practitioners* (pp. 421–438). New York: Wiley.

Shulman, A. D., Craick, J., & Wearing, A. J. (1983). A field investigation of new customer services. *Proceedings of the International Symposium on Human Factors, 10,* 1–8.

Shulman, A. D., & Steinman, J. I. (1978). Interpersonal teleconferencing in an organizational context. In M. Elton (Ed.), *The evaluation and planning of interpersonal telecommunication systems* (pp. 399–424). New York: Plenum.

Shulman, A. D., Wearing, A. J., & Craick, J. (1982). Conducting telecom Australia's field investigation of new customer services. In B. Brabet (Ed.), *L'experimentation sociale en telematique* (pp. 593–611). Montpellier, France: Le bulletin de l'IDATE.

Siegel, J., Dubrovsky, V., Kiesler, S., & McGuire, T. O. (1986). Group processes in computer medicated communication. *Organizational Behavior and Human Decision Processes, 37,* 157–187.

Sless, D. (1979). Image design and modification: An experimental project in transforming. *Information Design Journal, 1,* 74–80.

Sless, D. (1981). *Learning and visual communication.* London: Croom Helm.

Sless, D. (1985). Communication and the limits of knowledge. *Prometheus, 3,* 110–118.

Sless, D. (1986a). *In search of semiotics.* London: Croom Helm.

Sless, D. (1986b). Repairing messages: The hidden cost of inappropriate theory. *Australian Journal of Communication, 9–10,* 82–93.

Sless, D. (1988, August). *Ergonomics, computers and communication.* Paper presented at International Ergonomics Conference, Sydney.

Stigler, G. J. (1961). The economics of information. *Journal of Political Economy, 69* (3), 213–255.

Swanson, P. H. (1984). Research needs of industry. *Journal of Technology Transfer, 1,* 39–55.

Tompkins, P. K., & Cheney, G. (1985). Communication and unobtrusive control in contemporary organizations. In R. D. McPhee & P. K. Tomkins (Eds.), *Organizational communication: Traditional themes and new directions* (pp. 177–210). Beverly Hills, CA: Sage.

Tornatzky, L. G. (1986). Technological change and the structure of work. In M. S.

Pallak & R. O. Perloff (Eds.), *Psychology and work: Productivity, change and employment* (pp. 53–84). Washington, DC: American Psychological Association.

Toulmin, S. (1982) The construal of reality: Criticism in modern and postmodern science. *Critical Inquiry, 9,* 93–111.

Weick, K. E. (1969). *The social psychology of organizing.* Reading, MA: Addison-Wesley.

Weisband, S. P., & Kiesler, S. (1985, August). *New technology talk.* Paper presented at the American Psychological Association Annual Meeting, Los Angeles, CA.

Wiener, N. (1948). *Cybernetics, or control and communication in the animal and machine.* New York: Wiley.

Williams, E. A. (1974). *Summary of the present state of knowledge regarding the effectiveness of the substitution of face-to-face meeting by telecommunicated meetings. Type allocation revisited* (Technical Rep. #P/74294/WL). Communications Studies Group, University College, London.

Williams, F. (1984). *The new communications.* Belmont, CA: Wadsworth.

Yin, R. (1979). *Changing urban bureaucracy.* Lexington, MA: Lexington Books.

Intellectual Teamwork and Information Technology: The Role of Information Systems in Collaborative Intellectual Work

Jolene Galegher
University of Arizona

HP's R&D community partakes in one of the normal impossibilities of modern corporate life: it is now necessary for groups of people to hold continuing meetings in which the members cannot be together in the same place or even at the same time.
—Fanning and Raphael (1986)

Fanning and Raphael's (1986) description of the communication challenges at their firm, Hewlett-Packard, is a good example of the kind of problems people in large, distributed organizations face in sharing information and ideas with their co-workers. It is also a good example of the kind of problem that the technologies that have come to us as products of "the computer revolution" are designed to solve. This revolution encompasses not only the now widespread use of personal computers, but also systems that combine computers with telecommunications to create new ways of interacting—with people inside and outside one's own organization, with people who work at different times and places, and with people whose identity may be unknown to the communicator.

From a behavioral perspective, these technologies are interesting because they have the potential to affect the nature of the tasks people do and the way they interact to do them, directly impinging on the central phenomena in social psychology—human communication and other forms of social interaction. Specifying the properties of social interaction that are relevant to the design of new information technology and understanding the properties and the potential impact of technological innovations designed to affect human communication should thus be central concerns for social psychologists.

In this chapter, I intend to draw together theoretical analyses and empirical observations of work groups, general descriptions of some advanced information technologies (for more detailed descriptions of actual and potential tools for the support of cooperative work see Galegher, Kraut, & Egido, in press; Johansen, 1987; and the Proceedings of the Conference on Computer-Supported Cooperative Work, 1986, 1988), and empirical reports of experiences with some of these technologies as a means of examining the impact of particular information systems on the conduct of collaborative intellectual work. In so doing, I hope to demonstrate the mutual relevance of behavioral science and technology design. Ideally, this demonstration will encourage other social psychologists to consider how our knowledge about information processing, interpersonal communication, and group dynamics might inform the design of information systems and how those basic psychological and social psychological processes might be affected by specific technological interventions. Given our society's shift from a manufacturing to an information-based economy, building this understanding could be an important contribution to improving the quality of work and the quality of work life—both of which should be important goals for applied social psychologists.

INTELLECTUAL TEAMWORK: CHARACTERISTICS AND CHALLENGES

To talk sensibly about the mutual relevance of social psychology and technology design, and the relevance of that interface to performance at work, we need to delimit the focus of the conversation. Here, we discuss what my colleagues and I (Galegher, Kraut, & Egido, in press) call *intellectual teamwork*, a term that captures the idea of individuals working together to manipulate information or create "information-intensive" products. Examples of this sort of work are not hard to find. In industry, both basic research and new product development are typically carried out by teams of scientists, engineers, and designers (Ancona & Caldwell, 1987, in press; Burgelman, 1983; Burgelman & Sayles, 1986; Katz, 1982; Katz & Tushman, 1979; Keller, 1986; Tushman, 1978, 1979; Tushman & Katz, 1980). Other examples include the production of magazine articles based on information from geographically dispersed reporters, the design of complex software systems and the creation of multifaceted marketing campaigns.

Intellectual teamwork typically involves several specific activities requiring different kinds of expertise, both individual and joint problem solving, and substantial interpersonal communication; most often, it takes place over a relatively long time. This characterization draws together elements of several earlier analyses of work in groups, each of which deals with a part of the phenomena in which we are interested. First, it encompasses, but is not limited to, the single session, face-to-face group problem solving and task performance that social psychologists have most often studied (see McGrath, 1984, for a review that focuses on these studies). Second, it acknowledges McGrath's (in press) argument that researchers who study group processes have too often taken a too narrow view, focusing on the execution of well-specified, repetitive tasks, rather than on the completion of projects. Projects are sets of activities intended to fulfill a mission or achieve a goal of some sort; tasks are instrumental to the achievement of that goal. Projects are typically made up of a variety of tasks and extend over a "meaningful" period of time. Finally, this definition takes into account the complex information processing, communication, and coordination demands that arise from the mixture of people and tasks (Dhar & Olson, 1987).

The descriptions of scientific collaboration that my colleagues and I have generated reveal these facets of intellectual teamwork as it occurs in academic settings. In interviews about the collaborative process, we learned, first, that the typical project in the fields we studied takes about 18 months to complete, that each project involves the execution of many different kinds of tasks, and that there are important distinctions in the social modalities in which these tasks are carried out. Specifically, the inception of new projects may be highly informal, occurring as an almost accidental consequence of unstructured social interaction; project planning, on the other hand, involves coming to an agreement about the specific nature of the ɩ roject and seems to require extensive face-to-face discussion. Most other tasks involved in completing a research project are carried out individually (Kraut, Egido, & Galegher, in press; Kraut, Galegher, & Egido, 1987–1988). Drawing on this evidence, we characterized collaborative work as "threaded collections of jointly planned but individually executed products" (Kraut et al., 1987–1988, p. 44). Furthermore, our evidence suggests that informal communication between the members of the collaborative team is the thread that connects the researchers to each other and helps them move through the series of tasks involved in completing a research project.

Although scientific collaboration in academia differs from other kinds of work and work relationships in many ways, descriptions of collaborative intellectual work in other settings lead to similar conclusions. For instance, an associate whose work as a consulting engineer involves generating new chemical treatment processes as well as new applications for well-established techniques reports that most of these innovations begin in hallways, or even less formally, on walks into work from the company parking lot, in bars, or on the company's basketball court. The next steps are likely to involve a series of face-to-face, but still informal, discussions with people who "might be interested" in working on the project. Subsequently, three or four people might meet to plan an empirical test of their ideas, or, if specific organizational support is required, to construct a proposal justifying their plans. Assuming that the project involved conducting empirical analyses in-house, rather than, say, launching a marketing campaign to sell a new technique, the work would be divided up among those who are interested in pursuing the project or assigned to technicians. These individuals would then carry out the various tasks involved in executing the project individually, relying on the same kind of unplanned, informal interactions that gave rise to the project to monitor progress and coordinate tasks. Eventually, the pieces would come back together in a project report.

Another set of observations of the genesis and execution of a long collaborative project is available in Kidder's (1981) entertaining account of the development of a new computer. This documentary, which probably lies somewhere between our studies of research collaborators and the anecdotes provided by my engineering associate in terms of scientific credibility, also portrays the informal (but more intentional) mechanisms involved in formulating the project and recruiting its staff; in addition, his description emphasizes the importance of sharing information, tracking progress, and keeping records as ways of coordinating the work of the many individuals involved in this process. Burgelman (1983), Burgelman and Sayles (1986), Ancona (1984), and Ancona and Caldwell (1987, in press) have produced more scholarly accounts of this process that also emphasize the importance of communication within product development teams and between the teams and the organizations in which they exist. Taken together, these reports illustrate the centrality of informal communication, the need for extensive sharing of both substantive and procedural information, and the embeddedness of collaborative intellectual work in a web of personal and political relationships.

One might argue that this characterization of intellectual teamwork is too inclusive—that it incorporates everything people might do at work short of shoveling coal. Although there may be some truth to this charge, I do, in fact, want to emphasize the interrelatedness of different kinds of tasks, as an antidote to the narrower focus on performance of isolated tasks that is more typical in social psychology. The image of intellectual teamwork that I have tried to create here is quite different from the image associated with more familiar phrases such as *group problem solving* and *group decision making*. Those terms refer to activities that may be a part of collaborative intellectual work, but they do not convey the idea of people working to define goals and establish a sense of direction, and, subsequently, working together over a long period of time, sometimes by executing particular tasks individually, sometimes by meeting to discuss their progress and generate plans for the next part of the project, sometimes communicating face to face, other times passing documents back and forth or conducting "on-the-fly" meetings in hallways and lunchrooms.

The kinds of communication implied by this description pose two quite different challenges to systems designers who are interested in creating technology to support intellectual teamwork. On the one hand, the *initiation* of intellectual teamwork seems to require extensive face-to-face communication as group members strive to clarify the content and methods of their project, but does not necessarily present elaborate demands for document sharing or other kinds of text–graphic communication. On the other hand, the *execution* of collaborative work seems to require only minimal face-to-face interaction, but does require mechanisms that permit individuals to transmit text–graphic information to the other members of their project groups quickly, easily and in a form that the others will be able to interpret and operate on.

In this section I explain these challenges in more detail and examine research that speaks to the question of how well currently available technologies support each of these kinds of communication. This discussion focuses on the role of face-to-face communication in collaborative intellectual work and considers the suitability of other modes of communication for carrying out this kind of work. This focus is prompted by the centrality of face-to-face communication in some aspects of intellectual teamwork, by the intent to reduce or eliminate face-to-face contact that underlies the design of some information systems and by the frequent use of face-to-face communication as a comparison condition in studies of the impact of advanced information systems. This analysis ties empirical observations of the impact of electronic information systems to the conception of intellectual teamwork presented above as a way of specifying the advantages and disadvantages of current systems, and should, in turn, provide a basis for new designs that might provide additional benefits to people engaged in collaborative intellectual work.

Earlier, I noted that many instances of collaborative intellectual work involve joint planning and individual execution of specific tasks, with informal communication as a coordinating mechanism. We focus on these commonalities in the following discussion, but we begin with last things first; by shifting the sequence of initiation and coordination, we can proceed from discussion of a relatively straightforward task for which current information systems provide reasonable, if not wholly satisfactory, support to the more problematic enterprise of initiating collaborative work and the still more problematic enterprise of building information systems to support it.

INFORMATION TECHNOLOGY AND THE
COORDINATION OF INTELLECTUAL TEAMWORK

Coordination Mechanisms

When complex projects are partitioned into tasks and distributed among individuals—either because there is too much work for one person or because diverse kinds of expertise are needed—the added burdens of communication and coordination tend to counteract the benefits obtained by division of labor (Brooks, 1982). Social psychologists typically refer to these problems as process losses (Steiner, 1972), but, despite the inefficiency of group work, many projects could not be accomplished in any other way. Further, some authors (Hutchins, in press; McGrath, in press) have argued that group work may provide some nonobvious benefits. Opportunities for individuals to contribute, to be rewarded for their contributions, and to obtain enjoyment from their activities, may insure their continued willingness to participate in tasks necessary for the survival of the larger organization. Similarly, redundancy in skills within work groups permits individuals to take on each others' tasks should one member err or become incapacitated, thus insuring the group's ability to sustain itself and to carry out its tasks. The need to sustain both group productivity and these other aspects of group functioning creates a demand for techniques and technologies that will help group members work together, even, or perhaps especially, in difficult circumstances such as those described by Fanning and Raphael (1986).

Elsewhere (Kraut et al., 1987–1988), my colleagues and I have described mechanisms that scientists use to coordinate their work without the aid of sophisticated electronic technologies. For the most part, these methods consist of managing the allocation of tasks and the flow of information about the execution of those tasks in a way that minimizes the need for communication. For instance, research partners typically parcel out the tasks involved in conducting an empirical project; task assignments may be based on status, expertise or preference, but, in general, partners will trade off responsibility for shepherding the execution of successive tasks. This combination of division of labor and sequential processing means that most communication between partners takes place at points of transition to a new task.

At these transition points, the individual who is handing off a completed piece of work encapsulates information about the current status of the project prior to transmitting it to his or her partner(s); by confining their exchanges to the discussion of "finished products," the partners avoid having to share all the complex details of the procedures involved in reaching a particular transition point. To supplement this trilogy of division of labor/encapsulation/sequential processing, the researchers we studied occasionally exchange annotated drafts of interim documents and supervise each other's work through casual reminders and inquiries about the progress of the project. Although the extension of these observations to other examples of intellectual teamwork is, of course, speculative, mechanisms similar to these must be involved in coordinating most kinds of collaborative intellectual work.

Information Technology for Coordination

What then are the implications of this analysis for our concern with the role of information technology in collaborative intellectual work? Perhaps the most obvious conclusion to be drawn from these observations is that, at least with regard to actually accomplishing work (i.e., carrying out the production function; McGrath, in press), the amount of face-to-face discussion involved in these coordinative interactions is minimal. Most often, these meetings involve the exchange of noncontroversial information on topics about which group members already have considerable mutual knowledge; this mutual knowledge makes it relatively easy for individuals to shape their communications so that they can be readily understood by their listeners. Thus, for coordinating an already-defined project, the most fundamental determinant of the value of any information technology may be that it duplicate the capacity of face-to-face communication to exchange task-related information quickly and easily. Here, I describe evidence that one kind of information technology—electronic mail—meets this criterion and discuss its impact in studies of collaborative intellectual work.

Electronic Mail. Electronic mail (e-mail)—perhaps the most familiar and widespread of contemporary information technologies—combines text editing with telecommunications to make it possible for users to send and receive written messages by computer. Messages can be sent at any time to any individual who has an address on the system and can be retrieved at the convenience of the recipient; thus, e-mail clearly provides the possibility for asynchronous communication between geographically dispersed users that I have used as a reference point in this discussion.

Although there have been many studies of patterns of e-mail use (Eveland & Bikson, 1987; Feldman, 1986; Finholt & Sproull, in press; Sproull & Kiesler, 1986) in large organizations, only a few researchers have examined its utility as a mechanism for coordinating intellectual teamwork. The first of these studies (Finholt, Sproull, & Kiesler, in press) is particularly relevant to our concern with the question of whether computer-mediated communication can substitute for face-to-face interaction as a coordination mechanism. These authors analyzed patterns of interaction within teams of students carrying out software design projects, assessed the frequency of electronic mail use by each member of each of the teams in their study and also coded the content of each message. Their results reveal a positive association between frequency of electronic mail use and the group's performance on the project. Furthermore, their findings show that, to some extent, electronic mail use supplanted face-to-face communication; groups who used electronic mail more held fewer face-to-face meetings. Finally, their content analyses indicate that electronic mail was primarily used to handle coordination problems—to assign tasks, to schedule meetings, and to seek and provide reports about the status of individual work on the project.

Although not directly relevant to the substitution question, the results of two additional studies of groups engaged in collaborative intellectual work also provide positive evidence of the utility of computer-mediated communication as a coordination mechanism. In a study by Bikson and Eveland (in press), adult men were assigned to either a standard or a computer-supported task force to gather information relevant to and establish plans for retirement. The standard task force was allowed to communicate in face-to-face meetings or to exchange documents or phone calls; the other task force could use any of these means to share information with each other but was also supplied with the hardware, software and instructions needed to communicate by electronic mail. Subsequently, the participants were allowed to communicate in any way they chose. Bikson and Eveland (in press) report that the computer-supported group members became avid electronic mail users, were more likely than standard task force members to feel that their experimental assignment helped them complete their work and to be pleased with the work they produced. Although the authors do not report analyses of message content, much of the great volume of computer mail exchanged in this project must have been directed toward coordinating the work of individual members.

Finally, in a recently completed experiment (Galegher & Kraut, in preparation) student subjects were required to produce jointly authored writing projects using either face-to-face communication, a computer conference or a combination of the computer conference and the telephone. (Computer conferences are the electronic equivalent of a bulletin board; a close cousin of electronic mail, they differ from it in that users can read and write in a text file that is visible to all participants rather than transmitting messages between individuals.) In that investigation, the students reported that the computer conferences provided a useful forum for keeping track of the progress of other students, for reporting their own activities to their groupmates and for exchanging interim drafts of their work.

These results show that electronic mail may, in some circumstances, be an acceptable substitute for face-to-face interaction, but it is important to note that these findings mainly relate to the group's productivity. Its consequences for the "softer" dimensions of group effectiveness—the satisfaction of individual members and the group's ability to sustain itself (McGrath, in press)—

are less clear cut. In the studies where it was used in conjunction with other communication modalities, it seemed to provide a channel that permitted otherwise peripheral group members to participate more actively, increasing their commitment to the group (Finholt et al., in press) and the reported likelihood that group members would continue to see each other socially after completion of the task force project (Bikson & Eveland, in press). But, although they recognized its value as a coordination and exchange mechanism, the participants in the experimental study felt constrained and, eventually, irritated by the difficulties of conducting all their communication electronically. They reported that their interactions with their groupmates were limited to task-related communiques (cf. Siegel, Dubrovsky, Kiesler, & McGuire, 1986), and were hence "no fun."

Still, the basic message is that even a homely technology such as electronic mail can be a powerful aid to collaborative work. All collaborative work involves solving fundamental problems such as scheduling, reporting progress, and asking for help. These coordinative tasks are typically handled in fleeting, face-to-face conversations, and at least some of those conversations can be replaced by systems that make it possible for people who are not likely to bump into each other in an office corridor to work together. Moreover, systems developers are currently working to expand the capacity of these systems in two ways—by increasing bandwidth, making it possible for users to transmit graphics and voice messages as well as text, and by creating structured message systems designed to foster more effective collaboration (Flores, Graves, Hartfield & Winograd, 1988; Lakin, in press; Malone, Grant, Lai, Rao, & Rosenblitt, 1987; Olson & Atkins, in press). This new generation of technologies will make computer-mediated communication more available, orderly, and natural, hastening the day when distributed intellectual teamwork is seen as an ordinary occurrence.

Much more difficult than providing technological support for collaborative work in progress, however, is providing technological support for the initiation of that work. Here, then, we turn our attention to an analysis of the subtle, interactive communication apparently required to clarify the content and methods of a collaborative intellectual project.

INFORMATION TECHNOLOGY AND THE INITIATION OF INTELLECTUAL TEAMWORK

Initiation and Project Planning

Equivocality in the Problem Context. In the early stages of a collaborative intellectual project, the participants may have only the vaguest ideas of what they should be trying to achieve and how to go about it. This is especially likely for people who set their own goals (such as the researchers in my studies with Kraut and Egido), but may also be true when a general goal has been established by a project manager or some other organizational authority. Suppose, for instance, that a committee of urban transportation planners in a growing Sunbelt city is assigned to solve a problem defined as "too many traffic accidents." In this situation, the desired outcome, fewer accidents, is clear, but there are many potential explanations for the current accident rate which the planners will have to consider before they can begin to propose reasonable solutions.

Weick (1979) formulated the notion of equivocality to characterize information environments such as this where the problem people face is not simply the absence of some specifiable piece(s) of information (as is the case in an uncertain environment), but the absence of knowledge about what information is needed, or even how to interpret the information at hand. When equivocality is high, problem solving involves working to construct a shared interpretation of the problem that can provide a foundation for subsequent data gathering, evaluation, and action (Daft & Lengel, 1986; Weick, 1979). The attempt to carve out this shared interpretation is likely to be complicated by the diversity in disciplinary backgrounds, work experiences, and skills that characterizes most project teams; although this diversity is intended to provide the range of skills and perspectives needed to make the project a success, it is also likely to increase the difficulty of reaching a shared sense of the situation. In addition to coping with internal diversity, Ancona and Caldwell (1987, in press) suggest that shaping the work to be undertaken by a project team also involves considerable "foreign relations" activity; they point out that discerning the views of various constituencies in the environments (organizations) within which the team is embedded is an important part of the sense-making process that provides the basis for subsequent actions.

This analysis brings to mind the idea of convergence (i.e., somehow people "come in on" a sense of the current situation and a way to proceed). According to Daft and Lengel (1986), this convergence arises out of social interaction; their research has shown that in highly equivocal situations, people prefer "rich" sources of information such as face-to-face meetings that allow them to test definitions of the problem and obtain feedback that tells them whether their views are shared. In theoretical terms, this means creating, through interaction, a state of mutual knowledge that can serve as a foundation for subsequent actions. Although the researchers we studied described the face-to-face meetings in which they worked to define their projects as the most intellectually exciting and rewarding aspect of collaborative work (Kraut et al., 1987–1988), their enthusiasm should not obscure the challenge and the complexity of the social processes that transpire in these meetings; creating this shared understanding is not an easy or straightforward process.

The intricacies of establishing mutual knowledge are revealed in studies of referential communication that show that speakers use different terms to describe objects depending on their beliefs about the knowledge of their listeners (Krauss & Fussell, in press). These beliefs may be based on the speaker's knowledge about members of various social or occupational sub-groups (Krauss & Glucksberg, 1977), or may be derived directly from feed-back that the listener provides. This feedback (which may consist merely of the nods and "uh huhs" that conversation analysts call *backchannel communication*) plays a crucial signalling role in the development of a state of mutual knowledge. Backchannel signals permit the speaker to tailor his or her presentation to meet the needs of the listener (Krauss, Garlock, Bricker, & McMahon, 1977; Krauss, Vivekananthan, Weinheimer, 1968; Krauss & Weinheimer, 1966, 1967; Kraut, Lewis, & Swezey, 1982) and, in turn, this tailored presentation has a positive effect on the listener's comprehension. As evidence of this effect, Kraut et al. (1982) demonstrated that when a listener is able to provide feedback to a speaker, the listener's comprehension of the speaker's message is higher than when he or she is a passive listener.

A series of investigations by Chapanis and his colleagues (Chapanis, Ochsman, Parrish, & Weeks, 1972; Chapanis & Overbey, 1974; Chapanis, Parrish, Ochsman, & Weeks, 1977; Weeks & Chapanis, 1976) provides evidence that the absence of such on-line feedback can complicate communication. In summarizing the results of these experiments, Williams (1977) concluded that when people were able to hear each other, as is the case with the telephone, they were able to execute cooperative problem-solving tasks as efficiently as people who were in the same room communicating face-to-face, but subjects who could only communicate through written messages required substantially more time to solve the same problems. Although part of this difference is simply a function of the slowness of writing relative to speaking, the more important observation is that subjects in the face-to-face and audio-only conditions could simultaneously work on the problem and communicate about it, easily and immediately adjusting their communications to meet each other's needs for information as they carried out the task. The great difficulty of making these adjustments in writing caused those subjects to take longer to complete the task than subjects who could request or transmit information in face-to-face interaction or via a voice-only channel.

The observation that effective communication requires subtle adjustments based on the informational needs and information-processing capacities of one's listeners and one's own goals in the conversation (Kraut & Higgins, 1984) is important for our concern with the role of information technology in intellectual teamwork because the systems we are concerned about can and do intervene in social interaction. Interpersonal contacts that might have taken place in direct face-to-face conversations may instead by mediated by the exchange of text, or by audio and/or video connections. However, to develop and sustain collaborative intellectual work, information systems must permit people to assess and correct each other's knowledge, thus making it possible for them to come eventually to a state of mutual knowledge.

Uncertain Preferences in the Solution Context.   Related to the problem of equivocality in the problem context is the idea of uncertainty about preferences for alternative strategies, approaches, or designs in the solution context. For instance, in the example just given, the members of the transportation planning task force may be able to agree that they would like to see fewer accidents on the city's streets, but they may be uncertain about the desirability of various means of producing this outcome. That is, their uncertainty is not only about how *likely* it is that expanded freeways, a light rail system, new licensing regulations, or some combination of them would be the best approach to solving the problem, but also about the relative *desirability* of these approaches, because each is not only a means to an end, but also an outcome with potentially complex side effects.

Connolly (1987; Connolly & Wagner, 1988) argued that this uncertainty about the desirability of outcomes plays an important role in what people do (and should do) in making choices about how to solve problems. He observed that most models of human decision making are based on a "tree-felling" metaphor. In those models, the problem is assumed to be well specified, the goals are assumed to be clear, and the theorist's work is to describe how the decision maker selects an alternative to solve the problem. In contrast to this idea, Connolly proposed a model of decision making as "hedge-clipping" in which the elements of the problem are highly interactive, solutions are achieved iteratively rather than by selection of a well-specified alternative, errors produce few serious consequences and can be easily corrected, several alternative solutions are acceptable, and no specific sequence of problem-solving activities is required. Except that errors may sometimes be costly and not always easily corrected, this analysis captures the essential features of the idea generation and evaluation processes involved in intellectual teamwork.

Connolly and Wagner (1988) held that by taking small-scale actions guided by uncertain preferences, people can and do obtain experience that will enable them to select subsequent actions. Taking action not only provides information about the likelihood that particular choices will lead to particular final states; it also produces information about how desirable particular outcomes are. This view is, of course, in keeping with the recommendations of both popular and scholarly organizational theorists (Peters & Waterman, 1982; Quinn, 1980) who argue that a little experience at an early stage of project development can help people orient or re-orient their efforts so that the eventual outcome is more satisfactory. This analysis implies a second desirable property of information systems designed to support the initiation of intellectual teamwork—that they make it possible for people to approximate experience with particular approaches to problems as a way of reducing their uncertainty about preferences for alternative solutions.

Information Technology in Project Planning

Initiating a collaborative intellectual project usually requires that the project participants overcome a formidable set of intellectual, interpersonal and political problems. The preceding discussion suggests two mechanisms that help project participants overcome these problems—face-to-face discussion and creating approximations of alternative solutions. Face-to-face discussion helps group members reduce equivocality by creating a shared interpretation of the situation, and the opportunity to gain some experience with alternative approaches or outcomes makes it possible for group members to reduce the uncertainty of their preferences. Here, I discuss three different information technologies with a view toward determining how each of them affects the use of these mechanisms in confronting the challenges involved in the initiation of intellectual teamwork.

Electronic Mail. In two of the studies previously cited (Bikson & Eveland, in press; Finholt et al., in press), the researchers permitted participants to choose between face-to-face interaction and electronic mail as a means of communication during various stages of a long-term collaborative intellectual project. The results of these investigations show that in the early stages of work on their projects, the participants preferred face-to-face interaction over computer-mediated communication. For instance, Finholt et al. (in press) learned that the students they studied preferred face-to-face meetings over electronic mail for project planning and for subsequent decisions that required a consensus of the project team members. This preference for face-to-face interaction when progress on a group project requires establishing consensus also appears in the Bikson and Eveland results. Despite both experience with computer-mediated communication and considerable enthusiasm for it, as their project drew to a close and the participants were required to shift from reporting the results of individually executed tasks to creating a single, integrated document summarizing the results of their investigations, they chose to assemble in face-to-face meetings. These results appear to mean that the participants felt meetings of this type were necessary, or at least desirable, to converge on a common perspective that could provide a foundation for the rest of their work.

One might argue that these results merely reflect users's habits (i.e., people are used to getting together to talk things over when they are beginning a new enterprise and they continue that practice even when there are alternatives that could conceivably make such meetings unnecessary). However, preliminary observations from the related experimental study (Galegher & Kraut, in preparation) indicate that these preferences are unlikely to be overcome by imposing experience with the technology on project participants. Students who were restricted to using the computer conference reported that they found it very difficult to come to an initial agreement as to how to proceed, and those who were permitted to supplement their computer-mediated communications with telephone conversations reported carrying out almost all their planning work via the phone.

Taken together, these findings validate Fanning and Raphael's (1986) contention that "electronic mail . . . is more effective for distributing information than for discussing it" (p. 292). This liability is likely to be especially apparent at the early stages of a complex collaborative project. When participants are still working to clarify their goals and to develop a common understanding of how to proceed, they are likely to view a communication medium that does not permit them to obtain feedback and adjust or amplify their messages in response to it in real time as a major hindrance. Thus, even though electronic mail and computer conferencing do provide the asynchronous communication between geographically dispersed individuals that Fanning and Raphael (1986) described as necessary to contend with the "normal impossibilities" of corporate life, as systems to support the interactions necessary to launch a collaborative intellectual project, they do not seem to be totally satisfactory.

However, if we relax the requirement for asynchronicity, we can consider the usefulness of other technologies that could, in theory, make it possible for people at distributed work sites to initiate a collaborative project. Two such technologies are videoconferencing and the family of systems referred to as group decision support systems (GDSSs). These technologies have the potential to support the initiation of intellectual teamwork in different ways: by offering a technological bridge across distance that permits multiple users to conduct a free-flowing conversation, and by systematizing the analysis of problems and potential solutions. Unfortunately, we do not have well-controlled studies about the value or influence of either in the early stages of intellectual teamwork; instead, we must rely on our knowledge of their properties, the properties of collaborative intellectual work, and the limited evidence available about their utility and influence.

Videoconferencing. Videoconferencing systems provide for the transmission of sound and images across distance, making it possible for users to see and hear each other even though they are not physically co-present. They have typically been marketed as a way to hold meetings in which multiple participants can converse freely without actually meeting; thus, this medium appears to provide a distance-spanning mechanism to support the interactive discussion that the initiation of a collaborative project requires. However, they have not achieved the degree of commercial success that this potential suggests. Referring to the discrepancy between the optimistic claims and the small number of systems now in use, Egido (in press) characterized teleconferencing generally, and videoconferencing, in particular, as a technology that has been on the brink of success for 30 years.

Although there are several reasons for this limited commercial success, for our purposes, the most important is that the systems do not, in fact, allow users to converse as freely as they might in face-to-face conversation. To manage the problem of acoustic feedback, most systems operate in what is called half-duplex mode, meaning that only one person can speak at a time, imposing a rigid turn-taking sequence that constrains the free flow of ideas and interferes with the transmission of the kind of backchannel signals previously described. These limitations may be unimportant in some situations; for instance, videoconferencing is gaining popularity as a medium for training programs in organizations (Egido, in press) because it permits a standardized program to be widely disseminated at a fairly low cost. However, when the situation requires mutual adjustment as participants attempt to explain themselves and to understand each other, these limitations can make conversation awkward and irritating—hardly optimal for the difficult and delicate process of working through alternative perspectives on a complex problem.

Group Decision Support Systems. Unlike videoconferencing, which promises to transcend the physical barriers between people, group decision support systems promise to help people clarify their ideas and choose an optimal approach to solving a problem. Behavioral research on individual and group decision making has demonstrated that both cognitive biases and social constraints can (and often do) prevent people from behaving in ways that theories of rational choice would predict. To the extent that these problems shape people's discussions and choices, information systems that help them manage both the flow of data about the substantive problem and the flow of communication among project team members may be useful. DeSanctis and Gallupe (1987), Kraemer and Pinsonneault (in press), and Vogel and Nunamaker (in press) described systems that are meant to provide some or all of these advantages; although these systems differ in their specific features, they have in common the idea of minimizing the influence of the counterproductive features of group deliberation and decision making.

As noted earlier, there is little evidence about the role of GDSSs in collaborative intellectual work, perhaps because research in this domain presents unusually difficult methodological problems. Finding suitable control groups for teams and task forces engaged in planning complex projects is problematic, and broadly applicable measures of the quality of outcomes are impractical. Thus, this discussion mainly consists of speculations about probable outcomes based on the interplay of systems with particular features and the properties of intellectual teamwork just described.

Here, I assume a system that permits computer-mediated communication, allows users the option of participating anonymously, and also provides access to software versions of ranking systems, planning models, budgeting models, and utility and probability assessment models (cf. DeSanctis & Gallupe, 1987; Vogel & Nunamaker, in press). Typically, the users of such a system would spend some amount of time working to generate approaches to a problem (brainstorming) via computer, followed by one or more sessions to evaluate these alternatives and shape them into a statement, design, or set of procedures that would provide the foundation for subsequent actions. Thus, such a system would involve interventions in both the communication and information-processing aspects of group deliberation and decision making. It would not offer the option of asynchronous participation, but it could, and some systems do, support participation by users at different sites.

Conceivably, a system of this type could provide considerable benefit to people engaged in working out ways to approach a difficult problem or to structure a complex project, but the preferences for face-to-face interaction in these circumstances described by Daft and Lengel (1986) raise questions about this proposition. Of course, preferences for face-to-face interaction do not indicate that it is an inherently superior communication mode, but, given its importance in establishing a shared sense of the situation, it is important to show that the difficulty of converging on solutions without such interaction is offset by a gain in the quality of solutions that can be achieved using a GDSS. Yet, when equivocality is high it may be difficult to determine what criteria should be used to evaluate alternative solutions, or to reach any solution at all without face-to-face interaction.

This implies that there are important restrictions on one of the purported advantages of some GDSSs—that of improving the quality of deliberation and choice by permitting users to communicate anonymously. Proponents (DeSanctis & Gallupe, 1987) of GDSSs have argued that permitting users to exchange messages anonymously will encourage low status members or members with unusual ideas to participate without fear of ridicule or reprisal, thus reducing the likelihood of ill-considered decisions such as those described by Janis (1972). Some recent research suggests that computer-mediated communication can, indeed, have this effect: for instance, Siegel et al. (1986) have shown that participation rates are more nearly equal in computer-mediated discussions than in face-to-face groups and Jessup, Connolly, and Galegher (1988) have shown that anonymity does prompt group members to be more critical and to seek clarification of each other's proposals more often. Under equivocality, however, the benefits of anonymity may be limited to the very early stages of intellectual teamwork; in the absence of the shared views and values that result from working toward a consensual definition of the situation through interaction, it may be difficult to obtain the solidarity needed to enact controversial decisions. Once the parameters of a project or an approach to a problem have been identified, further progress will depend on whether project team members or managers are able to extract the resources they need from the organization.

This observation implies that, to support the initiation of collaborative intellectual work, GDSSs should have the capability of helping group members respond to the concerns of external constituents. Vogel and Nunamaker (in press) described such a system, a computer program called Stakeholder Identification and Assumption Surfacing, which is designed to be one part of a computer-mediated group decision or planning process. This program prompts users to specify constituencies who might contribute to or are likely to be affected by the plans the group is making and to clarify the likely response of each to those plans, thus encouraging them to think systematically about the group's needs for material and political support, potentially leading to more efficient information gathering and more effective coalition building. It might, of course, be possible to construct the same sort of analysis by listing the appropriate categories on a blackboard, but the computer-aided analysis yields a manipulable record that can be retained as a database to guide the group's subsequent activities.

Although there are, as yet, no clear data about the value of this GDSS feature, the preceding discussion suggests that it may provide a significant advantage to groups undertaking collaborative projects in the midst of complex organizations. Of course, it is important to be aware that the results of this analysis do not, in themselves, solve the "foreign relations" problems that confront work-group members; rather, they prompt users to seek particular interactions because they provide opportunities to gather information and build support for their projects. Those interactions would likely take the form of face-to-face discussions because acquiring the support necessary to carry the plan forward would require a combination of questioning, explaining, and cajoling that would be improbably difficult to carry off in any other medium. Whether these interactions result in the desired outcomes is likely to depend more on the persistence or persuasiveness of the person who initiates them, than on the fact that the interaction was prompted by a computer-aided analysis of the social environment. This explains why, as I previously argued, the benefits of anonymity in generating project ideas are likely to be limited to creating a more open environment that invites a broader range of suggestions, questions, and clarifications at the earliest stages of project development. Moreover, to the extent that such systems do add value to a project group's ability to understand and operate in its environment, it should be clear that this value stems from the congruence between what the system provides and the properties of the social system in which it is meant to intervene.

In addition to the political complexity associated with defining and enacting particular projects, the existence of uncertainty about the relative desirability of particular outcomes or solutions raises questions about the value of decision support systems based on the tree-felling model. A decision support system can easily be designed to reveal disagreements about preferences, or, perhaps less easily, to help people reach agreement about preferences. If, as Connolly (1987) suggested, preferences are likely to be altered by experience, then the most useful approach for builders of decision support systems may be to make it possible for people to obtain experience with particular alternatives. Thus, in addition to seeking to control the process of deliberation and choice, designers might strive to create systems that would help people envision the world given their choices. In fact, Salomon (personal communication, November, 1988) has argued that it is the ability of computers to create detailed, vivid alternative worlds (as in some current educational software), rather than their ability to serve as compact information repositories, high-speed calculators or alternatives to the telephone, that makes them uniquely valuable for intellectual work. This analysis provides the impetus for system designers to create computer tools that extend or exceed the capacities of the systems to support communication and modeling tasks that currently make up GDSSs.

In summary, this analysis of GDSSs raises several questions about the extent to which they help people solve the substantive and political problems associated with the initiation of collaborative intellectual work. Although GDSSs already appear in a variety of forms with a variety of specific features (Kraemer & Pinsonneault, in press; Vogel & Nunamaker, in press), increasingly sophisticated designs for new applications continue to evolve. The success of these developments is likely to depend, at least in part, on the extent to which they are based on a thorough understanding of the relationship between design characteristics and the characteristics of the work the system is intended to support. Here, I have identified several important properties of intellectual teamwork as a way of providing a theoretical foundation for these developments.

SUMMARY

This chapter is based on the premise that successful design and implementation of advanced information systems depends on understanding the tasks the information systems are intended to support and the organizational environments in which they will be implemented. I have argued that intellectual teamwork, a form of work that currently occurs in many different kinds of organizations, is likely to become more widespread as "the information age" unfolds and as organizations respond to competitive pressure by organizing workers in self-managed, project-oriented teams and task forces (Ancona & Caldwell, in press; Goodman, 1985). Thus, by constructing a detailed analysis of the cognitive and interpersonal challenges this kind of work presents, we gain considerable leverage in the effort to design useful information systems to support current and future forms of economic activity.

The description of intellectual teamwork presented here reveals three tasks that confront project group members as they attempt to plan and coordinate their work: reducing the equivocality that surrounds the definition of the project itself, resolving uncertainty about preferences for alternative approaches or outcomes, and achieving a smooth sequence of task activity. Our analysis demonstrates that currently available information technologies are better suited to helping people solve the latter problem than either of the former, thus defining areas that developers with an interest in collaborative work might fruitfully explore. First, they should be interested in creating systems to support the interaction needed to achieve a satisfactory state of mutual knowledge. In practical terms, this means improving the quality of audio and video transmission and resolving incompatibilities in text–graphic software systems to make it easier for people at distributed work sites to communicate with each other. The great difficulty of working out a satisfactory state of mutual knowledge and garnering adequate political support for a new project without on-line interaction suggests that asynchronous communication as a means of initiating intellectual teamwork may be permanently out of reach, but improvements of this sort would greatly reduce the obstacles that arise in communicating across distance. Second, they should be interested in creating systems to support efforts to resolve uncertainty about preferences for alternative approaches to problems by sampling simulated outcomes. Practically, this means building flexible, easy-to-use software systems that make it possible for people to construct alternative versions of whatever they are trying to create or achieve through their collaborative work, whether the product is a jointly authored document, a new computer, or an urban transportation plan.

Of course, some of the systems that might solve these problems already exist as prototype or demonstration projects. For instance, two high technology companies have piloted continuous video links between workers at different sites (Abel, in press; Goodman & Abel, 1986; Kraut, personal communication, December, 1988) as a way of fostering the informal communication that underlies most collaborative relationships, and the computer-aided design programs used in engineering are examples of the kind of software systems that help people envision alternative futures. But many more efforts of this sort are needed, and, perhaps, even more important, much more systematic research is needed to determine whether these and other systems do, in fact, help people confront the challenges of intellectual teamwork that I have specified.

Finally, it is important to note that although the discussion presented here does lead to some fairly specific observations about the utility of existing information systems for particular tasks and about desirable properties for new information technologies, it nonetheless represents a fairly narrow cut on the large problem of understanding the relationships among system design, task performance, user satisfaction and organizational effectiveness. I have concentrated on defining the conceptual properties of a single kind of work, albeit a kind of work that appears in many specific incarnations, and have devoted more attention to analyzing the task-related utility of a few reasonably well-developed (that is, either commercially available or used extensively in research settings) information systems than to examining users' affective reactions or to assessing the role of these systems in more remote organizational outcomes. However, the diversity of tasks that information systems designers might conceivably be interested in working on is so enormous that it hardly seems useful (or possible!) to attempt a more general analysis. And, finally, the conclusions resulting from this analysis underscore the utility of a conceptual approach to a narrow set of specific phenomena. By drawing on theoretical formulations derived from social psychology, human judgment, and organizational behavior, we have been able to identify the common properties of a variety of examples of intellectual teamwork and to spell out the implications of those commonalities for technology design. Thus, this approach seems justified both by the complexity of the problem and by its intellectual yield.

ACKNOWLEDGMENTS

The concept of intellectual teamwork that provides the foundation for this chapter grew out of my collaborative work with Robert E. Kraut and Carmen Egido, and reflects the small body of mutual knowledge that we have established over the last 2 years. I am grateful for their indirect contributions to this chapter. I am also grateful to John S. Carroll for his good editorial advice and his good humor.

REFERENCES

Abel, J. M. (in press). Experiences in an exploratory distributed organization. In J. Galegher, R. E. Kraut, & C. Egido (Eds.), *Intellectual teamwork: The social and technological bases of cooperative work.* Hillsdale, NJ: Lawrence Erlbaum Associates.

Ancona, D. G. (1984). Groups in context: A model of task group effectiveness. *Administrative Science Quarterly, 29*, 499–517.

Ancona, D. G., & Caldwell, D. F. (in press). Information technology and workgroups: The case of new product teams. In J. Galegher, R. E. Kraut, & C. Egido (Eds.), *Intellectual teamwork: The social and technological bases of cooperative work*. Hillsdale, NJ: Lawrence Erlbaum Associates.

Ancona, D. G., & Caldwell, D. F. (1987). Management issues in new product teams in high technology companies. In D. Lewin, D. Lipsky, & D. Sockell (Eds.), *Advances in industrial and labor relations* (Vol. 4, pp. 199–221). Greenwich, CT: JAI Press.

Bikson, T. K., & Eveland, J. D. (in press). The interplay of work group structures and computer support. In J. Galegher, R. E. Kraut, & C. Egido (Eds.), *Intellectual teamwork: The social and technological bases of cooperative work*. Hillsdale, NJ: Lawrence Erlbaum Associates.

Brooks, F. B. (1982). *The mythical man-month: Essays on software engineering*. Reading, MA: Addison-Wesley.

Burgelman, R. A. (1983). A process model of internal corporate venturing in the diversified major firm. *Administrative Science Quarterly, 28*, 223–244.

Burg n, R., & Sayles, L. (1986). *Inside corporate innovation: Strategy, structure and managerial skills*. New York: The Free Press.

Chapanis, A., Ochsman, R. B., Parrish, R. N., & Weeks, G. D. (1972). Studies in interactive communication: I. The effects of four communication modes on the behavior of teams during cooperative problem solving. *Human Factors, 14*, 487–509.

Chapanis, A., & Overbey, C. M. (1974). Studies in interactive communication: III. Effects of similar and dissimilar communication channels and two interrupt options on team problem solving. *Perceptual and Motor Skills, 38*, 343–374.

Chapanis, A., Parrish, R. N., Ochsman, R. B., & Weeks, G. D. (1977). Studies in interactive communication: II. The effects of four communication modes on the linguistic performance of teams during cooperative problem solving. *Human Factors, 19*, 101–126.

Connolly, T. (1988). Hedge-clipping, tree-felling and the management of ambiguity. In L. R. Pondy, R. Boland, & H. Thomas (Eds.), *Managing the challenge of ambiguity and change* (pp. 37–50). New York: Wiley.

Connolly, T., & Wagner, W. G. (1988). Decision cycles. In R. L. Cardy, S. M. Puffer, & J. M. Newman (Eds.), *Advances in information processing in organizations* (pp. 183–205). Greenwich, CT: JAI Press.

Daft, R. L., & Lengel, R. H. (1986). Organizational information requirements, media richness and structural design. *Management Science, 32*, 554–571.

DeSanctis, G., & Gallupe, R. B. (1987). A foundation for the study of group decision support systems. *Management Science, 33*, 589–609.

Dhar, V., & Olson, M. H. (1987 May). *The role of value-based assumptions for design of collaborative work systems*. Proceedings of the New York University Symposium on Technological Support for Work Group Collaboration, New York City.

Egido, C. (in press). Teleconferencing as a technology to support cooperative work:

Its possibilities and limitations. In J. Galegher, R. E. Kraut, & C. Egido (Eds.), *Intellectual teamwork: The social and technological bases of cooperative work*. Hillsdale, NJ: Lawrence Erlbaum Associates.

Eveland, J. D., & Bikson, T. K. (1987). Evolving electronic communication networks: An empirical assessment. *Office: Technology and people, 3,* 103–128.

Fanning, T., & Raphael, B. (1986, December). *Computer teleconferencing: Experience at Hewlett-Packard.* Proceedings of the Conference on Computer-Supported Cooperative Work, Austin, TX.

Feldman, M. (1986, December). *Constraints on communication and electronic messaging.* Proceedings of the Conference on Computer-Supported Cooperative Work, Austin, TX.

Finholt, T., & Sproull, L. (in press). Electronic groups at work. *Organization Science.*

Finholt, T., Sproull, L., & Kiesler, S. (in press). Communication and performance in ad hoc task groups. In J. Galegher, R. E. Kraut, & C. Egido (Eds.), *Intellectual teamwork: The social and technological bases of cooperative work*. Hillsdale, NJ: Lawrence Erlbaum Associates.

Flores, F., Graves, M., Hartfield, B., & Winograd, T. (1988). Computer systems and the design of organizational interaction. *ACM transactions on office information systems, 6,* 153–172.

Galegher, J., & Kraut, R. E. (in prep.). *Collaborative writing in a computer conference: A field experiment.*

Galegher, J., Kraut, R. E., & Egido, C. (Eds.). (in press). *Intellectual teamwork: The social and technological bases of cooperative work.* Hillsdale, NJ: Lawrence Erlbaum Associates.

Goodman, G. O., & Abel, M. J. (1986, December). *Collaboration research in the Systems Concepts Laboratory.* Proceedings of the Conference on Computer-Supported Cooperative Work, Austin, TX.

Goodman, P. S. (1986). Impact of task and technology on group performance. In P. S. Goodman and Associates (Eds.), *Designing effective work groups* (pp. 120–167). San Francisco, CA: Jossey-Bass.

Hutchins, E. (in press). The technology of team navigation. In J. Galegher, R. E. Kraut, & C. Egido (Eds.), *Intellectual teamwork: The social and technological bases of cooperative work.* Hillsdale, NJ: Lawrence Erlbaum Associates.

Janis, I. L. (1972). *Victims of groupthink: A psychological study of foreign policy decisions and fiascoes.* Boston: Houghton-Mifflin.

Jessup, L. M., Connolly, T., & Galegher, J. (1988). *The effects of anonymity on GDSS group process in an idea-generating task.* Unpublished manuscript, University of Arizona, Tucson, AZ.

Johansen, R. A. (1987, May). *A user view of computer-supported teams: What are they?* Proceedings of the the New York University Symposium on Technological Support for Work Group Collaboration, New York.

Katz, R. (1982). The effects of group longevity on project communication and performance. *Administrative Science Quarterly, 27,* 81–104.

Katz, R., & Tushman, M. (1979). Communication patterns, project performance, and task characteristics: An empirical evaluation in an R&D setting. *Organizational Behavior and Human Performance, 23,* 139–162.

Keller, R. T. (1986). Predictors of the performance of project groups in R & D organizations. *Academy of Management Journal, 29,* 715–726.

Kidder, T. (1981). *The soul of a new machine.* Boston, MA: Little, Brown.

Kraemer, K., & Pinsonneault, A. (in press). The impact of technological support on groups: An assessment of the empirical research. In J. Galegher, R. E. Kraut, & C. Egido (Eds.), *Intellectual teamwork: The social and technological bases of cooperative work.* Hillsdale, NJ: Lawrence Erlbaum Associates.

Krauss, R. M., & Fussell, S. R. (in press). Mutual knowledge and communicative effectiveness. In J. Galegher, R. E. Kraut, & C. Egido (Eds.), *Intellectual teamwork: The social and technological bases of cooperative work.* Hillsdale, NJ: Lawrence Erlbaum Associates.

Krauss, R. M., Garlock, C. M., Bricker, P. D., & McMahon, L. E. (1977). The role of audible and visible back-channel responses in interpersonal communication. *Journal of Personality and Social Psychology, 35,* 523–529.

Krauss, R. M., & Glucksberg, S. (1977). Social and nonsocial speech. *Scientific American, 236,* 100–105.

Krauss, R. M., Vivekananthan, P. S., & Weinheimer, S. (1968). "Inner speech" and "external speech": Characteristics and communication effectiveness of socially and nonsocially encoded messages. *Journal of Personality and Social Psychology, 9,* 295–300.

Krauss, R. M., & Weinheimer, S. (1966). Concurrent feedback, confirmation and the encoding of referents in verbal communication. *Journal of Personality and Social Psychology, 4,* 343–346.

Krauss, R. M., & Weinheimer, S. (1967). Effect of referent similarity and communication mode on verbal encoding. *Journal of Verbal Learning and Verbal Behavior, 6,* 359–363.

Kraut, R. E., Egido, J., & Galegher, J. (in press). Patterns of contact and communication in scientific research collaboration. In J. Galegher, R. E. Kraut, & C. Egido (Eds.), *Intellectual teamwork: The social and technological bases of cooperative work.* Hillsdale, NJ: Lawrence Erlbaum Associates.

Kraut, R. E., Galegher, J., & Egido, C. (1987–1988). Relationships and tasks in scientific collaboration. *Human-Computer Interaction, 3,* 31–58.

Kraut, R. E., & Higgins, E. T. (1984). Communication and social cognition. In R. S. Wyer, Jr. & T. K. Srull (Eds.), *Handbook of social cognition* (Vol. 3, pp. 87–127). Hillsdale, NJ: Lawrence Erlbaum Associates.

Kraut, R. E., Lewis, S. H., & Swezey, L. W. (1982). Listener responsiveness and the coordination of conversation. *Journal of Personality and Social Psychology, 43,* 718–731.

Lakin, F. (in press). Visual languages for cooperation: A performing medium approach to systems for cooperative work. In J. Galegher, R. E. Kraut, & C. Egido (Eds.), *Intellectual teamwork: The social and technological bases of cooperative work.* Hillsdale, NJ: Lawrence Erlbaum Associates.

Malone, T. W., Grant, K. R., Lai, K., Rao, R., & Rosenblitt, D. (1987). Semi-structured messages are surprisingly useful for computer-supported coordination. ACM *Transactions on Office Information Systems, 5,* 115–131.

McGrath, J. E. (1984). *Groups: Interaction and performance.* Englewood Cliffs, NJ: Prentice-Hall.

McGrath, J. E. (in press). Time matters in groups. In J. Galegher, R. E. Kraut, & C. Egido (Eds.), *Intellectual teamwork: The social and technological bases of cooperative work.* Hillsdale, NJ: Lawrence Erlbaum Associates.

Olson, G., & Atkins, D. (in press). Supporting collaboration with advanced multimedia electronic mail: The National Science Foundation EXPRES project. In J. Galegher, R. E. Kraut, & C. Egido (Eds.), *Intellectual teamwork: The social and technological bases of cooperative work.* Hillsdale, NJ: Lawrence Erlbaum Associates.

Peters, T., & Waterman, R. H. (1982). *In search of excellence.* New York: Harper & Row.

Proceedings of the Conference on Computer-Supported Cooperative Work. (1986). Austin, TX: December 3–5.

Proceedings of the Conference on Computer-Supported Cooperative Work. (1988). Portland, OR: September 26–28.

Quinn, J. B. (1980). *Strategies for change.* Homewood, IL: Irwin.

Siegel, J., Dubrovsky, V., Kiesler, S., & McGuire, T. W. (1986). Group processes in computer-mediated communication. *Organizational Behavior and Human Decision Processes, 37,* 157–187.

Sproull, L., & Kiesler, S. (1986). Reducing social context cues: Electronic mail in organizational communication. *Management Science, 1986, 32,* 1492–1512.

Steiner, I. D. (1972). *Group process and productivity.* New York: Academic Press.

Tushman, M. L. (1978). Technical communication in R&D laboratories: The impact of project work characteristics. *Academy of Management Journal, 21,* 624–645.

Tushman, M. L. (1979). Work characteristics and subunit communication structure: A contingency analysis. *Administrative Science Quarterly, 24,* 82–97.

Tushman, M. L., & Katz, R. (1980). External communication and project performance: An investigation into the role of gatekeepers. *Management Science, 26,* 1071–1085.

Vogel, D., & Nunamaker, J. (in press). Design and assessment of a group decision support system. In J. Galegher, R. E. Kraut, & C. Egido (Eds.), *Intellectual teamwork: The social and technological bases of cooperative work.* Hillsdale, NJ: Lawrence Erlbaum Associates.

Weeks, G. D., & Chapanis, A. (1976). Cooperative versus conflictive problem solving in three telecommunications modes. *Perceptual and motor skills, 42,* 879–917.

Weick, K. E. (1979). *The social psychology of organizing.* Reading, MA: Addison-Wesley.

Williams, E. (1977). Experimental comparisons of face-to-face and mediated communication: A review. *Psychological Bulletin, 84,* 963–976.

Author Index

Subject Index